DOCTRINAL STANDARDS IN THE WESLEYAN TRADITION

DOCTRINAL STANDARDS
IN THE
WESLEYAN TRADITION

THOMAS C. ODEN

FRANCIS ASBURY PRESS
of Zondervan Publishing House
Grand Rapids, Michigan

DOCTRINAL STANDARDS IN THE WESLEYAN TRADTION
Copyright © 1988 by Thomas C. Oden

FRANCIS ASBURY PRESS is an imprint of
Zondervan Publishing House
1415 Lake Drive, S.E.
Grand Rapids, Michigan 49506

Library of Congress Cataloging in Publication Data
Oden, Thomas C.
    Doctrinal standards in the Wesleyan tradition / Thomas C. Oden.
        p.   cm.
    Bibliography: p.
    Includes index.
    ISBN 0-310-75240-X
    1. Methodist Church—Doctrines. 2. Methodist Church—United
States—Doctrines. 3. United Methodist Church (U.S.)—Doctrines.
4. Authority (Religion) I. Title.
BX8331.2.O34   1988
230'.7—dc19   87-24640
                                                                  CIP

Printed in the United States of America

88 89 90 91 92 93 94 / AH / 10 9 8 7 6 5 4 3 2 1

For Tal and Jane

CONTENTS

The Systematic Structure of the Twenty-five Articles; How the Thirty-nine Articles Were Amended to Twenty-five

PREFACE

This is a little like a long-delayed, newsy, circular letter to members of a widely scattered family. I speak of the vast family of those who regard themselves as sons and daughters of John Wesley—members of the Wesleyan family.

As in any long letter to insiders, they do not mind if those outside the family find its details less interesting. For insiders are eager to hear news from those with whom they have long been out of touch. There is a growing hunger for roots in the wider Wesleyan family and for news from those who have lived in distant parts. The family is divided and there is much catching up to do.

The crisis in the family now has to do with whether the older traditions of the family should be followed, amended, or abandoned. The specific issue focuses upon what Wesleyans have for almost two hundred years called "doctrinal standards" or "our doctrines."

This review of the question seeks two closely interrelated objectives— first, to sort out the state of affairs in the "mainline" or "oldline" branch of the family, the *United Methodist Church,* especially as to how basic teaching is defined textually (Part One); and second, to provide a clearing for *other Wesleyan-rooted churches,* other branches of the extended family, to enter this debate significantly (Part Two).

Hence our agenda is not limited to a *denominational* issue but broadens into preliminary treatment as an *ecumenical* issue. The heavy investment by United Methodists in ecumenical dialogue may have been diminished by tending to neglect some partners in dialogue, especially those in the more closely proximate family of Wesleyan-related churches who have strikingly similar doctrinal standards, despite differences.

We will first show why the issue of doctrinal standards has again become a matter of intense debate— actively within the United Methodist Church, and potentially within the Wesleyan family as a whole. Chapter 1 shows the historic roots of the contemporary debate, indicating how doctrinal standards were first formed, narrowing the question conceptually and chronologically. This in turn becomes the basis for retracking the historic debate on doctrinal definition through its major phases leading to the present crisis. That is the primary concern of Part One (Chs. 2–5), a concise résumé of evidence of major events, decisions, and personae of doctrinal standards definition from 1763 to the present. These chapters will show how Wesleyan doctrinal standards became transplanted to America in 1763–84 (Ch. 2), maintained as established standards in 1785–1808 (Ch. 3), and constitutionally protected from 1808 to the present (Ch. 4) in the expanding Wesleyan tradition. Chapter 5 explores continuing issues of Wesleyan doctrinal standards—pluralism, enforceability, distinction between types of sources, and the questions of apostasy and schism—all issues that have reverberating analogies in various Wesley-related churches.

Part Two follows with an analysis of key doctrinal documents of the Wesleyan tradition. Chapter 6 serves as a bridge chapter between the history of the standards debate and contemporary varieties of Wesleyanism. It presents various documents that show how Wesley's *Explanatory Notes upon the New Testament* have uniquely functioned as doctrinal standards; it introduces key themes of Wesley's *Standard Sermons*; and it clarifies the documentary history of the *Articles of Religion.* Chapter 7 presents a selection and analysis of documents embodying doctrinal standards from various churches of the Wesleyan tradition, revealing similarities and differences. This provides in a convenient, comparative form the texts of key documents of many churches of the Wesleyan family on doctrinal standards. The book concludes with an outline of a lay study course on the *Articles of Religion,* with classic annotations from Thomas Coke and Francis Asbury of 1798.

Hence the book begins by focusing more strictly upon the *American Methodist tradition,* then broadens to include the whole *worldwide Wesleyan family of churches.* Our purpose is to show how the Wesleyan standards were originally shaped and derived, how they have functioned through varying Wesleyan traditions, and how they might be reappropriated for instructional use today.

Regardless of which modern branch of the Wesleyan tradition of churches one might belong to, the historical evidence needs to be carefully sifted. Whether one approaches the issues from the perspective of the A.M.E., C.M.E., A.M.E. Zion, Free Methodist, Nazarene, the former E.U.B. tradition, Salvation Army, Wesleyan Church, or a dozen other groups, the earlier historical issues remain much the same, since the same theological root stem is under investigation.

Surprisingly, no definitive, comparative doctrinal study has yet been made of these influential groups. These bodies worldwide comprise, according to one reckoning, over twenty million members (Africa: 2,658,199; Asia: 3,586,986; Central America and Caribbean: 235,337; Europe: 749,090; North America: 15,242,564; Pacific: 941,790; South America: 282,510; total: 23,696,476. *World Methodist Council Information, 1982–86,* 127.) Broader definitions of the Wesleyan family, inclusive of various Holiness church traditions or embracing various Charismatic and Pentecostal movements and traditions, yield figures much larger. The extended family, however defined, is larger by far worldwide than many other church connections, yet has been grossly neglected as a subject of comparative ecumenical study.

Both the terms *Wesleyan* and *Methodist* will be used here, not to describe a particular church body, but generically to refer to the larger family of churches that have grown out of the Wesleyan movements of the last two centuries.

I wish to thank colleagues who have critically examined drafts of portions of this study at various stages, whose judgment I greatly value—Albert C. Outler; Kenneth Rowe; Charles Yrigoyen; Thomas W. Ogletree; Robert Cushman; Ted Runyon; John B. Cobb, Jr.; Schubert M. Ogden; Charles Cole, Jr.; Thomas Langford; Kenneth Kinghorn; John Deschner; Young Ho Chun; and Bishops Nolan B. Harmon; Olë E. Borgen; William Cannon; W. T. Handy, Jr.; John Wesley Hardt; Earl G. Hunt, Jr.; Jack M. Tuell; and Herbert Skeets. Scholars from various Wesleyan traditions to whom I am deeply indebted include Timothy L. Smith, Paul Bassett, Donald W. Dayton, Melvin E. Dieter, Charles White, Vincent Synan, John Tyson, Stephen Seamands, Donald Thorsen, David Eaton, and Darius Salter. My assistants David C. Ford, Stephen M. Maret, and Leicester R. Longden have helped immensely with difficult tasks. Drafts at every stage have been shared with, and helpful responses received from, Richard P. Heitzenrater, with whom the discussion at several points is principally concerned.

Debatable aspects of our question make it all the more imperative that this case be made with the descriptive clarity required of a careful résumé of historical evidence. I welcome responses from all who share these concerns, especially from ordinands and ordinal examination committees and Boards of Ministry in the Wesleyan tradition, who struggle often with these issues.

Especially to the ones to whom this book is affectionately dedicated do I feel deepest gratitude—my brother Tal, levity personified, experienced ecclesial legislator, delegated (more often than any lay person of our generation) to eight United Methodist General Conferences, who has constantly oriented me toward the serving church, caring brother, and wise counselor; and to Jane who beautifies and ennobles everything she touches.

Thomas C. Oden
Drew Forest
Madison, New Jersey
Epiphany, 1987

INTRODUCTION:
Why the Debate on Doctrinal Standards Has Reappeared

A *standard* is literally a flag, a banner, an ensign distinctive of a community. It is metaphorically that which is set up visibly and established by authority as a rule for the measure of value of something.

Something is standard if it maintains the prescribed degree or quality specified by some rule. A *standard* is a criterion of judging, a rule or test by which something is tried in forming a reasoned judgment about it, "an authoritative or recognized exemplar of correctness," "a measure."[1] It comes from the Old English *standan,* meaning to stand, to take or occupy a position, to remain erect on one's feet in a stated condition. It implies adhering to an avowed policy, abiding, holding a course at sea, or enduring.

Doctrinal pertains to that which is taught or believed. It comes from the Latin *doctrina,* which means teaching or instruction, that which is taught or laid down as true, a body of principles taught by a body of believers.

At issue: Does doctrine in the Wesleyan tradition have a definable textual standard, a specifiable criterion?

While being examined for ordination, every United Methodist minister is asked: "Have you studied the doctrines of the United Methodist Church? After full examination do you believe that our doctrines are in harmony with the Holy Scriptures? Will you preach and maintain them?" (*Disc., 1984,* 212). But what are "our doctrines"? If one is going to promise to maintain them, must not one know where they are, to study them? Is there textual clarity about what is meant by "the doctrines of the United Methodist Church"? That is what we will try to discover in Part One.

Has the Momentum of "Doctrinal Pluralism" Been Reversed?

The period between 1968 and 1988 has been one of considerable confusion for United Methodists. Part of this confusion emerged out of the understandable adjustments required for the union of the Methodist Church and the Evangelical United Brethren Church. More of it emerged out of the vast confusions that characterized American society during the social experimentation of

15

that period. But a significant part of it emerged as a result of doctrinal diffusion, or lack of centeredness.

In the heyday of social experimentation, the 1972 Doctrinal Statement of the *Discipline* confidently asserted that "pluralism should be recognized as a principle" (*Disc., 1972,* 69). This elicited a wrenching debate after 1972 about whether United Methodism had any doctrinal standards at all. By 1980 the language of the *Discipline* had been sobered to a simple statement of empirical fact that "we recognize the presence of theological pluralism" (*Disc., 1980, 72*). The doctrinal pluralism, which had been glowingly defined in the glossary of the 1976 *Discipline,* and which had seemed to be so enriching that it had become a United Methodist principle, had by 1980 elicited such ambivalence that it was simply recognized as an ambiguous fact (*PP,* 3–9).

By 1984 resistance to theological indifferentism had strengthened to the point that the General Conference once again cautiously revised the doctrinal introduction of the *Discipline* to read: "We recognize *under the guidance of our doctrinal standards* and guidelines the presence of theological pluralism" (*Disc., 1984, 72,* italics added). If theological pluralism is recognized in United Methodism but firmly placed under the constraint of doctrinal standards, it is crucial that the church understand what texts specifically define those standards. That is what Part One of this book is about.

As further evidence of a hunger for theological roots, two hundred years after the founding Conference a Committee of the General Conference was appointed to work to revise paragraphs 66–69 of the 1984 *Discipline,* entitled "Part II—Doctrinal Standards and Our Theological Task." That Committee, known as the Committee on Our Theological Task (C.O.T.T.), has at this time of writing published its preliminary report to the church for critical responses leading to the General Conference of 1988. We hope that what follows will help readers understand the issues underlying this legislative debate.

After having textually stable doctrinal standards for over two hundred years, United Methodists have lived through a period of doctrinal instability accompanied by institutional decline and diminished numbers of United Methodists (1972–88). Whether these are correlated is a matter of urgent concern to many. Now the United Methodist Church is deliberately asking its theologians for greater clarity about the precise nature of its doctrinal standards. This requires careful historical inquiry, for the question cannot be answered without asking precisely what happened in 1763, 1784, and especially 1808, for our constitution binds us to decisions made then.

It may seem as though current discussions are unprecedented, yet in 1881 the definitive work on *Wesley's Doctrinal Standards* began with this statement: "It has come to be asserted with great assurance in our day, and perhaps, by some sincerely believed, that doctrinal standards are no longer necessary" (Burwash, *WDS,* v.). Hence our present discussions are not wholly new and may be illuminated by understanding previous rounds of similar debates. The only thing new is the history we have not read.

The aged John Wesley wryly confessed his anxiety—not that Methodists would cease to exist, but that they should only exist as a dead sect having the form of religion without the power; and that this undoubtedly would be the case, unless they held fast both the doctrine, spirit, and discipline with which they first set out.[2] The Wesleyan family is once again being put to the test as to whether it will "hold fast."

The Pivotal Issue

When I became a "licensed preacher" (West Oklahoma Methodist Conference, 1951), I was presented a copy of *Sermons on Several Occasions* by John Wesley and was told by the superintendent that these "standard sermons" constituted the "criterion of Wesleyan preaching." Later, in seminary, I discovered that the *Articles of Religion,* along with these sermons and Wesley's *Explanatory Notes upon the New Testament,* were protected as doctrinal standards by the First Restrictive Rule of the church's constitution. When in 1968 the E.U.B. *Confession* of 1962 was included under this protection, there was no great flurry of debate, and most agreed that doctrinal standards were consensually defined.

In 1985 Richard P. Heitzenrater (general editor of the Bicentennial Edition of the works of John Wesley) rekindled the doctrinal standards issue in a way that has invested it with urgency and consequence by challenging the prevailing assumption of over a hundred years, arguing that Wesley's *Sermons* and *Notes* are not legal doctrinal standards at all and have not been since 1785. The fact that everyone thinks they are, he says, is a mistake of historical judgment. It is ironic that little interest focuses upon doctrinal standards *unless* they are challenged.

Having now been challenged,[3] the standards have become charged with extraordinary significance. Doctrinal standards could be a major issue in future legislative and constitutional deliberations, among not only United Methodists but also the larger Wesleyan family of churches.

Some observers believe that these standards have never been textually defined or specified satisfactorily enough to be consensually received. If their opinion or Heitzenrater's should become generally accepted, it would constitute *the* pivotal revolution of the century in this hitherto quiescent arena of doctrinal standards in the Wesleyan tradition. Hence, it is imperative that this challenge be carefully answered.

The Wesleyan tradition has not been accustomed to rigorous historical or theological debate and may have suffered from the lack of it. The challenge before us is sufficiently important that the response must be circumspect, historically documented, and reasonably argued. These long-neglected problems deserve fresh debate by both laity and clergy, based upon a new look at the historical evidence, which has remained relatively unexamined for decades. The last major studies of Methodist doctrinal standards were completed seven decades ago: James Monroe Buckley's *Constitutional and Parliamentary History of the Methodist Episcopal Church* (Buckley, *CPH*) and Thomas B. Neely's *Doctrinal Standards of Methodism* (Neely, *DSM*).

The continuing debate hinges on an innocent-sounding sentence written in 1808: "The General Conference shall not revoke, alter, or change our Articles of Religion or establish any new standards or rules of doctrine contrary to our present existing and established standards of doctrine" (*Disc., 1984,* 25). This is usually called the First Restrictive Rule. The same sentence is in every *Discipline* of the United Methodist Church and its predecessors from 1808 to the present. To what "standards" does this crucial sentence refer? Part One of this study seeks to answer that question.

The most common interpretation is as follows: "The *Discipline* seems to assume that for the determination of otherwise irreconcilable doctrinal disputes, the Annual and General Conferences are the appropriate courts of appeal, under the guidance of the first two Restrictive Rules (which is to say, the Articles and Confession, the *Sermons* and the *Notes*)" (*Disc., 1984,* 49). But is this interpretation historically correct and accurate in its textual specification of what the Rules protect? That is what we shall try to answer.

PART ONE:
The Historical Debate in Contemporary Focus

1.
The Formation of Wesleyan Standards of Doctrine

A doctrinal standard is a normative form of Christian teaching. The final standard of Christian teaching is Scripture. Additional standards of doctrine seek to assist the Christian community in gaining clarity concerning the accountability of that community to Scripture. No valid Christian doctrinal standard is separable from Scripture.

Those who seek to be accountable to Scripture must develop a method of interpretation appropriate to Scripture. In listening carefully to the divine address in Scripture, the serious reader makes integrative judgments about what unifies the varied statements of Scripture and what enables Scripture to be a cohesive statement of God's saving action. Serious traditions of Scripture interpretation have sought to develop some unified norm of teaching, some assessment of the central truth of Scripture, without which Scripture would lose its center-edness, internal cohesion, and intrinsic unity. This view does not seek to identify a canon within the canon (for that implies arbitrary selectivity), but rather it recognizes the cohesive center of the canon (which implies integrity and internal congruence in the canon). "The Bible is the rule of faith (*regula fidei*); the confession, the rule of doctrine (*regula doctrinae*)."[1]

Doctrinal standards seek to assist us in developing this accountability to Scripture in six complementary ways in the Wesleyan tradition: (1) The standards serve as an authoritative *guide* to one seeking the essential and central truth of Scripture. (2) They serve as an authoritative *standard* to which appeal can be made in matters of controversy. (3) They serve as an authoritative *source* from which the truth is received (cf. Burwash, *WDS,* viii). (4) Doctrinal standards serve to regulate the teaching office of the church, for essential Christian teachings ought to be clearly understood by those whose ordination distinctly calls them to such instruction.

Doctrinal standards serve in two additional ways related to their legal and sociological function: (5) They *unite* a diverse church body in a common doctrinal purpose. And (6) they *defend against abuses* (such as the misuse of church property) by those who would not hold these views.

These six functions appear in the confessional statements and church teachings of most Christian traditions. All six play a crucial role in Wesleyan doctrinal standards.

The earliest summaries of Christian teaching, and hence the earliest summaries of the teaching of the Scriptures, are found in three complementary types of sources: (a) the apostolic preaching of the New Testament, (b) commentaries on biblical teaching, and (c) the ancient baptismal formulae, which later formed the basis for instruction of catechumens. *These three basic forms of instruction have been passed on to the Wesleyan tradition so as to become integral to Wesleyan doctrinal standards in Wesley's Sermons, Notes, and Articles—one is homiletic, one exegetical, and the third systematic in approach and method.* These three forms correspond to major divisions of theological curriculum: homiletical, exegetical, and systematic theology.

Is There a Distinctive Wesleyan Form of "Doctrinal Standard"?

Did Wesley create a new type of "doctrinal standard" or did he revise available older types? It is useful to review briefly these three types of standards—both in their origin and development—in order to understand how Wesley received and adapted them.

Apostolic Preaching

The earliest form of doctrinal standard was the apostolic *preaching* itself, such as that of Peter and Paul in Acts, Paul in Romans, and Paul's recollection in 1 Corinthians 15 of the tradition of preaching that had been passed on to him. This form of preaching was passed on to Timothy, who was urged to preach according to "the pattern of sound teaching" (2 Tim. 1:13), to urge others "not to teach false doctrines" (1 Tim. 1:3), and to preach as one "brought up in the truths of the faith and of the good teaching that you have followed" (4:6). It is this apostolic standard and type of preaching that Wesley sought to reappropriate when he set forth his *Sermons on Several Occasions* as doctrinal standards for Methodist preachers.

In doing so, Wesley was following a distinctively Anglican pattern, which had developed a form of doctrinal standard relatively unfamiliar within the sixteenth-century Lutheran and Reformed traditions. For Anglicans, church-appointed homilies were designed to be read and used as a model doctrinal standard for preaching. Wesley stood in this tradition when he designated certain sermons as "the substance of what I have been preaching" (*SSO*, preface). Wesley gave his followers "not merely the outlines of a system of truth to be subscribed and believed, but the method and substance of doctrine in the form of sermons delivered from the pulpit" (Harrison, *WS*, 7). The forms of error addressed in these sermons have been perennial, not limited to a particular age. "That which was to be tested by them was the *pulpit in every Methodist Church*. This was to be the type of preaching for which these houses were created" (Sugden, *WSS*, xviii).

Early Commentaries

The apostolic preaching was soon followed by *commentaries* on Scripture. Origen, John Chrysostom, Ambrose, Augustine, and Jerome wrote extensive annotations, interpretations, and expositions of Scripture texts. Wesley continued this tradition in his *Notes,* as a model for the Methodist people of the use of the best available linguistic, textual, and critical resources for the translation and interpretation of Scripture. By introducing the *Notes* along with the *Sermons* into every Trust Deed in the Methodist connection, Wesley also sought to assure, "so far as human means can do so, an Arminian evangelical preaching and exposition of God's Word" (Sugden, *WSS,* xviii).

Conciliar Formulae

During the classical period of ancient ecumenical orthodoxy, carefully constructed formula statements by Ecumenical Councils summarized Christian teaching and erected a defense against its distortions. This third pattern—quite different in form from either preaching or exegesis—was continued in the Reformation, wherein *articles of faith* were articulated and agreed upon by a confessional community as the basis for a confession of faith. These articles were then used as the basis for catechisms of Christian instruction, as a rule and guide for Christian confession and preaching accountable to Scripture. In this way, the baptismal formula was expanded into ecumenical creedal definitions that formed the basis for Confessions of the Protestant Reformation. Of these, the Anglican•Thirty-nine Articles became the basis for Wesley's *Articles of Religion.*

A summary of the Wesleyan adaptation of these three types of doctrinal standards was concisely formulated by Nathaniel Burwash in a memorable, oft-quoted statement:

The Wesleyan standards of doctrine . . . are three-fold, viz.:

I. The Standard of Preaching— the fifty-two sermons embraced in the four volumes.

II. The Standard of Interpretation—the notes on the New Testament.

III. The Standard of Unity with the Sister Churches of the Reformation—the Twenty-five Articles (Burwash, *WDS,* xi).

The Sermons set before us that great, distinctive type and standard of gospel *preaching,* by which Methodism is what she is as a great, living Church. When she ceases to preach according to this type and standard she will no longer be Wesleyan Methodism. . . .

The Notes . . . open up to us the mode of *interpretation* by which the grand type of preaching contained in the Sermons was derived from its fountain-head—the New Testament of our Lord and Saviour Jesus Christ. They are thus the link which binds our subordinate standard to the original Apostolic standard. . . .

But the Articles of Religion have their own appropriate place in our doctrinal foundations. They indicate that which we have received as our common heritage from the great *principles of the Protestant Reformation,* and from the still more ancient conflicts with error in the days of Augustine and Athanasius (Burwash, *WDS,* x, italics added).

This threefold complementarity in the development of Methodist doctrinal standards may be pictured as follows:

Standards of:	Preaching	Interpretation	Unity
Early Church	Apostolic preaching	Exegesis	Baptismal Formula
Reformation	Homilies (Anglican)	Commentaries	Confessions
Wesley	Sermons	Notes	Articles

In none of these three types of standards do we find any attempt at theological novelty or presumptuous innovation. The steady focus is rather upon fidelity to the faith once delivered. "The student should keep in mind the important truth that there is no new principle in Christian theology. While the modes of interpretation, the terms by which the Word of God is explained and illustrated, will in different ages vary according to the degree of enlightenment and the environment of the ministry and the laymen of the Church, yet the truth is always *old*" (Harrison, *WS*, 13). Accordingly, our theological task is not to fancy that we can improve upon the substance of apostolic teaching, but to remember and interpret it accurately and accountably within our own ever-emergent cultural settings. Progress in doctrinal reflection is possible, therefore, but is best viewed as moving further toward a more reliable and adequate interpretation and re-presentation of apostolic teaching.

The ecumenical balance of the Wesleyan doctrinal synthesis was not exaggerated by the Victorian rhetoric of Nathaniel Burwash:

This full-orbed conception of scriptural religion embraced the great scriptural verities of all ages and schools of Christian thought. It grasped the wideness of God's love with the old Greek Christian and the modern Arminian, and it sounded the depths of the human heart with Augustine. It maintained the necessity of good works with the Roman Church, and it recognized the peculiar import of faith with Protestantism. With the Churchman it held the importance of means, and with the evangelical mystic, it recognized the peculiar office of inward grace; and it built the doctrines of inward holiness and Christian perfection of the English mystics upon their true foundation, by uniting them to the evangelical principle of saving faith (Burwash, *WDS*, xiii).

Those today who are most deeply committed to the recovery of ancient ecumenical Christian teaching may also take pleasure at the extent to which Wesley himself participated in such a recovery in his own time:

The fundamental principle of Wesley's doctrine, the impartial universality of God's provision of grace in Christ, was clearly apprehended and taught by all the Greek fathers, and has been unquestioned in all the eastern Church down to the present time. It was obscured, though not directly denied by Augustine; but firmly held by the great body of the Latin Church, both before and since the Reformation. . . . In fact, during Mr. Wesley's student days, the whole strength of the English Church divines had been devoted for nearly half a century to the formation of a system of theology on the basis of the first five centuries. This was evidently the School of Divinity from which Mr. Wesley most largely received his opinions, and this revival of patristic theology held as tenaciously as did the ancients to the dogma of human freedom and responsibility (Burwash, *WDS,* xiv–xv).

"Our Doctrines" and the "Doctrinal Minutes"

It is noteworthy that "our doctrines" were first specified through a dialogical process ("conversations") as reported in minutes of extended colloquies between Wesley and his associates. This was done through:

doctrinal declarations which were published in the Minutes of Wesley's yearly Conference, the first of which was held in 1744, one year after the General Rules were prepared, and which Conferences continued thereafter from year to year. In these Minutes, particularly in the earlier years, much space was given to the definition and statement of religious doctrine, and in 1749, Mr. Wesley took from the Conference "Conversations" of 1744, 1745, 1746, 1747, and 1748, the matter relating to doctrines, and printed his combination under the title of "Minutes of some late Conversations . . .", and this publication, because of the specific nature of the contents, was popularly called "The Doctrinal Minutes." This presentation of Wesleyan doctrines doubtless had a position of authority (Thomas B. Neely, *DSM,* 104).

The *Minutes* of these dialogues were designated "our doctrines" long before the Twenty-five Articles were compiled by Wesley. The rationale for the development by which these standards initially emerged—first from conference minutes and then to include Wesley's *Sermons* and New Testament commentary—was aptly described by the United Methodist Theological Study Commission on Doctrine and Doctrinal Standards in their "Interim Report to the General Conference, 1970," edited by Albert C. Outler (hereafter *TSC*):

The doctrinal guidelines hammered out in these first conferences served the Methodists in England and America throughout their formative years. . . . Wesley then conceived the idea of supplementing the conference progress with a collection of exemplary sermonic essays in which he attempted to sum up *all* the "essentials" of his doctrine and most of his "opinions," putting his written word in place of his personal presence. In 1746, he published the first of four volumes of *Sermons on Several Occasions* in which he sets forth his basic method of theologizing and suggests, indirectly, that the *sermons* are a more nearly adequate medium for doctrinal teaching than "confessions," on the one hand, or formal theological treatises, on the other! . . .

However, if doctrinal teaching is to be truly "biblical," then preachers and hearers need guidelines for their exegesis and interpretation of Scripture; therefore, Wesley undertook to provide them with yet a third standard reference: his *Explanatory Notes Upon the New Testament* (*TSC,* 9, 10).

Chronologically, the sequence of doctrinal definition moved from *Minutes* (beginning 1744) to *Sermons* (beginning 1746) to *Notes* (1754) to *Articles* (1784).

The familiar Methodist code phrase, "our doctrines" (*Disc., 1984,* 212), has remained a weighty, traditional Wesleyan phrase for over two centuries (*WJW,* 8:275ff.; cf. Outler, *John Wesley,* 136ff.). In "Conversation I" of the "Minutes of Some Later Conversations Between the Rev. Mr. Wesley and Others, Monday, June 25th, 1744," the questions that first brought the conversants together (the first minute of the first Conference) were: "1. What to teach; 2. How to teach; and 3. What to do; that is, how to regulate our doctrine, discipline and practice" (*WJW,* 8:275).

"Our doctrines" came to refer to the early editions of the Minutes, which required the preacher "To preach the *old Methodist doctrines,* and no other, as contained in the Minutes of the Conferences" (*Large Minutes, 1780,* 588). These "Doctrinal Minutes" explicated the very teachings that were central concerns of Wesley's *Sermons* and *Notes:* justification by grace through faith, atonement, assurance of pardon by the witness of the Spirit, sanctification, free grace, and holiness of heart and life (*WJW,* 8:275–339; Outler, *John Wesley,* 134–77).

If one possessed only the *Articles of Religion* without the *Minutes, Sermons,* or *Notes,* one would have general Anglican teaching without specific Methodist teaching. The *Articles of Religion* affirm what is commonly held in Protestant religion, which Wesley also clearly affirmed, such as the sufficiency of Scripture, the triune God, and justification by faith. When Wesley amended the Thirty-nine Articles in 1784, he made them align more closely to distinctive Methodist teaching. Yet these *Articles* are not the best place to discover doctrine that is distinctively Methodist, for Methodists share them with Protestantism generally. Wesley did not characteristically use the term "our doctrines" to refer to the Thirty-nine Articles, although he affirmed them (with certain preferred revisions). Rather, the phrase "our doctrines" referred to those teachings that have from the beginning characterized and distinctively defined the people called Methodists.

The *Discipline* does not attempt to make fine distinctions between four key phrases: "established standards of doctrine" (*Disc., 1984,* 659), "the doctrines of the United Methodist Church" (Ibid., 212), "our doctrines" (Ibid., 212), and "our doctrinal standards" (Ibid., 85). They are all requisite to the ministry and are required by Methodist discipline. All four phrases point to the same, not different, teachings. "Established standards of doctrine" designates the standards protected by the First Restrictive Rule of 1808. "The doctrines of the United Methodist Church" and "our doctrinal standards" are those defined and consensually assumed by the Rules. They include, but are not limited to, the *Articles of Religion.*

In 1968 the Plan of Union of the Methodist Church and the Evangelical United Brethren, the E.U.B. *Confession* of 1962 was included under the Restrictive Rules of the United Methodist Church. The *Confession* is now protected just as firmly as the other standards by the Second Restrictive Rule: "The General Conference shall not revoke, alter, or change our Confession of Faith" (*Disc., 1984,* 25). Since the status of the *Confession* is unambiguous and not presently under challenge or debate, it will not be our primary concern, though in Part Two its complete text appears in the section comparing variants of the *Articles of Religion.*

Note that doctrinal criteria for *laity* are not principally at question in the discussion of Wesleyan doctrinal standards; instead, they apply to *clergy* charged with the task of preaching. No direct doctrinal tests were prescribed for preliminary entry into the early Methodist societies. Rather, as the *General Rules* declared: "There is only one condition previously required of those who desire admission into these societies: 'a desire to flee from the wrath to come, to be saved from their sins'" (*WJW,* 8:279; *Disc., 1984,* 69). This assumed that members would manifest the seriousness of this intent by Scripture study, prayer, mutual accountability, and attendance upon the ordinances of God. Although the *General Rules* do not require of members positive subscription to a doctrinal formula, they do imply and assume doctrinal beliefs (see Tigert, *CH,* 144).

Hence our question focuses essentially upon doctrinal standards for preaching in the Wesleyan tradition: Are they textually defined? Does the traditional definition enjoy a long and uninterrupted history of consensual reception? Is this historic definition applicable today?

The thesis to be investigated: *From 1763 onward (and from 1773 on in America) it has been generally assumed by preachers throughout the connection that to preach contrary to "our doctrines" would be to preach counter to and against Wesley's teachings as defined textually in the Sermons and Notes (and after 1784, the Articles of Religion).* Do the facts warrant this conclusion?

2.

The Transplanting of Standards to America, 1773–84

The question of doctrinal standards recurs in the early documents of American Methodism from their inception in the 1770s to their constitutional settlement in 1808. A brief chronicle of key documents will recount the story of how Wesley's doctrinal standards were transplanted to America.

The doctrinal criteria of the British *Minutes* were transferred immediately and directly into the American *Minutes,* and into deeds defining the right use of Methodist properties in the United States. Evidence of this transfer may be found by examining actual deeds of this period. For example, the original deed to the John Street Methodist Church in New York City, dated November 2, 1770, provides:

> that the said person or persons, so from time to time to be chosen as aforesaid, preach no other doctrine than is contained in the said John Wesley's Notes upon the New Testament and his four volumes of Sermons (*CS,* 118–19)[1]

Similarly, the deed for the first Methodist meeting house in Philadelphia—St. George's, June 14,

1770, before John Street—contained precisely the same proviso (Neely, *DSM,* 139). Hence these doctrinal criteria remained in place, although with language revised according to changing American property laws, during the period following 1773. Borgen concludes that "The earliest deeds of record in America followed Wesley's form of 1763" (Borgen, *SDUMC,* 2).

The Pattern Set: First American Conference, 1773

The very first "query proposed to every preacher" of the first American Conference (at St. George's Church, Philadelphia, July 14, 1773) was:

> Ought not the authority of Mr. Wesley and that Conference to extend to the preachers and people in America, as well as in Great Britain and Ireland? Yes.

Second question:

> Ought not the doctrine and discipline of the Methodists, as contained in the [British] minutes, to be the sole rule of our conduct, who labor in the connection with Mr.

Wesley in America? Yes. (*MAC*, 1:5; cf. *MMC, 1773*, Q. 1, 2).

These two questions established from the outset three key principles that would enter deeply into the spirit of early American Methodism:

(1) Wesley would exercise authority within the connection as long as he would live, and the distance to America did not weaken or diminish that, so that Wesley or his authorized representatives would govern personally as Wesley did in Britain and Ireland.

(2) The doctrine taught in Europe and America was the same. Hence there was not thought to be a Methodist doctrine taught in one country distinguishable from that in another.

(3) More importantly, Methodist doctrine had a specifically defined textual basis and reference. It was defined by the received *Minutes,* which excluded from the Methodist preaching houses any preaching that was contrary to Wesley's *Sermons* and *Notes.*

The first of these three principles would be interrupted by the Revolutionary War, when anti-Tory feeling was strong and some Methodist leaders associated with Wesley were viewed as being surrogates of British influence. The other two—the principles of the doctrinal unity of the connection and the textual specification of its doctrinal standards— were sustained through and beyond the Revolutionary period without challenge.

The Status of the Minutes

The "minutes" to which the Conference of 1773 referred were the *Large Minutes* of 1770. Can it be assumed that the *Large Minutes* were actually taken with detailed seriousness by American Methodists? The rigor of these doctrinal constraints as applied to American Methodists was stressed in the third question of the Conference of 1773: "If so, does it not follow that if any preachers deviate from the minutes we can have no fellowship with them till they change their conduct? Yes" (*MAC, 1773*, Q. 3).

But was it to be supposed that every American Methodist preacher had indeed read and was prepared to follow in detail the *Large Minutes*? The injunction is exceptionally specific: "And remember! A Methodist Preacher is to mind every point, great and small, in the Methodist discipline! Therefore you will need all the sense you have, and to have all your wits about you!" (*WJW*, 8:310). Francis Asbury wrote a crucial memorandum of the first Annual Conference of 1773, which revealed the preachers' determination to hold strictly to the doctrinal standards of the *Minutes*:

The following propositions were agreed to: 1. The old Methodist doctrine and discipline shall be enforced and maintained amongst all our societies in America. 2. Any preacher who acts otherwise, can not be retained amongst us as a fellow-laborer in the vineyard (Asbury, *J&L,* 1:85).

In the same Conference of 1773, one of the rules "agreed to by all the preachers present" was: "None of the preachers in America is to reprint any of Mr. Wesley's books without the authority (when it can be gotten) and the consent of their brethren" (*MAC, 1773*, 5). This directive indicates that Wesley's writings were esteemed of such central importance in America as to require that they stand under the legal control of the Conference. In order rightly to protect and present them, they were not to be published indiscriminately, but only by Conference authorization.

Wesley sent a three-volume presentation set of his *Explanatory Notes upon the New Testament* to all American preachers attending the 1775 Conference. Frank Baker noted that "It seems quite probable that Wesley also presented them with copies of his *Sermons*" (Baker, *FWA*, 171n).

The darkest and most uncertain period of Methodist history in America was 1775–80. Following the third Annual Conference of 1775, which met at Philadelphia at the same time as the Second Continental Congress, the preachers had been put somewhat on the defensive by Wesley's publication of "A Calm Address to our American Colonies." Virtually all British-born Methodist leaders except Asbury returned to England. During much of 1778–80 Asbury was in semi-hiding in Maryland.

Phillip Gatch kept a record of the Annual Conference of 1777, which shows that under these very trying circumstances the preachers still pledged to follow the doctrine of the *Sermons* and *Notes*, "to preach the old Methodist doctrine and no other, as contained in the Minutes."[2] Among the "articles of agreement" signed by twenty-five preachers, they further pledged "to observe and enforce the whole Methodist Discipline, as laid down in the said Minutes."

Asbury remained the principal leader of American Methodism from 1773 until his death in 1816.

There is no official record at any Conference between 1773 and 1808, or in any of Asbury's journals or in the memoirs of other eyewitnesses (such as Lee, Whatcoat, or Bangs) that suggests that these early doctrinal commitments were ever overtly revoked, formally amended, or even seriously contested.

The Subscription of 1781:

To Preach the Doctrine of the Sermons, Notes, and Minutes

By the Conference of 1780, some semblance of regularity had returned to American Methodism. That Conference formalized the pivotal principle (already commonly in effect) that "all the deeds shall be drawn in substance after that in the printed [British] Minutes" (*MAC, 1780,* 12; cf. Tigert, *CH,* 113; Buckley, *CPH,* 162, 163). Tigert called this the "*earliest* recognition, in the official transactions of the American Conferences, of the doctrinal standards of Methodism. The American chapels and meetinghouses had been generally settled according to the form of the deed used in England since 1750" (*CH,* 113). This procedure required that trustees meet regularly and keep a record of their proceedings, and that every American deed should follow precisely the printed *Large Minutes,* which defined that those appointed could preach no other doctrine than that contained in Wesley's *Sermons* and *Notes.* (Tigert, *CH,* 113; see full record of the deed, 589ff.; cf. Tyerman, *Life and Times of the Rev. John Wesley,* London: Hodder, 1876, 2:478, 3:417). Tigert commented on this development:

This question is of far-reaching importance, and will come up again. Only in recent times, by those who have permitted the history to drop out of their memories, has the question been raised as to the scope and intention of that part of the first Restrictive Rule which forbids the General Conference to "establish any new standards or rule of doctrine contrary to our present existing and established standards of doctrine." For American Methodism the progress of our history will tend to establish that these standards of doctrine are (1) the Twenty-five Articles, (2) Wesley's Notes on the New Testament, and (3) his four volumes of Sermons (Tigert, *CH*, 114).

Three actions of the following Conference of 1781 indicate that if Wesley had been a liability to American Methodism during the war, he was not perceived as such following the hostilities.

First, at the top of the agenda was the question of doctrinal standards—not so much their definition (for they had already been defined), but the integrity and depth of earnest preaching and following them. The first entry in the 1781 *Minutes* reads: "Ques. 1. What preachers are now determined, after mature consideration, close observation, and earnest prayer, to preach the old Methodist doctrine, and strictly enforce the discipline as contained in the Notes, Sermons, and Minutes published by Mr. Wesley. . . ?" (*MAC, 1781,* 13). Then follows a list of preachers who answered yes: "Francis Asbury, William Watters, etc. . . ." This list is thought to have implied a formal subscription: "The thirty-nine preachers assembled in the Conference subscribed their names to an affirmative answer" (Buckley, *CPH,* 163). Curtiss agrees that the response was "signed" (*SC,*

115). Jesse Lee entered this record of the ninth Conference of 1781: "They also agreed that they would preach the old Methodist doctrine and enforce the discipline which was contained in the Notes, Sermons, and Minutes published by Mr. Wesley" (*HM,* 75). What was meant by "old Methodist doctrine" was precisely that contained in the *Notes, Sermons,* and *Minutes.*

Second, Asbury wrote in his journal of October 18, 1781: "We have come to a conclusion to print the four volumes of Mr. Wesley's Sermons" (*J&L,* 1:413). This decision meant that the Methodists had come out of the darkest period of the revolutionary conflict with their doctrinal standards intact.

Third, a supplementary level of doctrinal study—but not of the same level of legal accountability as that required by the deed—was reflected in question 8 of the 1781 *Minutes:* "Ought not the preachers often to read the 'Rules of the Societies,' the 'Character of a Methodist,' and the 'Plain Account of Christian Perfection,' if they have got them?" (*MAC, 1781,* 14). None of these items were included in the *Sermons on Several Occasions.* This conditional language suggests that the other sermons were commended as optionally additional to the normative *Sermons* and *Notes* specified in the *Minutes.*

Summary of Doctrinal Instructions to 1784

After the Peace of Paris, Wesley wrote a letter "To the Preachers in America" (sent through Jesse Lee), received at the Conference of 1783, which once again made a special point of precisely defining "Methodist doctrine and discipline" textually, so there could be no further possible doubt about his views:

1. Let all of you be determined to abide by the Methodist doctrine and discipline, published in the four volumes of *Sermons,* and the *Notes upon the New Testament,* together with the *Large Minutes* of the Conference.

2. Beware of preachers coming from Great Britain or Ireland without a full recommendation from me. . . .

3. Neither should you receive any preachers, however recommended, who will not be subject to the American Conference, and cheerfully conform to the Minutes both of the English and American Conferences. . . .

Undoubtedly the greatest danger to the work of God in America is likely to arise either from preachers coming from Europe, or from such as will arise from among yourselves speaking perverse things, or bringing in among you new doctrines, particularly Calvinism. You should guard against this with all possible care, for it is far easier to keep them out than to thrust them out (*LJW,* 7:191; Lee, *HM,* 85, 86; Bangs, *HMEC,* 1:148; Stevens, *Hist. MEC,* 2:131, 132).

Several conclusions may be drawn from this letter: (1) This action affirmed the conjoint authority of both the British and American *Minutes.*[3] This establishes that the textual norm for established standards of doctrine (*Sermons, Notes, Minutes*) in the British and American connections was precisely the same and could not be viewed as distinguishable. (2) The formula was now positively stated—to "abide by the

doctrine published in"—rather than the negative syntax of the Model Deed that "persons preach no other doctrine than is contained" in the *Sermons* and *Notes.* (3) The rigor of the directive is extraordinary; it is not conceivably interpretable in a latitudinarian direction. (4) Exclusion from the connection was the result of rejecting these established doctrinal standards.

Asbury confirmed this in his journal entry for Christmas Eve, 1783: "Here I received a letter from Mr. Wesley, in which he directs me to act as general assistant, and to receive no preachers from Europe that are not recommended by him; nor any in America who will not submit to me and to the Minutes of the Conference" (*Journal,* 1:363; cf. Tigert, *CH,* 134; Neely, *GCM,* 210).

More crucially, in April and May of 1784, the twelfth Conference (held at Ellis's Chapel, Virginia, and Baltimore) set forth four specific provisos under which European preachers could be accredited: "If they [1] are recommended by Mr. Wesley, [2] will be subject to the American Conference, [3] preach the doctrine taught in the four volumes of Sermons and Notes on the New Testament, and [4] be subject to Francis Asbury as general assistant, whilst he stands approved by Mr. Wesley and the Conference, we shall receive them; but if they walk contrary to the above directions, no ancient right or appointment shall prevent their being excluded from our connection" (*MAC,* 1785, 21, numbers inserted).

The Spring Conference of 1784 instructed circuits to "read one of Mr. Wesley's Sermons" in the absence of a preacher (*Minutes,* 1784, sec. 17). It also directed preachers to "read the Scriptures, with Wesley's Notes" (Ibid., sec. 18).

Summarizing thus far, on five occasions between 1773 and 1784, supported by unambiguous documentation, the established standards of doctrine were clearly and textually defined as Wesley's *Sermons* and *Notes*: (1) the Conference of 1773, (2) the Conference of 1780, (3) the Subscription of 1781, (4) Wesley's letter to the Conference of 1783, and (5) the Conference of May, 1784. All of these documents, criteria, and actions were well known to American preachers when they met at the Christmas Conference in 1784.

If there had been some rescinding or amendment of these standards in the period from 1784 to 1808, one would expect to find some record of it. There is no record of it whatever, either in Conference minutes or private memoirs; and furthermore, there is no record of any debate that would indicate these established standards were under challenge or even being questioned.

Articles of Religion Added to Established Doctrinal Standards:

The Founding Conference,
Christmas, 1784

By 1784 Wesley submitted his plan for the reorganization of American Methodism. He was eighty-one, and there was no time for delay. The appeals were urgent for American clergy who could baptize and administer the Lord's Supper, since most of the Church of England clergy had left during the War.

The *Articles of Religion,* which Wesley revised from the Thirty-nine Anglican Articles, were recommended and accepted by the American Conference and later became bound into the constitution (an article-by-article analysis is in Part Two). The Christmas Conference of 1784 received twenty-four articles from Wesley, accepted them as standards for the new church, and added to them a twenty-fifth (numbered 23 in the final arrangement), which affirmed the sovereignty and independence of the United States of America.

The *Articles* sought to define, not the doctrine that distinguished Methodism from Protestantism generally, but that which was held in common with Reformation teaching, especially in its Anglican-Arminian form. Coke and Asbury, in an early advocacy of ecumenism, commended these *Articles of Religion* as describing doctrines which were "maintained more or less, in part or whole, by every reformed church in the world" (*Disc., 1798,* Notes, Preface).

A service book was at the same time prepared by Wesley for the American Methodists; this revision of the *Book of Common Prayer* was entitled, *The Sunday Service of the Methodists in North America, with Other Occasional Services* (London: 1784). Richard Whatcoat, Thomas Coke, and Thomas Vassey brought the *Articles* and *Sunday Service* with them in loose sheets to the Baltimore Conference of 1784. This edition of the *Articles* included the twenty-four articles that Wesley had reduced from the Thirty-nine. The second edition (London: Frys and Couchman, 1786) had the twenty-fifth article added by the American Conference, concerning obligation to American civil authority.

Among Wesley's notable amendments of the *Book of Common Prayer* were his omission of the Office of

Confirmation and his changing of the terms *priest* and *bishop* to *elder* and *superintendent*. Whatcoat's memoirs recorded: "We agreed to form a Methodist Episcopal Church, in which the Liturgy, as presented by the Reverend John Wesley should be read and the Sacraments be administered by a superintendent, elders and deacons, who shall be ordained by a presbytery using the episcopal form as prescribed in the rear of Mr. Wesley's Prayer Book" (*A Short Account*, 1806; cf. Tigert, *CH*, 44). Although the reading of prayers soon was bypassed by the anti-formalism of American Methodism,[4] nonetheless eight offices of the service book would be largely retained by regular American usage: the Service of Holy Communion, Baptism (infant and adult), Matrimony, Burial of the Dead, and three services of Ordination. The *Discipline* of 1792 contained amended offices taken from the *Sunday Service*.

Strong internal evidence in Wesley's *Articles of Religion* indicates that he did not intend for the Twenty-five Articles to substitute for the *Sermons* and *Notes*, but to supplement them. This point was shrewdly intuited by Abel Stevens but now deserves sharpening:

In omitting certain articles from the Thirty-nine, Wesley "eliminates the supposed Anglican Calvinism, but he does not introduce his own Arminianism" (Stevens, *HMEC*, 2:208). Only if one takes the premise that Wesley assumed that his *Sermons* and *Notes* would continue to be viewed as normative by Methodists does this decision make sense. For there was no need to state in the *Articles* what was already so clearly stated in the *Sermons* and *Notes*— namely, the doctrines of the witness of the Spirit and Christian perfection. If, however, Wesley had considered the twenty-four articles to be a substitute for the *Sermons* and *Notes,* it is reasonable to suppose that he would have taken an entirely different stance by amending the articles along these lines. For "no doctrines more thoroughly permeate the preaching, or more entirely characterize the moral life, of Methodism than his opinions of the universal salvability of man, assurance, and sanctification" (Ibid., 1:209).

Hence we conclude that neither Wesley nor the American preachers thought of the *Articles of Religion* as discontinuing the force of the *Sermons* and *Notes*. " 'Our Articles of Religion' were superadded to 'our present existing and established standards of doctrine' at the Christmas Conference of 1784" (Wheatley, *MQR*, 1883, 32).

Complementarity of the Articles, Homilies, and Prayerbook

Note these analogies: Wesley's *Articles, Sermons,* and *Sunday Service* stood in broad analogy and correspondence to the Anglican Thirty-nine *Articles, Homilies,* and *Book of Common Prayer*. Viewed schematically:

Anglican Practice:	Articles	Anglican Homilies	Prayerbook
Methodist Practice:	Articles	Wesley's Sermons/ Notes	Sunday Service

Hence if one of these three were abstracted from the rest, as if one could select the Anglican *Articles* and omit the *Homilies,* that would skew the balance of sources received and transmuted from the Anglican tradition. Similarly, if one selected only the Twenty-five Articles and omitted the *Sermons, Notes,* and *Sunday Service,* the threefold structure would fall into imbalance.

In Wesley's own theological development, the Edwardian-Elizabethan *Homilies* and *Book of Common Prayer* were probably more persistently influential than the Thirty-nine Articles. In Wesley's writings, the *Articles* were less often quoted than the *Homilies* or *Prayerbook,* but they remained acknowledged doctrinal boundaries for him. It is to these *Articles* that he assented *ex animo* (from the soul, earnestly) in receiving his Anglican orders.

In American Methodism, the *Sermons* and *Notes* have exerted far more pervasive influence on preaching than have the *Articles.* Phrases from Wesley's *Sermons* are familiar to lifelong Methodists ("If your heart is as my heart, give me your hand"; "the almost Christian"; "plain truth for plain people"; "scriptural Christianity"; "give all you can"; "prevenient grace"; etc.). But few can quote a line from the *Articles of Religion.* Yet the *Articles* have remained uncontested doctrinal standards consistently throughout American Methodist history after 1784.

The post-Revolutionary American Methodists viewed themselves as heirs of the Episcopal Church tradition in a period in which Anglican sacraments were almost nowhere to be found, since Episcopal ministers had largely fled this country during and after the Revolution. Abel Stevens wrote:

> The Methodist bishops were the first Protestant bishops, and Methodism the first Protestant Episcopal Church of the New World; and as Mr. Wesley had given it the Anglican articles of religion (omitting the seventeenth, on predestination), and the liturgy, wisely abridged, it became, both by its precedent organization and its subsequent numerical importance, the real successor to the Anglican Church in America (Stevens, *Hist. MEC,* 2:215).

Since the Episcopal Church had very nearly disappeared after the Revolution, and hence "there then existed in America no organized Episcopal Church from which to separate" (Tigert, *CH,* 207, exaggerating), the American Methodists after 1784 had some reasonable claim to viewing themselves as the bearers of the Episcopal Church tradition in America. Hence they denominated themselves the Methodist Episcopal Church, assuming that *Episcopal* is the genus and *Methodist* the species (Ibid., 205ff.).

This correlation reinforces the telling parallelism that makes clearer the crucial role of the *Articles:* Wesley's *Articles of Religion* stood in direct continuity with and succession to the Anglican Articles, just as the *Sunday Service* was successor to the *Book of Common Prayer.* Something would be notably missing in this picture if the *Articles* and *Sunday Service* were accepted and the *Sermons* omitted or rejected. There would be no American Methodist complement or successor to the Edwardian-Elizabethan *Homilies*.

Two books of *Homilies* were issued by the Church of England—in the reigns of Edward VI and Elizabeth I.[5] They provided for the clergy sermonic models for preaching along the lines of the English Reformation. Authorized by the Convocation of 1542, the twelve homilies of the first book were collected and edited by Thomas Cranmer, who wrote several of them. Revoked by Mary, they were reinstituted by Elizabeth and included with the second book, written chiefly by John Jewel and published in 1562–63. Just as the Anglican homilies provided a sermonic model for addressing key themes of Protestant theology, Wesley's *Sermons* (e.g., "Salvation by Faith," "Original Sin," "Scriptural Christianity," "The Righteousness of Faith," and "The Law Established Through Faith") served a similar purpose for Methodist theology, being enriched by Wesley's special attention to teachings especially laid upon the Methodists.

This stands as corroborating evidence for our central premise. It makes the argument less convincing that the *Sermons* and *Notes* were abruptly separated or detached from the body of Methodist teaching during this period between the Founding Conference (1784) and the Constitutional Conference (1808). They were all the more urgently needed, not only to fill out the lacuna that would have been left in analogy to the *Homilies,* but also because they had been firmly established for two decades as the "old Methodist doctrine" that stood in continuity with and as a complementary Wesleyan version of Anglican teaching.

Nothing in the record would suggest that the *Articles of Religion* were intended to uproot or supplant previous doctrinal standards of American Methodism (i.e., the *Sermons* and *Notes*). Rather, the *Articles* were added to prevailing standards of 1773–84; the *Articles* supplied the American Methodists with a document that would perform a function analogous to the Anglican Articles, just as the *Sunday Service* provided a liturgy grounded in the *Book of Common Prayer.*

How did these three sources (*Articles, Sermons,* and *Notes*) in time come to complement each other so as to form an integral pattern? Nathaniel Burwash propounded a memorable formula that reveals a rich complementary cohesiveness, probably intuited or implied by Wesley from the outset: The *Sermons* constitute the STANDARD OF PREACHING, the *Notes* the STANDARD OF INTERPRETATION, and the *Articles* the STANDARD OF UNITY with the churches of the Reformation (*WDS*, xi).

In only one special context were the *Articles* arguably treated as separable from the *Sermons* and *Notes,* and that for a very good reason. It was in the case of *trial* of ministers, where the church needed a concise text for legal accountability, much shorter than the *Sermons* and *Notes.* There is no evidence that any early Methodist figure desired to stretch the usefulness of the *Articles* into a fully adequate doctrinal model for Methodist preaching. Aside from this one point—trial (to be thoroughly examined later)—there were no instances in constitutional Methodism in which the *Articles* were viewed as standing alone, apart from the "old Methodist doctrines."

In all of these documents, Scripture was regarded by Wesley and the preachers as the primary source of doctrine. In his preface to the *Sermons,* Wesley depicted himself as *homo unius libri (WJW,* 5:3). He sought to "try every Church and every doctrine by the Bible" *(LJW,* 3:172). He considered his *Explanatory Notes upon the New Testament* (1754) to be a help for ordinary readers to hear the divine address in and through Scripture in the service of preaching.

Did the American Conference Become Doctrinally Alienated From Wesley?

Was there evidence of such tension between Wesley and the American preachers as to warrant some discontinuity in established doctrinal standards? The recent contention that the *Sermons* and *Notes* were not retained as binding doctrinal standards after 1784 hinges on the assumption that there were encumbering differences between Wesley and the American preachers that affected not only polity but doctrine. To respond to that case, it is necessary to consider carefully this relationship.

Wesley's plan for the future of American Methodism was clearly spelled out in a letter to the American Methodists, which set forth his case for ordination of ministers who would care for the special needs of American Methodists, which differed so widely from those in England, where the sacraments of the Anglican Church were readily available:

Bristol, September 10, 1784

To "Our Brethren in North America,"

. . . the case is widely different between England and North America. Here there are bishops who have legal jurisdiction; in America there are none, neither any parish ministers; so that for some hundred miles together there is none either to baptize or to administer the Lord's Supper. Here, therefore, my scruples are at an end. . . . As our American brethren are now totally disentangled both from the State and from the English hierarchy, we dare not entangle them again either with the one or the other. They are now at full liberty simply to follow the Scriptures and the primitive Church, and we judge it best that they should stand fast in that liberty wherewith God has so strangely made them free. John Wesley *(LJW,* 7:238, 239).

There are two ways of interpreting this. Most early Methodist historians (Thomas Ware, Freeborn Garretson, Nathan Bangs, et al.) viewed it as Wesley's intention at this stage to liberate the American Methodists from "entanglements" with the Anglican hierarchy. Hence they believe he intended, desired, approved, directed, and rejoiced in the founding of the Methodist Episcopal Church in 1784. They stress both Wesley's personal initiative in the founding and the shared desire for unity of doctrine and discipline by both Wesley and the American Conference of preachers. Others, however, stress the American initiative in breaking away from Wesley, the relative impotence and resignation of Wesley, and an embittered struggle for independence. Thus, they see an analogy between the American Revolution and the Christmas Conference. Wesley's letter of September 10, 1784 (quoted above) seems more to support the former opinion.

The degree of alienation between Wesley and the American Conferences impinges indirectly upon the issue of doctrinal definition. For if one assumes the American Methodists were profoundly alienated from Wesley, it is easier to argue that they might have circumvented, shelved, or reduced his *Sermons* and *Notes* from binding doctrinal authority sometime between 1784 and 1808. But if one sees this relation as occasionally strained on polity but never on doctrine, as the written record seems to indicate, then such an argument is implausible.

The Conference record shows that both factors—Wesley's commendation and the Conference's self-determination—were significant elements in the decisions of the organizing Conference of 1784:

> Therefore, at this Conference we formed ourselves into an independent Church, and *following the counsel of Mr. John Wesley,* who recommended the episcopal mode of Church government, we thought it best to become an Episcopal Church, making the episcopal office elective, and the elected superintendent or bishop amenable to the body of ministers and preachers (*MAC,* 1785, 22, italics added).

The synergism between Wesley and the Conference was also demonstrated in Asbury's insistence that he could accept Wesley's proposal that he be ordained only if it were approved by a called meeting of Methodist preachers.[6] By this means, Asbury transmuted the ethos of American Methodism by shifting authority from Wesley's personal direction *only* to the synergism of Wesley *and* the Conference of preachers in concord, as long as he lived.

Considerable evidence attests the view that Wesley affirmed the development of a separate Methodist Episcopal Church in America. This stands against the more recent view that the creation of a separate Methodist Church in America never gained Wesley's consent or that the Methodist preachers had to struggle vigorously against Wesley in order to achieve it. Numerous memoirs of eyewitnesses clarify this delicate point:

1. One of the attending preachers in 1784, William Watters, recorded this memoir: "We formed ourselves into a separate Church. This change was *proposed to us by Mr. Wesley* after we had *craved his advice* on the subject; but could not take effect till adopted by us. . . ."[7]

2. Eyewitness Thomas Ware thought that the intent of the Conference was to "receive and follow the advice of Mr. Wesley."

3. Freeborn Garretson stated even more candidly: "I am fully of the opinion that the Christmas Conference was authorized by Mr. Wesley, to organize themselves under an episcopal form of church government. . . . I doubt not but that we followed his wishes to a punctilio."[8]

4. Coke and Asbury's notes to the *Discipline* reflect the same theme: "The late Rev. John Wesley recommended the episcopal form to his societies in America."[9]

The "Binding Minute":
Union Grounded on Connection With Wesley

The most important doctrinal decision of the Christmas Conference was in fact its first decision. Its placement in the order of minutes indicates its exceptional importance. It was the "Binding Minute" of the Christmas Conference—a decisive, risk-laden act of loyalty to Wesleyan doctrine among American Methodists. According to this "Binding Minute" at the outset of the 1784 Founding Conference (Question 2), the preachers publicly avowed their continuing indebtedness and loyalty to Wesley and their rigorous determination to maintain doctrinal union between Methodists of Europe and America. Notice their unequivocal language:

> What can be done in order to the future Union of the Methodists? A. During the Life of the Rev. Mr. Wesley, we acknowledge ourselves his Sons in the Gospel, ready *in Matters belonging to Church-government,* to obey his Commands. And we do engage after his Death, to do every Thing that we judge consistent with the Cause of Religion in America and the political Interests of these States, to preserve and promote our Union with the Methodists in *Europe.*[10]

Wheatley remarked: "Could their engagement 'to preserve and promote union with Methodists of Europe' be construed in any other sense than that of continuous adherence to 'our established standards of doctrine'?" Could this pledge have been "voluntarily made by those heroic and truthful men if they had not intended to embrace doctrinal matters within its scope?" (*MQR, 1883,* 38; cf. Curtiss, *SC,* 117). Three years later, this "Binding Minute" would become the source of controversy, but not concerning any aspect of doctrine. Rather, it would be a controversy over Conference rights.

Hence it is hazardous to argue that the Founding Conference overturned Wesley's long-established doctrinal standards. Lacking evidence, such an assertion can only be a matter of remote speculation. To the contrary, the record of this Conference shows that preachers were specifically urged to "Be active in dispensing Mr. Wesley's Books" (*CH,* 27), and this minute was retained in subsequent issues of the *Discipline* from 1784 to 1808.

The direct use of Wesley's writings is clearly evidenced in the early Conference Minutes. For example, the *Minutes* of 1785 included a verbatim reprint of Wesley's account of the rise of Methodism, which would reappear in revised form in Methodist *Disciplines* until 1948. The 1787 *Discipline* contained sections by Wesley "Against Antinomianism" (Sec. 16) and "On Perfection" (Sec. 22).

The intense interconnectedness of the British and American Conferences even after the Revolution is seen in the fact that the American *Discipline* of 1786 was printed in England under Wesley's direction!

> Coke also took to England the American Minutes and they were printed on a press which Wesley used, and under his own eye. The Baltimore proceedings were therefore known to Wesley, but we hear of no remonstrance from him. They soon became known, by the Minutes, to the public: and when Coke was attacked publicly for what he had done, he replied, as we have seen, through the press, that "he had done nothing but under the direction of Mr. Wesley." Wesley never denied it (Stevens, *Hist.*

MEC, 2:227; cf. Bangs, HMEC, 2:191).

The opinion that the American preachers were at this time giving determined resistance to Wesley's leadership is a view that has been repeatedly espoused for over a century, perhaps first by Alexander M'Caine, who was answered in 1827 by Bishop John Emory: "But if he can believe that the omission [of an account of Wesley's death in the American Minutes] resulted from 'contempt' of Mr. Wesley we must leave him to enjoy his opinion. The adoption of such a sentiment requires a strong predisposition, and desire to believe it."[11] The argument that "Wesley never intended to originate an American General Conference" (Tigert, CH, 71) was successfully challenged by T. A. Kerley (CR, 74–83). Bishop Emory further countered M'Caine's assertion:

> Now there is every reason to believe that Mr. Whatcoat had a correct acquaintance with the intentions of Mr. Wesley; and when Dr. Coke stated the design of forming the Methodists in America into an "independent Episcopal Church," if Mr. Whatcoat knew that this was contrary to Mr. Wesley's intentions, it was his duty to express it. The universally admitted character of Mr. Whatcoat is a sufficient guarantee that he would have done so.[12]

The Legal Principle of Non-Abrogation and Its Doctrinal Relevance

The legal principle of non-abrogation impinges upon this discussion. It states that *laws not repealed are laws in force:*

The Church in 1784 was organized with these expressions as a part of her law, and so continued to 1808, when they were in fact reenacted. Hence these became standards of doctrine in the Methodist Episcopal Church. In order for these laws in force in American Methodism, when it was organized independently, to become null and void, it was necessary to repeal them by a distinct act. Until so repealed, they would be laws of the Church. This follows all legal analogy. Now, who can show that at any time, from then to this time, they were repealed, or any attempt ever made to repeal them? Since there is no record of such an act, it is enough for us to say, they have *not been repealed*. They stand to-day as the real standards of the Methodist Episcopal Church in doctrine (Curtiss, SC, 115–16).

Richard Wheatley accurately formulated this pivotal legal principle, upon which the continuity of any doctrinal tradition must be based:

> All laws imposed by rightful authority are valid until repealed by rightful authority; and *as the law repeatedly accepting certain specified writings of Mr. Wesley as the doctrinal standards of American Methodism has never been repealed, it follows that they must be such at the present day* (MQR, 1883, 37).

This maxim remains a familiar rule of law:

> The principle which obtains in the State and Federal Courts, by which the British laws in force in the Colonies at the time of the assumption and Declaration of Independence of the Colonies shall be in force in the new condition of the States, until altered and amended or repealed by subsequent legislation.

Such a principle is sound legal doctrine. It is also equally sound ecclesiastical doctrine (Curtiss, *SC,* 106–7).

By this rule it becomes unnecessary for the Congress to re-pass every previous bit of legislation every year. Accordingly, the actions of Conference of 1773, 1781, and of May and December of 1784 "have been acknowledged as legal by the tacit consent and by the uniform procedure of their successors. Their enactments in relation to the essentials of Methodist doctrine and discipline have neither been repealed nor virtually annulled by antagonistic legislation" (Wheatley, *MQR, 1883,* 37). On this decisive principle of non-abrogation, Wheatley and Curtiss have been followed by the mainstream of leading interpreters (Harrison, Wheeler, Tigert, Buckley, Neely, Lewis, and Outler).

The preface to the first separate edition of the Articles stated: "These are the doctrines taught among the people called Methodists. Nor is there any doctrine whatever, generally received among the people, *contrary to* the articles now before you" (italics added). Accordingly, the *Sermons* and *Notes* were not judged *contrary to* the Articles. This commendation of the Articles, far from putting in question the "old Methodist doctrines" (*Sermons* and *Notes*), sought to show that the Articles were not contrary to these already existing standards.

3.

The Maintenance of Established Standards of Doctrine, 1785–1808

If the standards defined in 1763 were still firmly in place after the Christmas Conference of 1784, what happened thereafter? If it could be shown that between 1785 and 1808 these standards were gradually eroded or rejected by some formal action, then it could more easily be argued that the constitution of 1808 did not place the *Sermons* and *Notes* on a par with the *Articles of Religion*.

The Discipline of 1785

The more obvious reason that we know the *Sermons* and *Notes* were not neglected, relegated, or rejected as doctrinal standards in 1784 is that the American *Discipline* of 1785 itself made numerous references commending Mr. Wesley's *Sermons* and *Notes*. Among specific instances, here are two examples:

> We advise you . . . from five to six in the Evening, to meditate, pray, and read, partly the Scripture with Mr. *Wesley's* Notes, partly the closely practical Parts of what he had published. . . . Frequently read and enlarge upon a portion of the Notes (*Disc.*, *1785*, quoted by Tigert, *CH*, 562, 567).

Again:

> Searching the Scriptures, by (1) Reading; *constantly*, some Part of every day; *regularly*, all the Bible in order; *carefully*, with Mr. *Wesley's* Notes . . . (Ibid., 576; for the *Discipline's* similar references to themes of Wesley's sermons, see *CH*, 535, 548, 550, 585; and for references to Wesley's writings generally, *CH*, 562, 600.)

It seems unlikely that a document that commends such diligent study of the *Notes* could be at the same time deliberately rejecting them as doctrinal standards.

Wesley's Model Deed of 1763 mandated that *Sermons* and *Notes* be used to determine the doctrinal adequacy of any Methodist preacher (*WJW*, 8:331). Heitzenrater believes the Model Deed was intentionally omitted from the 1785 *Discipline* as a signal that the post-Revolutionary American Methodists did not accept the *Sermons* and *Notes* as legal standards.[1] Yet the principal reason for the omission of Wesley's Model Deed from the *Discipline* of 1785 lies in the transitional nature of deed-making in the emergent post-Revolutionary American political situation. It has nothing whatever to do with amending doctrinal standards. Recall that each state had its own property laws. The Anglican or Congregational Church remained the tax-supported church in some states, compounding the confusion, and these "establishment issues" were not to be settled quickly. The property laws of various states required deeds dissimilar in form to the original Model Deed. It required some years for the dust to settle and the legal environment to become more stable. During this post-revolutionary interim, it was probably impossible for any single deed to apply to many state property laws, themselves in transition.

Moreover, the deed in the *Large Minutes* had numerous references obviously not pertinent, and probably offensive, in the newly emergent United States. For example, the British deed required that property claims be filed with New Stamps, quite different from the process of legal filing required by U.S. courts. The British deed was drawn up by London lawyers, using language and protocols of British chancery, which were viewed as inappropriate in the post-Revolutionary setting.

Frank Baker attributes no doctrinal rejection to these omissions. Rather, he argues that haste contributed to the omissions: "The early neglect of these two 'standards' [*Sermons* and *Notes*] does not seem to have been deliberate, but the result of the hasty preparation of the 1785 *Discipline* from Wesley's large *Minutes* of 1780—the reference to them was buried in a clause in the lengthy Model Deed, which was not reproduced" (*FWA*, 170).

It is stretching the case to argue

from silence that the simple absence of the Wesleyan standards in the Model Deed constitutes a direct disapproval of them or withholding of approval from them; nor does it necessarily imply a permanent, deliberate, and conscious rejection of standards specified in the deed.

Doctrinal Changes Disavowed

Most crucial for our narrative: Four years after the Christmas Conference, the Conference of 1788 officially served notice that its doctrine had not changed. The 1788 Conference declared that it had taken actions "such as *affect not in any degree the essentials of our doctrines*" (*MMC, 1788*, italics added).

American Methodist preachers before 1784 had long been bound to the clear rule that they "preach no other Doctrine than is contained in Mr. Wesley's Notes upon the New Testament, and four Volumes of Sermons" (*WJW*, 8:331; Tigert, *CH*, 591). It is difficult to imagine that any American Methodist preacher in 1784 could have been ignorant of that standard. Indeed, there is substantial evidence to refute the conclusion that American Methodists thought their doctrines were significantly different in content from the British counterparts. Numerous resolutions from General Conferences stressed that "Wesleyan Methodism is one everywhere—one in its doctrine, its disciplines, its usages" (Bangs, *HMEC*, 3:259, cf. 115ff.). Thomas B. Neely accurately summarized the continuity in doctrinal standards in the period following 1784:

Those who organized the new Church already had standards of doctrine which they had accepted, and to which they were committed, and these standards were the Wesleyan Standards contained in Wesley's Fifty-two Sermons, Wesley's Notes on the new Testament, the Minutes, and we may say, the General Rules, which all recognized. . . . It is plain that the reorganizers carried over with them their existing and continuing doctrinal convictions, and, unless there was some action to the contrary, their accepted doctrines and standards of doctrine went with them into their reorganization.

The fact is that, in the organizing Conference, there was no formal or informal repudiation, or discarding of their old doctrines. There was no action of any kind doing away with their old doctrinal standards, and there was no informal action that could be construed as an abandonment of their Wesleyan doctrines which they had had from the beginning (*DSM,* 154).

When, in the Conference of 1787, Wesley's name was temporarily removed from the *Minutes* and reinserted in 1789 (see accounts of the "Binding Minute" by Neely, *GCM,* 281ff., and Buckley, *CPH,* 56ff.), the issue was not in any sense over doctrine, but over church government or, as Asbury thought, over "Mr. Wesley's absolute authority over the American Connection. . . . The Americans were too jealous to bind themselves to yield to him in all things relative to Church government. Mr. Wesley was a man they had never seen—was three thousand miles off; how might submission in such a case be expected?" (Neely, *GCM,* 289, 290). Coke had held that the "Binding Minute" of 1784 obligated the Conference to approve Wesley's nomination of Whatcoat as joint superintendent with Asbury, a move opposed by most preachers. Asbury candidly declared:

I never approved of that binding minute. I did not think it practical expediency to obey Mr. Wesley, at three thousand miles distance, *in all matters relative to Church government;* neither did Brother Whatcoat, or several others. At the first General Conference I was mute and modest when it passed, and I was mute when it was expunged. For this Mr. Wesley blamed me, and was displeased that I did not rather reject the whole connection, or leave them, if they did not comply. But I could not give up the connection so easily, after laboring so many years with and for them (Asbury, *J&L,* 2:106, italics added).

The controversy over the "Binding Minute" hinged essentially upon the extent to which the American Conference was directly reportable to Wesley in explicit details concerning church governance; but there is no evidence that the controversy was about doctrinal definition, as some have supposed.[2] Asbury specifically rejected the view that the striking of the minute implied "a rejection of Mr. Wesley" (*J&L,* 2:106). The *Minutes* of 1789 further clarified the relationship of Wesley to the Conference: "*Question 1.* Who are the persons that exercise the *episcopal office* in the Methodist Church in Europe and America? *Answer.* John Wesley, Thomas Coke, Francis Asbury" (*MAC, 1790,* 36; cf. Neely, *GCM,* 296ff.; Tigert, *CHAEM,* 234ff.). Jesse Lee's record here adds: "by regular order and succession" (*HM,* 142).

The *Discipline* of 1789 did not hesitate to acknowledge John Wesley as one who "under God, has been the father of the great revival of religion now extending over the earth by the means of the Methodists" (*Disc., 1789*, 3). This language would be repeated in the *Disciplines* of 1790 and 1791. In the "Notes" written by Coke and Asbury for the *Discipline* of 1798, which were prepared on request of the General Conference of 1796 and reconfirmed by the General Conference of 1800, the encomium toward Wesley would increase. They regarded him as "The most respectable divine since the primitive ages, if not since the time of the apostles" (*Disc., 1798*, 7). This does not sound like the language of those who had just circumvented Wesley's standards of doctrine.

The Corresponding British Pattern

A slightly revised Chapel Model Deed that preserved the textual specification of the doctrinal standards of the 1763 deed and followed its essential principles was adopted by British Methodism in 1832. The revision came to be employed as a Reference Deed, from which various model deeds of British branches of Methodism derived their pattern (Methodist New Connection in 1846; Bible Christians in 1863; United Methodist Free Churches in 1842 and 1865; and Primitive Methodists in 1864). When the united church evolved in 1932, it was on the basis of the "essential similarity of the Trust Deeds," which preserved the doctrinal and connectional unity of British Methodism from Wesley's time. John Lawson concisely summarized the legal status of the British deeds in relation to doc-

trinal standards since 1832 and showed their profound relevance for ministry:

The Methodist Conference of 1832 adopted the "Chapel Model Deed," to be used henceforth for all Methodist Chapels. This contained: (i) an account of the origin and constitution of Methodism; (ii) detailed provisions for the government of the property by the Trustees in accordance with the rules of the Conference. . . .

The purpose of these arrangements was: (i) to secure that Methodist Trusts should everywhere be drawn up on a uniform and approved plan, and that the Trustees be bound to administer them on behalf of the whole Methodist Church, in accordance with Methodist law; (ii) to secure legal power to exclude from ministerial office any person not recognized by Conference as a Minister; (iii) to secure legal power to exclude from Methodist pulpits any person holding opinions alien to the genius of Methodism; (iv) to secure that if in any local Church a discontented section wishes to sever itself from the Methodist Church as a whole, and from Conference, it shall not have the power to take possession of the trust property. To have these considerable legal powers in reserve is a valuable and necessary factor in maintaining the life of our Church as an ordered Connexion. When other branches of Methodism came into existence they adopted various model deeds of their own, for the same purpose of safeguarding connexional discipline. At Methodist Union provision was made in the Methodist Union Act, 1932, for a New Model Deed. In line with the long tradition of our Church, this repeats the clause regarding Wesley's Sermons and Notes. These circumstances are the basis of the rule of our Church, that all preachers shall read, and give general approval of, the Notes on the New Testament and Wesley's Sermons. It is hoped that this explanation will help the young preacher to feel that this reading which is set him is no mere formality, no dull piece of hide-bound tradition. It is an integral part of a discipline which admirably expresses a very vital spiritual principle, namely, that the Church is one cohesive body with a definite witness. Every member owes allegiance to one Lord and one Faith, and to every other member.[3]

The Deed of Settlement:
General Conference of 1796

Four doctrinally-conserving actions were taken by the General Conference of 1796 that sustained established doctrinal standards and resisted their amendment:

1. Their first action was to reassure all American Methodists that *no doctrinal changes* had been made and that, however the disciplinary language had been prudently readjusted for the American situation, its intent was not to alter doctrine. This was the third time (1784, 1788, and now in 1796) since the founding of American Methodism that such official Conference assurances had been articulated.

The language of its Prefatory Address to Members was so distinctively Wesleyan that it could hardly have been referring exclusively to the *Articles of Religion* as its standard:

We can truly say that we have been *fearful of making alterations*. We have made none which we do not believe to be highly necessary, or evidently useful. . . . Our grand object is to raise and preserve *a holy and united* people. *Holiness* is our aim (*JGC, 1796,* 7, italics added).

Note that the *Articles* contained no reference to the doctrines of holiness. If the *Articles* were not the only doctrinal standards assumed in 1796, then the only other plausible standards or rules to which they could have referred were Wesley's *Sermons* and *Notes.* The Preamble further stressed: "We think we have been as cautious as the nature of our case will admit, *to prevent hasty innovations*" (Ibid., italics added).

2. Immediately following this reassurance, the second action taken was to provide a revised plan for "a deed of settlement"—the standardized, legal, post-Revolutionary American version of the Model Deed. It was a legal instrument enabling properties to be set aside for one particular use: Methodist preaching. We are given additional insight into the deed's purpose by two further actions that were taken by the same Conference:

3. The Conference of 1796 specifically appended to the deed of settlement an explanation of its meaning. There it became clear that the central purpose of the "general deed for the settlement of our preaching houses" is to maintain "The *union* of the Methodist society" (Ibid., 15, italics added). The concept of "union" of the Wesleyan connection cannot be separated from doctrinal considerations. *The union was in order to preserve the doctrinal teaching, not vice versa.* Hence the stated purpose of union already presupposed the existence of doctrinal standards. Although the trustees were to be granted the right to mortgage, buy, and sell, the surveil-

ling of doctrine and appointment of ministers remained in the hands, not of local trustees, but of the Conferences: "But the preservation of our union, the progress of the work of God indispensably require that the free and full use of the pulpit should be in the hands of the General Conference and the yearly conferences authorized by them" (Ibid.).

The "rules and discipline" to which the deed of settlement bound the trustees at that time had long assumed that no preacher could join the connection without agreeing to "abide by the Methodist doctrine and discipline published in the four volumes of sermons and the notes" (*MMC, 1783*; see Lee, *HM,* 85).

In this official explanation we learn the key to the 1796 deed: The writers feared that the deed might be rejected in the courts if it was unnecessarily detailed (*JGC, 1796,* 15, 16). For these reasons, the attorneys and deed-writers chose a simpler, parsimonious form of writing the deed, rather than a more elaborate one. Their purpose was not to change doctrine but to write a deed that could be accepted uniformly in the courts of various states—no easy matter. The key phrase that encompassed this simplicity was "according to the rules and discipline" of the church.

Our contention is that those rules, insofar as they implied standards of doctrine, were never changed, amended, or abrogated after their earliest specification in 1763, the *Articles* being added to them in 1784. In order to prove that the deed rejected the *Sermons* and *Notes,* one would have to show in the record of the "rules and discipline" of the church some indication that these

crucial rules (so decisive that they repeatedly headed the agenda of minutes) had been at some point abrogated.

This deed of settlement became further embedded in church law by the following instruction incorporated in the 1820 *Discipline,* concerning church deeds: "That from this date no house of worship under our charge shall be built, or the building commenced, until the site or ground on which such house or houses are to be located is secured to the church as our deed of settlement directs, and said deed is legally executed" (Bangs, *HMEC,* 3:139). Accordingly, it was assumed (though not explicitly stated) that trustees would surveil preaching so that nothing contrary to "our doctrines" would be allowed, just as they had prior to 1796.

4. Intrinsically connected with the promulgation of this deed, the Conference of 1796 made a telling point once again of underscoring its *doctrinal unity with British Methodism.* The Conference included in its minutes an "Address of the British Conference to the General Conference of the People Called Methodists in America." The printed record of the General Conference conveys this message clearly: "We see an absolute necessity of strictly adhering to our first principles, by firmly maintaining our original doctrines" (*JGC, 1796,* 9). These could be no other than those textually specified as the *Sermons* and *Notes.* "Herein, we doubt not you are like minded with us. . . . We trust, dear brethren, that you will join us in frequently calling to mind our original design" (Ibid., 9–10).

The Doctrinal Tracts Incorporated With the Discipline, 1788–1808

This still leaves at issue the status of doctrinal tracts that were inserted in the *Disciplines* between 1788 and 1808. They are:

1. *The Scripture Doctrine of Predestination, Election, and Reprobation* (Wesley's abridgment of Henry Haggar, *The Order of Causes,* 1654, which was first abridged by Wesley in 1741). This tract was inserted in 1788, 1789, 1790, 1791, 1792, 1797, 1801, 1804, and 1805.

2. Wesley's *Serious Thoughts on the Infallible, Unconditional Perseverance of All that have Once Experienced Faith in Christ.* This was the new title the editors gave to *Serious Thoughts upon the Perseverance of the Saints.* This tract was inserted the same years as above.

3. *A Plain Account of Christian Perfection,* which was inserted in the *Disciplines* of 1789, 1790, 1791, 1792, 1797, 1801, 1804, and 1805.

4. *A Treatise on the Nature and Subjects of Christian Baptism, extracted from a late author.* This had been extracted from Moses Hemmenway, *A Discourse on the Nature and Subjects of Christian Baptism* (Philadelphia: John Dickens, 1790). The tract was inserted in *Disciplines* of 1790, 1791, and 1792.

5. *Of Christian Perfection,* inserted in 1792, 1797, 1798, 1801, 1804, and 1805.

6. *Against Antinomianism,* also inserted in 1792, 1797, 1798, 1801, 1804, and 1805.

In order to avoid confusion with other tracts added after 1808, we will refer to these as the "six tracts (1788–1808)." All were temporarily displaced in the 1798 *Discipline* for an economic reason: to allow the printer enough space for the "Notes" on the *Discipline* by Coke and Asbury. The tracts were restored in the following editions of 1804, 1805, and 1808.

The General Conference of 1808 had these six tracts before them since they had been included in previous books of *Doctrine and Discipline.* Question: Were these tracts the doctrinal standards referred to in the First Restrictive Rule, which would make them binding on all subsequent General Conferences and all future Methodism? Our reasons for answering no to this should be carefully considered.

It remains a glaring fact that these six tracts were never reprinted in the nineteenth century in their 1808 form. It is unconvincing to argue that the 1808 writers of the *Rule* (which would be binding on all future Methodist doctrine) would change their minds at the very next Conference and shift the definition of doctrinal standards to include other documents and eliminate some of the previous ones.

It should be further remembered that not one of these six tracts was included in the *Sermons on Several Occasions.* This is why they were viewed as "other useful Pieces annexed," a title that distinguished them from the *Sermons* and that suggested they were being "annexed to" (rather than added to) the established disciplinary and doctrinal standards. The most decisive evidence that they were not recognized, perduring doctrinal standards is that they had no history of subsequent consistent consensual reception.

A redefined group of tracts appeared in 1817, a third in 1825, with yet another revision in 1831,[4] and further revisions in 1832 and 1862. Such a checkered, uncertain, variable history of publication and reception does not argue for their inclusion in the First Rule, which spoke of unalterable "established standards." Buckley's reasoning seems most plausible:

> The question has arisen whether these Doctrinal Tracts were included in the other existing Standards. But as they were not recognized Standards by Wesley or by the Wesleyan body, and as the *Sermons* of Wesley were specified, and also his Notes; and the Conference of 1808 knew this to be the fact, and as they also knew that Wesley had sent over the Articles of Religion and said nothing whatever about the *Doctrinal Tracts,* the most natural conclusion is that it was not intended to regard them as Standards. Nevertheless, like the "Notes" written by Asbury and Coke, they were valuable "advices" so far as they discussed subjects harmonious with and explanatory of the general doctrines and principles of Methodism. This seems the more reasonable as little or no proof can be adduced that they were ever regarded as official Standards (*CPH*, 164; for another view, see Baker, *FWA*, 182).

Tigert reasoned that the second clause of the First Rule must refer either to the *Sermons* and *Notes* or to the *Six Tracts*. His ambivalent judgment was cautiously stated: "If there is any express and decisive evidence *ad rem,* enabling us to choose with certainty and finality between these two views which appear to be the only *definite* ones we have historical warrant for entertaining, I have not been able to find it. My judgment rather inclines to" the Tracts. Ti-

gert's judgment in this particular case, however, hinged too unilaterally upon a simple verbatim comparison of the title pages of the Disciplines of 1784–1808.

Albert Outler rightly summarized the doctrinal decisions leading to the 1808 Conference:

> What can a modern Methodist make of the first Restrictive Rule, in the light of the circumstance in which it was framed? In the first place, he must recognize the conjoint authority of both the Articles of Religion and the "standards of doctrine." It is this latter half of the duplex norm which requires further clarification.

The six tracts could hardly have been regarded as "a fixed and invariable body of 'standards,'" because they in turn

> rest upon a smaller nucleus of authoritative teaching which had been normative for Methodists in England since the Model Deed and in America from at least 1781. These are the "four volumes of Sermons" and the *Notes on the New Testament.* This is the non-compressible core of "our present existing and established standards of doctrine"—and it is still in legal force to this day. Together with the Articles of Religion, the Sermons and Notes furnish us with a valid and ample yardstick for determining our Wesleyan heritage and tradition (*HSCC,* iv, 6).

Entering the Nineteenth Century

American Episcopal Methodism was indeed an independent church in governance, but there is no indication that it thought of itself as doctrinally distinguishable from the

British connection. Further signals would be given in the years between 1796 and 1804 that the American Methodists of this period understood themselves in a solemn and meaningful doctrinal union with European Methodists. Seventeen years after the Christmas Conference, the minutes of the American Annual Conferences were still reporting statistics of European Methodists, indicating a deep sense of shared mission, correspondence, and unity of the Wesleyan connection felt by the American preachers (*MAC, 1801,* 98).

In 1798 Coke and Asbury appended their interpretive "Notes" to the *Discipline.* They also provided detailed biblical references for the *Articles of Religion* (see Chapter 8 for the full text). In their "Notes," Coke and Asbury championed "the doctrines of holiness" and resisted "heretical doctrines," noting especially Arianism, Universalism, and Socinianism, and other views contrary to Wesley's teaching (*Disc., 1798,* 113). Recall that if the *Articles* had been considered the sole doctrinal standard during this period, they would have provided no basis for dealing with those who oppose "the doctrines of holiness."

The Coke-Asbury 1798 "Disciplinary Notes" further explained the necessity of making proper deeds of conveyance of Methodist properties. They explained why the power of appointment would lie not in local, but Conference hands. This polity was doctrinally significant: "The property of the preaching houses is invested in the trustees" (*Disc., 1798, with Notes,* 40), but the power of appointment was not. Local trustees retained the rights to convey and administer church property but only

"according to the rules and discipline" adopted by the Conference (*Disc., 1804,* 202), rules that by long and unabrogated tradition had specifically prohibited preaching contrary to Wesley's *Sermons* and *Notes.*

The Discipline of 1805

The *Discipline* that the Conference of 1808 had in hand when it wrote the Constitution and Restrictive Rules was the *Discipline* of 1805.[5] When they constitutionally limited subsequent General Conferences from establishing new standards contrary to "our present existing and established standards of doctrine," they surely must have assumed that the Discipline of 1805 was consistent with then present standards.[6] For if the standards were "present and existing," it is inconceivable that they would not be embodied in the 1805 *Discipline.*

Neely guardedly dissected the phrase "present existing and established standards" to explain that they were

> standards that had been duly established by legal and constitutional enactment, or in some other equivalent way, if there was any such other way, and which were existing at that time, or in other words, if they once had been constitutionally established, had not been abrogated, but existed legally, and were legally in force in that "present," namely, when the Constitution was adopted in 1808, that is to say, the doctrines that were then recognized (*DSM,* 223, 224).

If the standards referred to in the Constitution were already legally in force in that "present," then a careful examination of the *Discipline* of 1805 is crucial for American Methodist doctrinal definition. Such an examination yields four conclusions:

1. That Wesley is venerated, not resisted and ignored, is clear from numerous generous references to him—"our venerable friend, who under God, had been the father of the great revival of religion now extending over the earth" (*Disc., 1805,* 5).

2. That the *Explanatory Notes upon the New Testament* were assumed as normative seems to be indicated in Section 12, Question 2 on the "Duty of Preachers," who are required to read the *Notes* carefully, "seriously" and "with prayer," "every day" (*Disc., 1805,* 30). "From four to five in the morning and from five to six in the evening, to meditate, pray, and read the Scriptures with notes, and the closely practical parts of what Mr. Wesley has published" (*Disc., 1805,* 38). This means that the "rules and discipline" assumed by the deeds of settlement made the extraordinary requirement on the American Methodist preacher that he spend over forty hours per month studying the Scripture with Wesley's *Notes* and selected *Sermons.* (The "practical parts" referred to are largely found in the last half of the four volumes of *Sermons.*)

3. The reason Wesley's *Sermons* and *Notes* were not physically included in the early *Disciplines* was an economic, not doctrinal one, as suggested by the editors in the 1805 Preface: "We know you are not in general able to purchase many books" (*Disc., 1805,* 4). The *Sermons* and *Notes* were already available in various American and British editions. So there was no compelling need to make an enormous book of the *Discipline* by including the *Sermons* and *Notes,* which were widely distributed already and obviously did not need legislative updating, as did the "rules and discipline."

4. A fourth point is less definite, but intriguing: There appears to be an anticipation in the 1805 *Discipline* of a two-clause or dual track of doctrinal definition (*Articles* + *Sermons* and *Notes*), which would appear in fuller form in the First Restrictive Rule of 1808. The Preface to the 1805 *Discipline* said that the *Articles of Religion* were "maintained, more or less, in part or in the whole, by every reformed church in the world" (*Disc., 1805,* 4). These *Articles* were not thought to stand alone, however, but were linked with and complemented by "our plan of Christian education," embodied in the entire book of *Doctrines and Discipline.*

These four aspects of the 1805 *Discipline* further reinforce the conclusion that the *Articles* alone were not the sole source of binding doctrine at the time the Constitution spoke of "our present existing and established standards of doctrine" (*JGC, 1808*).

Having reviewed doctrinal standards documents and issues to 1808, the stage is now set for the careful constitutional protection of these standards of doctrine that had been so circumspectly established and preserved.

4.

The Constitutional Protection
of Established Standards:
1808 to the Present

Three previous chapters have presented a résumé of historical evidence of how Wesleyan doctrinal standards became textually defined, transplanted to America, established, and maintained until 1808. The narrative now takes a decisive turn in the constitutional protection of these same standards. This chapter shows how the established standards were confirmed and guarded in exceptionally imaginative ways by the writers of the American Methodist Constitution in 1808, and how later major interpreters of the Constitution viewed their continuity and transmission.

The Preamble of the General Conference of 1808

Before the 1808 Conference met, a preparatory committee "relative to regulating and perpetuating General Conferences" studied the needs of the growing denomination and prepared for vast changes to come. Its report indicates how important it was to them to constrain future General Conferences from changing their well-known, consensually received doctrinal standards.

Their strong determination against reconceiving or reworking received standards of doctrine is seen in their preamble, which began on a rigorously conserving tone: "It is of greatest importance that the doctrines, form of government, and general rules of the United societies in America be preserved sacred and inviolable" (Buckley, *CPH,* 105–6). It was principally for this purpose that the Constitution was written. The preamble shows that matters of doctrine were *not* being debated at this time but were generally understood and viewed in a settled way as assuming previously "established standards of doctrine."

Such a consensus could not have occurred quickly. Consensual reception does not develop or become "established" in a single month or year, but only over decades of continuity through change, and this had in fact occurred during the years between 1770 and 1808. What other understanding of doctrine could have been assumed than that which had been consensually shared for thirty-five years (in the case of the *Sermons* and *Notes*) and twenty-four years (in the case of the *Articles*)?

When Daniel Hitt suggested that a committee be appointed "to modify certain *exceptional expressions* in the General Rules" (*JGC, 1808*, 89), the motion was defeated. The Conference of 1808 was not of a mind to tinker with doctrinal formulations that had long been settled.

The Construction of the First Restrictive Rule

The principal means by which the Conference's doctrinal conservation occurred was a single sentence known as "the First Restrictive Rule"—a rule to restrict the General Conference from altering established doctrinal standards.

There were two different early formulations of the First Restrictive Rule between which the Conference had to choose. Both were formed around a dual clause, assuming two major types of documents of doctrinal definition ("Articles" and "standards of doctrine"). The earlier language (first *proposed* on May 16, 1808) appears in the first column, while the revised language (which was *carried* and became accepted Methodist church law) appears in the second column:

Simpler Language First Proposed	Complex Language Later Accepted
May 16, 1808	*May 24, 1808*
The General Conference shall not revoke, alter, or change our Articles of Religion, nor establish any new standards of doctrine (*JGC, 1808*, 82).	The General Conference shall not revoke, alter, or change our Articles of Religion, nor establish any new standards or rules of doctrine contrary to our present existing and established standards of doctrine (*JGC, 1808*, 89).

The second version is the intriguing sentence upon which this study largely focuses. Why was the latter wording preferred and carried—especially since the first column seems simpler? Several reasons may be discerned:

1. The accepted version stressed, more than the rejected version, that Wesleyan standards of doctrine were already "established," hence not needing to go through a process of authentication or consensual validation. Moreover, they did not need

debate, for they had been repeatedly defined without record of dissent or debate since the 1770s (as *Sermons* and *Notes* and, after 1784, the *Articles*). The word *established* refers to that which is a settled arrangement, stable or firm, immovably fixed (from the Latin *stabilis*, meaning firm or stable). The word was not lightly chosen, and it appeared twice in the approved version.

2. The approved language conveyed more pointedly that these standards of doctrine were indeed

"our present existing" (hence familiar) standards, not standards that had yet to gain consensus or that this Conference had lately developed. It was evidently expected that every informed Methodist present would know precisely what those standards were. There was no ambiguity, unconscious or intended, in the minds of the framers of the Rule.

Note this irony: The most perplexing aspect of the First Rule that gives *us* such trouble today is its absence of textual definition. That silence was precisely a mark of deliberate confidence and moral certainty on the part of the 1808 writers who assumed that anyone, even a novice, would know exactly the specified texts referred to as "present existing and established standards of doctrine." What was then so familiarly known that it could be left silent (in order to avoid redundancy) has become for us a complex problem of historical reconstruction.

3. Why did the revised language add the term *rules* to standards? To reinforce and amplify the intent of the restriction. For a "rule of doctrine" is not precisely synonymous with a "standard of doctrine." The English word *rule* comes from the Latin *regula,* meaning a regulation, a prescribed guide for conduct, or a directive. A *standard* is something held up for measurement, while a *rule* is something to follow. Both were protected by the First Rule from contrary alteration by the General Conference.

4. The amended version conveyed more pointedly than the first that new contrary standards were prohibited; hence no new rules that were contrary to the well-known and established standards of doctrine could be embraced by the General Conference. The restriction focused precisely upon "new" standards or rules that might be intended to supercede or compete with the previously established standards. This reveals the conserving spirit of the 1808 Conference, as opposed to the view that it was in some way doctrinally innovative.

One may envision the structure of the received version of the First Rule in this way:

Methodist Doctrinal Standards:	Prohibitions Against:
1. Articles of Religion	Revocation Alteration Change
2. Established Standards—by inference, Wesley's *Sermons* and *Notes*	
Present Existing Established	Any new standard or rule contrary to present existing and established standards

The Dual Clauses Point to Two Types of Texts

Having devised this particular language, the Conference of 1808 resisted further amendment. Bangs reported that the Rule was passed unanimously (*HMEC,* 2:233).

In this way, the language of the First Restrictive Rule came to contain two clauses: the first clause specified the *Articles of Religion* received from Wesley, as distinguished from the older criteria of the second clause, the "standards of doctrine," which by long consensual and legal tradition had been textually specified as Wesley's *Sermons* and *Notes.*

"It is evident that the 'standards of doctrine' here alluded to are not the Articles of Religion, for these have been previously mentioned. The reference is undoubtedly to the Sermons and Notes" (Harrison, *WS,* 6). "That means that the Church has doctrines, and has 'standards or rules of doctrine,' besides the 'Articles of Religion.'"[1] That the Judicial Council also has accepted the two-clause interpretation of the First Rule seems evident from its ruling on the Theological Study Commission's Report, where it distinguished between making "changes in our Articles" or Confession and establishing "new standards or rules of doctrine contrary to our present existing standards of doctrine" (Judicial Council, Decision No. 358).

These two clauses conceptually distinguish the two norms of classical Methodist doctrine: the tightly constructed twenty-five sections of the *Articles of Religion,* as distinguished from the extensive four volumes of *Sermons* and *Explanatory Notes upon the New Testament.* Most leading constitutional historians (McTyeire, Tigert, Buckley, and Neely) have subsequently read this rule as indicating a "duplex norm" (Outler, *HSCC,* iv, 6):

First Clause: "The General Conference shall not revoke, alter, or change our articles of religion,"

Second Clause: "nor establish any new standards or rules of doctrine, contrary to our present and existing and established standards of doctrine."

The two distinguishable clauses have doctrinal significance: The Rule required two clauses to convey the two complementary dimensions of Methodist doctrinal accountability: first, to the teachings of the Reformation (expressed by the *Articles*), and secondly, to the more specific Methodist teachings (embodied in Wesley's *Sermons* and *Notes*). It is precisely these doctrinal norms that the 1808 Conference was determined to protect, insuring that they could not be casually revoked.

The two clauses are best compared and contrasted as follows:

Articles of Religion	Sermons and Notes
Confessional form	Homiletical-exegetical form
The Ecumenical Consensus	The Methodist Emphasis
Anglican Theology	Wesleyan Themes

Concise	Five Volumes
Criterion for Trial	Criteria for Preaching
Shorter History of Consensual Reception (Since 1784)	Longer History of Consensual Reception (Since 1763)
Textually Specified by the Constitution	Recognized by the Constitution and Known by "plain historical inference"

Bishop McTyeire formulated a concise summary of the sequence leading to this distinction: "American Methodists (1781) vowed to 'preach the old Methodist doctrine' of Wesley's 'Notes and Sermons.' May, 1784, 'the doctrine taught in the four volumes of the Sermons [the first fifty-two of our edition] and Notes on the New Testament' was reaffirmed. The Deed of Declaration (February, 1784) legally established these standards in the parent body. The Rule (1808) guards them equally with the Articles" (McTyeire, *MD,* 131).

To the above statement of doctrinal standards, McTyeire correctly added a cautious statement on "usage," distinguishing canonical standards from interpretative and supportive works of "high expository authority" by general consent: "Usage allows Watson's Theological Institutes and the authorized Catechisms and Hymnbook to be high expository authority" (*MD,* 131), but these do not have the same level of consent as the *Sermons, Notes,* and *Articles,* and obviously could not have been intended by the writers of 1808, because they were not yet written.

Thomas B. Neely was perceptive enough in 1918 to anticipate much of our dilemma today:

Some one may ask whether the adoption of the Articles of Religion could automatically do away with the doctrines and the doctrinal standards that existed among the American Methodists before they were organized into a regular Church, or did the former doctrines continue with the Articles as an addition to the former standards? . . . The Articles did not annul anything in the old standards and there was no act of abrogation (*DSM,* 206–7).

Why did the 1808 Conference not spell out the textual definition of the phrase "established standards of doctrine"? The most decisive reason, in my view, is a rhetorical one: *The principle of parsimony ruled the legislative language of the period.* The standards were so generally known by every Methodist preacher that it was thought redundant and unnecessary to declare the obvious.

Why did the restatement of doctrinal standards not occur in subsequent General Conferences? Because once settled, and having once entered the definition unalterably in the Constitution of American Methodism, there was no need (and indeed no way) to return to it, unless one wished to try to amend the Constitution. This is why the absence of reference to the *Sermons* and *Notes* in subsequent minutes is not by any means an indication of their neglect or rejection. The opposite is true: The presence of the First Restrictive Rule is precisely what guaranteed in the most decisive and unequivocal way the inclusion of the *Sermons* and *Notes* in all subsequent doctrinal definition. Once decided, as it was in 1808, the matter of doctrinal standards needed no further mention or definition because this matter was decided as absolutely and irrevocably as any constitution-making body could possibly act— i.e., by strictly limiting the ability of the legislative process to amend these "established standards of doctrine." (For a discussion of the 1808 motion by Francis Ward to include John Fletcher's writings among established doctrinal standards, see Appendix.)

After 1808 the preoccupation of General Conferences understandably turned away from doctrinal definition, for that issue had been once for all rigorously settled. So the General Conferences turned more intently toward development and improvement of the constitutional system that had been inaugurated in 1808 but which would need periodic modifications. A system of polity as functionally detailed as the Methodist Episcopal Church and its successors could not be created overnight. Rather, it required responses to new historical situations to clarify and implement its mission. But the best testimony to the fact that formal doctrinal standards have not changed since 1808 is that virtually no serious attempts to amend the First Restrictive Rule have ever been made, and the few that were have never come close to succeeding. Hence the constitution writers have been eminently successful in their protective intent.

Did the Conference of 1808 assume that previous Conference minutes were rejected by this Conference's action (a crucial issue in any discussion of the status of the deeds)? For this question we have a definite answer:

> Moved by Daniel Hitt, and seconded by John Pitts, that every part of the Discipline that stands in contrast with any of the rules and regulations adopted at this sitting of the General Conference be repealed (*JGC, 1808,* 94).

Here the Conference was being given an opportunity to say that the present minutes would repeal all previous minutes that stood in contrast with its present legislation. This is the principle that has been dubiously applied to explain the omission of the Model Deed in 1792 (i.e., the principle that its omission by one Conference implied its negation as a binding standard by subsequent Conferences). Now the Conference could act deliberately on that principle. The motion lost (*JGC, 1808,* 94).

The Surveillance of Established Standards

The General Conference of 1816 resolved that the "General Conference do earnestly recommend the superintendents to make the most careful inquiry in all annual conferences, in order to ascertain whether any doctrines are embraced or preached contrary to our established articles of faith, and use their influence to prevent the existence and circulation of all such doctrines" (*JGC, 1816,* 157). The Committee of Safety had reported its investigation of charges that "doctrines contrary to our established articles of faith" (Ibid., 155) were being disseminated.

Might the Conference *Journal* be referring here to doctrines contrary to the *Articles of Religion*? This cannot be the case because of the issues to which they were primarily attending, which focused upon the defense of Wesleyan doctrines not included in the *Articles of Religion*. Among these doctrines "as defended by Wesley" were the doctrines of "the direct witness of the Holy Spirit, and of holiness of heart and life, or gospel sanctification" (Ibid., 156). The committee's report dealt extensively with issues treated in Wesley's *Sermons* but not the *Articles*, such as "the duty of constant communion," "experimental religion," "love-feasts, class and society meetings," assurance, and perfection (Ibid., 156–58). The doctrinal offenses cited here could not have arisen out of a failure to follow the *Articles*, since these doctrines are not mentioned in the *Articles*. Hence the phrase "articles of faith" in this instance could not have referred exclusively to the Twenty-five *Articles of Religion* but must have referred generically to the *Sermons* and *Notes*. If not, then some alternative hypothesis must be devised.

Nathan Bangs, who was present at the Conference of 1808, wisely interpreted the meaning of its Restrictive Rules in this way:

> The unanimity with which these restrictive regulations were adopted by the Conference shows the deep sense which was very generally felt of the propriety of limiting the powers of the General Conference. . . . Call these rules, therefore, *restrictive regulations*, or a *constitution of the Church*—they have ever since been considered as sacredly binding

upon all succeeding General Conferences, limiting them in all their legislative acts, and prohibiting them from making inroads upon the doctrines, general rules, and government of the Church. . . . Under this state of things, knowing the rage of man for novelty, and witnessing the destructive changes which have frequently laid waste churches, by removing ancient landmarks, and so modifying doctrines and usages as to suit the temper of the times, or to gratify either a corrupt taste or a perverse disposition, many had felt uneasy apprehensions for the safety and unity of the Church and the stability of its doctrines (*HMEC*, 2:233, 234).

Accordingly, subsequent Conferences were prohibited from making inroads upon the doctrines of the church. If the fundamental concern of the Conference of 1808 was, as Bangs suggests, to conserve the stability of Methodist doctrine as well as church government, then it seems wholly implausible that the same Conference could have made the most radical revision of doctrine in the history of Methodism (which would have been the case if the *Articles* alone were so exclusively affirmed as to eliminate the doctrinal force of the *Sermons* and *Notes*).

The First Restrictive Rule Becomes Virtually Unamendable:
The Exception of 1832

An even more fixed and determined constitutional structure to secure the *Sermons, Notes,* and *Articles* as inviolable against devaluation or amendment was devised in the Exception of 1832. This allowed for a method of amending the constitution by "the concurrent recommendation of three-fourths of all the members of the several annual conferences who shall be present and vote on such a recommendation, then a majority of two-thirds of the General Conference succeeding" (*JGC, 1832,* 378).

One crucial exception, however, was made to this procedure: It could not apply to the First Restrictive Rule.

> The insertion of the words "excepting the first article," made it impossible by the above process to change the Restrictive Rule in regard to the doctrines of the Church. . . . The new provision for amendment created a double process. First, it would be necessary to amend the provision for amendment by striking out the words "excepting the first article." This, according to the constitution, could be done by the action of the Ministers in the Annual Conferences and the concurrence of the next General Conference, or by the action of two-thirds in the General Conference and the concurrence of three-fourths in the Annual Conference. If this was agreed to, then the first restriction would no longer be an exception and it could be amended just as any other restriction (Neely, *GCM,* 405).

Following 1968, the procedure for constitutional amendment of the First, Second, and Seventh Restrictive Rules required "a three-fourths majority of all the members of the Annual Conferences and Missionary Conferences present and voting" (*Disc., 1984,* 38–39). In this way, the E.U.B. *Confession* of 1962 has been included under the same procedural Exception. Thomas B. Neely

further commented on the Exception:

> The General Conference cannot revoke, or call back, any article, or anything in any article. It cannot alter any article in any way, or any degree, in whole or in part. Then, to cover every possible thing, the broad and generic word "change" is used, so that the General Conference cannot modify the Articles of Religion in any possible way, directly or indirectly. It cannot change by abrogating, or rescinding; it cannot change by eliminating or inserting; it cannot change by modifying in any way the meaning of the wording; it cannot modify by shifting sentences or phrases, even though every word and every letter were preserved; it cannot take out old articles and put in new ones, as it cannot add any articles; and it cannot change the titles, number, and order of the Articles. In other words, the General Conference cannot amend the Articles of Religion in any way, or in any degree. That is to say, the General Conference must not touch the Articles of Religion, but must let them stand unchanged. The General Conference, of itself, must let them stand precisely as they were when the first restrictive rule was made, which is to say, that the General Conference cannot make them different in any particular from what they were in 1808, which means, what they were at the beginning of the denomination (*DSM,* 220).

Note the progression: *Before 1808* the General Conference "possessed unlimited powers over our entire economy" and "could alter, abolish, or add to any article of religion or any rule of discipline." "This depository of power was considered too great for the safety of the Church, and the security of its government and doctrine" (Bangs, *HMEC,* 2:177, 178). *After 1808* the Restrictive Rules were provided, but with the proviso that they could be amended "upon the joining recommendation of all the Annual Conferences, then a majority of two thirds of the General Conference" (Ibid., 2:233). This meant that after 1808 there still remained a possible avenue, however remote, for the General Conference to alter Methodist doctrine. This is what the Exception of 1832 further resisted with this extraordinary procedure. *After 1832* the amendment procedure became even more arduous. If the Restrictive Rules are analogous to the Bill of Rights (in the sense that they limit the legislature from intruding into certain arenas), the Exception of 1832 is analogous to a brilliant procedural defense to protect the Bill of Rights.

What meaning can we draw from such an unlikely—practically impossible—procedure? It signifies the seriousness of intent of the constitution writers and legislators of 1808, 1832, 1939, and 1968 to prevent any change of Methodist doctrinal standards, so as to build a fortification of procedural defenses around them that would be virtually impenetrable. Therefore no General Conference can strike the Exception on its own authority (without the overwhelming concurrence of the Annual Conferences), no matter what its majority. To date these procedural defenses have been eminently successful.

Wesley's Continuing Influence

A list of advocates of Wesleyan doctrine during the first half of the nineteenth century is a stellar list of Methodist notables. Nathan Bangs, Timothy Merritt, Abel Stevens, and Thomas Summers are among many examples of scholarly preachers who were strongly influenced by Wesley during this period. Early bishops known particularly as stalwart defenders of the "old Methodist doctrine," in addition to Asbury and Coke, were Richard Whatcoat, Elijah Hedding, and John Emory. Among active bishops in the middle of the nineteenth century who wrote and spoke widely on the Wesleyan doctrine, discipline, or history with a strong and overt indebtedness to Wesley were Leonidas L. Hamline, Edmund S. Janes, Matthew Simpson, Osmon C. Baker, Holland N. McTyeire, Randolph Sinks Foster, Stephen Merrill, Gilbert Haven, and Jesse T. Peck. Over sixty editions of Wesley's *Sermons on Several Occasions* were published in the years 1784–1860.

One way to track the continuing influence of the Wesleys in mid-nineteenth-century American Methodism lies in the unusual number of editions required for *A Collection of Hymns For the Use of the People Called Methodist, largely written by Charles and John Wesley, with a Preface by John Wesley.* The first American edition was published in 1814 (Baltimore: Pomeroy, 562 hymns). There followed edition after edition, in most cases published by the official organs of the General Conference, in 1821, 1822, 1824, 1826, 1829 (606 hymns), and 1830.

Then came *A Supplement to the Collection of Hymns for the Use of the People Called Methodist,* which went through numerous American editions in 1832, 1834, 1835, 1836, 1838 (three editions), 1839, 1842 (two editions), 1843, 1844, 1845 (three editions), 1846 (two editions), 1847, 1848, 1849, 1850, and following years.

The General Conference at the beginning of the nineteenth century had ordered publication of a book of hymns largely taken from the Wesleys. Republished in 1808, this hymnal was substantially revised in 1820 by the order of the General Conference. It is significant to note a determination on the part of the General Conference of 1820 to restore Wesley's original language to hymns whose wording had been changed in 1808, as Bangs reported:

> An improved edition of our Hymn Book was ordered by this [1820] General Conference to be printed by the book agents. The first hymn book printed in this country for the use of the members and friends of our Church was small, containing, to be sure, a choice selection, but not a sufficient variety. . . . This had been remedied, as was supposed, by adding, in 1808, a second book, consisting chiefly of hymns taken from the original hymns of John and Charles Wesley; but unhappily, those who made this selection had taken the liberty to alter many of the hymns, by leaving out parts of stanzas, altering words, shortening or lengthening hymns, without much judgment or taste. By this injudicious method the poetry was often marred, and the sentiment changed much for the worse (*HMEC,* 3:133).

In 1830 Nathan Bangs wrote an extended defense of Methodist doctrine and discipline against various critics, which he entitled *The Reviewer Answered; or, The Discipline and Usages of the Methodist Episcopal Church Defended Against the Attacks of the Christian Spectator* (New York: Emory & Waugh, 1830). In this book Bangs responded to charges against "Wesley's Testament"— that it supported "heretical doctrines" and that it presented "a mutilated copy of the Holy Scriptures" (*RA,* 7). Bangs' defense of Wesley's *Explanatory Notes upon the New Testament* proceeded on the basis of "the doctrines of our church" (Ibid., 8). In his defense, Bangs appealed to "the learned, the holy, the evangelical, the indefatigable Wesley" (Ibid., 29). "The effects of the doctrines so powerfully promulgated by Wesley and his helpers, have been felt less or more by almost every denomination of Christendom" (Ibid., 91). He defended the premise that "a *Methodist* preacher is bound to preach *Methodist* doctrine" (Ibid., 80); apparently this fact was troubling Congregational and Presbyterian ministers of the 1820s. "We advise them, therefore, to let John Wesley alone. He is an overmatch for their strength. Though his ashes sleep in the dust, his spirit breathes in his works, he lives in the affections of thousands, and his voice may be heard yet speaking for him in the numerous testimonies to his worth which are scattered through the invaluable defences which he has left behind him" (Ibid., 83).

Were the doctrinal standards functionally inert during this period? In defending "the standards of doctrine" of Methodism, Bangs referred repeatedly to the *Articles* (Ibid., 50–53), *Sermons* (Ibid., 106), and *Notes* (Ibid., 7, 114–24). "The doctrines which they preach require holiness of heart and life" (Ibid., 94). He chided his opponents, asking "whether they have ever read Mr. Wesley's sermon entitled 'A Caution

Against Bigotry', or that which immediately follows it, entitled 'A Catholic Spirit'? . . . We beg them to read those sermons" (Ibid., 106).

Doctrinal Union With British Methodism Conspicuously Reaffirmed

The unity of American, Canadian, and British Methodist doctrinal standards was repeatedly reaffirmed and publicly stated by official actions of American General Conferences during the early nineteenth century. In 1820 the General Conference affirmed: "The British and American connections have now mutually recognized each other as one body of Christians, sprung from a common stock, *holding the same doctrines*" (*HMEC*, 3:131, italics added).

There can be no doubt that the *Sermons* and *Notes* were legal standards in Britain and Canada. The American affirmations of doctrinal unity with Canadian and British Methodism stand as striking evidence against the view that the *Sermons* and *Notes* had been defaulted as binding standards during the early nineteenth century.

The General Conference of 1828 at Pittsburgh adopted an even more rigorous statement of American doctrinal affinity with British Methodists: "We are, with you, dear brethren, endeavoring to maintain the purity of our doctrines, and are not conscious that we have suffered them in any instance to be *changed or adulterated* in our hands. As they are the doctrines which have proved to so many, *both in Europe and America,* the power of God unto salvation, we deem them to be the gospel of God our Saviour; and while he owns

them we will never give them up" (*HMEC,* 3:281, 282, italics added). If these doctrines were understood to be precisely the same in the entire Wesleyan connection, and if their purity was thought to have been maintained unadulterated, then it could scarcely be argued that the doctrinal *standards were changed* or revoked by the 1784 or 1808 Conferences so as to circumvent or eliminate the *Sermons* and *Notes* as binding standards.

The *Doctrines and Disciplines of the Methodist Church of Canada,* 1882, began the first section of its *Discipline* with a precise definition of "Standards of Doctrine": "The doctrines of the Methodist Church of Canada are declared to be those contained in the Twenty-five Articles of Religion, and those taught by the Rev. John Wesley, M.A., in his Notes on the New Testament, and in the first fifty-two Sermons of the first series of his discourses, published during his lifetime" (p. 9). Tigert wistfully commented: "It were well if some such declaration as this formed the first section of the first chapter of the first part of the Discipline of every Methodist Church in the world" (*CH,* 139).

Official statements of American-British doctrinal union were recurrent: "*Wesleyan Methodism* is one everywhere—one in its doctrines, its discipline, its usages" ("Address to the General Conference," *HMEC,* 3:259). "The credentials furnished by our brethren in Europe, either to their ministers or members, are recognized and honoured by us here, as entitling them to every privilege of our church. The credentials which we furnish are also acknowledged by them" (Emory, *Defense of Our Fathers,* 78). If

American and British Methodists had viewed themselves as possessing two different doctrinal standards, then these official actions might have seemed inappropriate. If there was *only one recognized international standard,* as it appears from these quotations, then the *Sermons* and *Notes* must have been American doctrinal standards during this disputed period. The British and American connections thought of themselves as synchronous and doctrinally identical.

Doctrinal Criteria for Preaching and Trial

Note how different are two major contexts in which doctrinal standards apply: (1) the recurrent and primary task of *preaching* and (2) the rare and exceptional situation of the *trial* of a minister.

Most would agree that the more important of these two arenas for application of doctrinal standards is *preaching,* which includes the teaching office. In early American Methodism, clergy trials were extremely rare; yet preaching was central to Methodist worship. The criteria that more naturally and readily applied to Methodist preaching were Wesley's *Sermons,* themselves models of Methodist homily, and his *Notes,* which support the study of Scripture and biblical preaching (see Sugden, *WSS,* Introduction). The less frequent, yet necessary, arena in which doctrinal standards applied is the conflicted and extraordinary situation of *trial.* Here a much tighter, more concise, specific definition was needed than could be functional for preaching.

Among early chargeable offenses was the specific charge of "dissemi-nating false doctrines." Even here it is unlikely that early American Methodists would have intentionally ruled out any reference whatever to the "old Methodist doctrines." Keep in mind that the *Sermons* and *Notes* had been designated as doctrinal standards for preaching three decades before the *Articles* were designated as standards that have special applicability to trial (1763 as opposed to 1792).

In Methodist legislation with respect to trial, a high value has been placed upon justice through due process, tolerance, and protection of the rights of the accused. In *A Digest of Methodist Law,* Bishop Stephen M. Merrill set forth the criteria and procedure for trial for dissemination of false doctrine as generally understood in 1885:

The Methodist Episcopal Church has always been liberal with regard to doctrines, not entering into the minutiae of personal opinions privately held, particularly upon speculative points in theology; but she does, nevertheless, require subscription to the substantial doctrines of the Gospel, such as are essential to the Christian life. Especially does she require her ministers to "banish and drive away all erroneous and strange doctrines contrary to God's Word," and to teach only in accordance with the twenty-five articles of religion, the Methodist Catechism and such other standards as meet the general approval of the denomination. Private members may become liable to accusation and trial by "Inveighing against our doctrines," but it is of much greater importance to keep the preachers within the lines of permissible beliefs. Their teaching office makes the difference. . . . But doctrines contrary to the articles of religion and the catechism are easily detected, and it is seldom necessary to proceed against parties whose teachings do not antagonize these standards. In the event of a minister disseminating doctrines contrary to these standards of doctrine, he is to be arraigned at once, and proceeded against in the form of trial, as if accused of gross misconduct (Merrill, *DML,* 186–87).

The Extension of Chargeable Offenses to Include "Established Standards"

The Methodist Episcopal Church (North and South) had other doctrinal standards besides the *Articles* throughout the nineteenth century. By 1880 the northern church decided to make this legislatively clear. It did so by adding a telling phrase to the list of chargeable offenses for clergy: "When a Minister or Preacher disseminates, publicly or privately, doctrines which are contrary to our Articles or Religion *or established standards of doctrine . . .*" (*Disc., 1880,* 140), borrowed directly from the First Restrictive Rule.

This trend was further intensified in 1912 when the word *other* was added to the phrase "established standards of doctrine." The preacher may be "charged with disseminating, publicly or privately, doctrines which are contrary to our Articles of Religion, or our other existing and established standards of doctrine" (*Disc., 1916,* 181). This wording was carried into the *Disciplines* after union in 1939. This had the effect of underscoring the intention of the General Conference that there exist *other* established standards of doctrine than the *Articles of Religion* alone. Borgen rightly concludes that

the *other* established standards "cannot be anything but Wesley's Notes on the New Testament and his . . . sermons" (*SDUMC,* 4).

Thomas Neely in 1918 pointed to the steady stream of continuity in these rulings: "These laws coming down without a break from the very early days of the church show a very strong and persistent determination to protect its doctrinal standards . . . to say that they are not obligatory, or binding, is to display ignorance of the law of the Church and of its history" (*DSM,* 215–16).

By 1939 the list of chargeable offenses had been once again slightly amended: The preacher could be tried for "Disseminating, publicly or privately, doctrines which are contrary to the Articles of Religion, or the established standards of doctrine" (*Disc., 1939,* 188), dropping the word *other* but retaining the two-clause premise. Yet the *other* language reappeared in the *Discipline* of 1944, which stated that a preacher could be tried for disseminating doctrines contrary to (a) the *Articles* or (b) "other established standards of doctrine of the church" (*Disc., 1944,* 209).

Only out of this history of revisions we can rightly understand the present language of the *Discipline,* which since 1968 has designated this chargeable offense: "dissemination of doctrines contrary to the established standards of doctrine of the Church" (*Disc., 1984,* 659). This language deliberately brings the two previous clauses together so as to view both the first clause (referring to the *Articles of Religion*) and the second clause (referring to "other established standards of doctrine") under a single phrase, yet in such a way as to include the E. U. B. *Confes-*

sion of 1962, which by 1968 had been incorporated by the Plan of Union. The intention of the General Conference to include Wesley's *Sermons* and *Notes* under the rubric of "established standards of doctrine" is very clear from the Preface to the doctrinal documents: "The phrase, 'our present existing and established standards of doctrine,' . . . included as a minimum John Wesley's forty-four *Sermons on Several Occasions* and his *Explanatory Notes on the New Testament*. Their function as 'standards' had already been defined by the 'Large Minutes' of 1763, which in turn had been approved by the American Methodists of 1773 and 1785. To these *Sermons* and *Notes* the Conference of 1808 added *The Articles of Religion*" (*Disc., 1968*, 35).

Doctrinal Obligation of Church Members

How have doctrinal standards applied to church members in our history? It is clear that church members have a right to expect that their clergy have given consent to established doctrines of the church. But has any form of assent been required of Methodist church members? Is any member

> at liberty to hold and advocate any doctrine, and to disavow and antagonize the doctrines and the doctrinal formularies . . . ? The result of this would be doctrinal anarchy. . . . It is inconceivable that any body, religious or otherwise, would deliberately incorporate within itself the seeds of its own dissolution. . . . Being in, or coming into an organization, be it a Church, or any other organization, creates the presumption that those who are in, or come in, will conform to the rules and

regulations of the body (Neely, *DSM*, 249–50).

The 1792 form of this obligation read: "If a member of our Church shall be clearly convicted of endeavoring to sow dissension in any of our Societies, by inveighing against either our doctrines, or discipline, such person so offending shall first be reproved" and expelled if he persists (*Disc., 1792*, quoted in Neely, *DSM*, 252).[2]

During most of Methodism's first two centuries, the gist of these provisions remained in effect. As late as the *Discipline* of 1964 (prior to union with the Evangelical United Brethren), the "Offenses for Which a Lay Member May be Tried" included "Disseminating doctrines contrary to the Articles of Religion or other established standards of doctrine of the church. . . . If a member of the church shall be accused of endeavoring to sow dissension in the church by inveighing against its doctrines or discipline, its ministers or members, or in any other manner, he shall first be reproved by the pastor or church lay leader. If he shall persist in such practice, he shall be brought to trial" (*Disc., 1964*, 300–301). After the Plan of Union (1968), the language was pared down, but the core of the provision remained. A member could be charged with "disseminating doctrines contrary to our established standards of doctrine of the Church" (*Disc., 1968*, 494). This language remains in the current *Discipline* (*Disc., 1984*, 659–60).

Church trials have always been regarded as an expedient of last resort in the Wesleyan tradition, after every reasonable effort has been otherwise made to correct a wrong. In the early Methodist societies, the worthiness of members to continue in fellowship was decided by the local society under Wesley's guidance and sometimes with his direct intervention. In the earliest American Methodist societies, the preachers continued to exercise the right to exclude offending members. But by 1789, some preliminary rules were devised to deal with those members accused of serious lapses of discipline. After 1800, the responsibility shifted from the pastor to a committee. The Fifth Restrictive Rule of 1808 provided a right to a fair trial of both clergy and laity. It stated that the General Conference cannot "do away privileges of our ministers or preachers, of trial by committee, and of appeal; neither shall they do away the privileges of our members of trial before the society, or by a committee, of an appeal" (*JGC, 1808,* 89).

The General Rules state: "There is only one condition previously required of those who desire admission into these societies—'a desire to flee from the wrath to come, and to be saved from their sins.' " Yet as early as 1738 Wesley had established a probationary period (two months —in 1789 extended to six months) for all who would be received into his societies. Probationers were further required to satisfy the local society as to their fitness before they were received into full connection. Hence the first sentence of the General Rules has often been held to refer to entrance upon probationary membership, not to final acceptance as full members.

This probationary membership rule remained in effect during much of the history of American Methodism. Persons who became Method-

ists from other denominations, however pious, were required to join on a probationary status. The *Discipline* of 1840 asked: "How shall we prevent improper persons from insinuating themselves into the Church?" Initiates were required to "give satisfactory assurances both of the correctness of their faith, and their willingness to observe and keep the rules of the church" (*Disc., 1840,* sec. 2, Q3). Until 1864, however, there was no ritual provision for members' being formally asked for doctrinal accountability. Rather, this was left to the inquiry and judgment of the pastor both as to faith and practice. In 1864 the General Conference gave form to this long-established procedure by placing in the ritual for admission of probationers this formal question: "Do you believe in the doctrines of Holy Scripture, *as set forth in the Articles of Religion* of the Methodist Episcopal Church?" (*Disc., 1864,* 155, italics added). This constituted a doctrinal test for admission to the church.

There was little debate on this matter until 1920, when the General Conference was petitioned to assess the constitutionality of the 1864 test. Its Committee on Judiciary made a majority report against the test, on the grounds that the General Conference had no power to change the General Rules, which say, "There is only one condition previously required." Hence they proposed that no further doctrinal test be ritually required. On May 25, 1920, after pathos-laden debate, the General Conference voted by a slender majority (375 to 359) that the 1864 doctrinal test for membership was unconstitutional. Three days later, an opportunity was given to absentees to vote and to members to change their votes, and the Conference reversed itself, deciding that the test was constitutional. The Minority Report of the Judiciary Committee, who won this vote, argued that the church never meant the provisions of the 1864 test "to stand as the 'One condition' of reception into full membership, but only of admission into preparatory membership" (Shipman, *DT,* 37). The Minority Report further held that "One seeking the privilege of full membership cannot claim the rights without assenting to the requirements" (Ibid., 39). Joseph C. Nate observed that the ritual test had been "in general and accepted use for more than a half century, and by virtue of such long and accepted use has fair claim to being an established standard of custom if not of law" (Ibid., 28).

The Judiciary Committee of the next Conference (1924) sharply distinguished between the way in which doctrinal standards function for clergy and for church members: "The phrase 'established standards of doctrine', has always been interpreted to include, besides the Articles of Religion, Wesley's *Notes on the New Testament,* the so-called *Large Minutes* of Conference, and four volumes of Wesley's Sermons. . . . But none of these standards are ever referred to, either by John Wesley or any contemporary minister, as conditions of membership in the Church. They are always and everywhere used as norms of teaching and therefore doctrinal requirements for preachers."[3] This interpretation prevailed.

After 1924, "The Order for Confirmation and Reception into the Church" of the *Book of Worship and Methodist Hymnal* contained no specific reference to the *Articles of Religion;* and so it remains today. In the period following 1964, persons seeking admission "profess publicly the faith into which they were baptized" by answering this question: "Do you receive and profess the Christian faith as contained in the Scriptures of the Old and New Testaments?"[4]

Summarizing: Insofar as trial of church members is concerned, laity can be charged for "disseminating doctrines contrary to the established standards of doctrine of the Church." Insofar as Methodist ritual is concerned, the profession of Christian faith "as contained in the Scriptures" is the sole doctrinal requirement.

5.
Continuing Issues of Wesleyan Doctrinal Standards

We have reviewed the formation and transplanting of Wesleyan doctrinal standards, their early maintenance and constitutional protection, the ways they have functioned and have been guarded through their first two centuries. This brings us to a consideration of six continuing issues:

1. How are we wisely to treat the questions of cultural, doctrinal, and theological pluralism in interpreting Wesleyan doctrinal standards?

2. Does the United Methodist *Discipline* textually specify established doctrinal standards?

3. Are the standards enforceable?

4. How is their binding character to be defined?

5. Can constitutional protection of the standards continue?

6. What if the "worst case" scenario occurs within United Methodism?

Can Cultural, Doctrinal, and Theological Pluralism Be Accommodated?

We are well-served by making careful distinctions between *cultural pluralism* (which has always been celebrated in the Wesleyan tradi-

tion), *doctrinal pluralism* (which is problematic and confusing unless rightly defined), and *theological pluralism* (which requires and guards academic freedom in the context of the free pursuit of ideas in the university).

Cultural pluralism is intrinsic to the universal scope of Christian witness and koinonia. It cannot be denied without a denial of the Christian gospel. Doctrinal pluralism can be affirmed, provided it moves generally within the frame of the church's doctrinal standards and does not inveigh against the standards. A doctrinal pluralism that would ignore or contest these standards is constitutionally rejected. The term *theological pluralism* finds its rightful home in the university, where the values of free inquiry are definitive of the nature of the university.

Theological pluralism means diverse theological viewpoints—i.e., views that may wish to speak to the church or affect the church, but if so they must proceed on the basis of the ground rules set by the church.

The church needs critical theological reflection; but if the fruit of that theological reflection is to find a place within official church teaching, it must take seriously the doctrinal context in which the church has historically found itself. Hence a disciplined and chastened theological pluralism or diversity is welcome; but if the ideas thus articulated seek to become official church teaching, they must do so within the framework of the church's historic and constitutional standards.

Cultural Pluralism

Christianity is a universal human community, embracing all languages and cultures. Cultural diversity is essential to its universality. The Wesleyan tradition shares with classical Christianity this understanding, reaching out to embrace every class, every culture, every race, every historical and social situation, while seeking to maintain union with Christ. The world being the object of God's love (John 3:16), the church's ministry must care not only for the church but also for the world, the *saeculum,* the secular sphere. The heavenly city (characterized by the selfless love of God) and the earthly city (characterized by the godless love of self) interact in history, wheat and tares being mixed together in the visible church.

> This heavenly city, then, while it sojourns on earth, calls citizens out of all nations, and gathers together a society of pilgrims of all languages, not scrupling about diversities in the manners, laws, and institutions whereby earthly peace is secured and maintained, but recognizing that, however various these are, they all tend to one and the same end of earthly peace. It therefore is so far from rescinding and abolishing these diversities, that it even

preserves and adapts them, so long only as no hindrance to the worship of the one supreme and true God is thus introduced.[1]

Doctrinal and Theological Pluralism

In enclaves where doctrinal pluralism has been regarded as a virtue, and toleration the epitome of virtues, there is good reason to listen carefully to the warnings arising in the early church—warnings not about cultural pluralism, but about an undisciplined doctrinal pluralism. The essential cultural pluralism of ecumenical Christianity was early and repeatedly affirmed. Many cultures, languages, and classes were embraced and transformed by Christianity; but amid this variety, there was a rigorous commitment to the unity of the body of Christ under apostolic teaching. There has been proximate unity in liturgy and sacrament, and a strong resistance to doctrinal pluralism: "Where diversity of doctrine is found, *there,* then, must be the corruption both of the Scripture and the expositions thereof."[2] Similarly, Wesley fought hard to maintain doctrinal cohesion within the diversity of Methodist societies.

It is precisely because the Wesleyan tradition has come alive in varied cultural situations, speaking many languages, addressing diverse historical challenges with flexible means, that all the more energy must again be given to ensure its fundamental unity, its direct continuity with the ministry of Jesus, its visible, organic cohesion in ancient ecumenical teaching. This requires a continuing battle with self-determined views different from (Gk., *hairesis*) the apostolic witness. It also requires a steady commitment to nurture in each new historical situation a living sense of participation in the one body of Christ. Wesley, like the early Christian writers, was just as adamant against schism as against heresy, because schism displayed lack of care toward the church through divisiveness.

The more subtle problem of doctrinal pluralism arises when it in fact ceases to be sufficiently pluralistic, when it becomes narrowly dogmatic and ideologically skewed and forces out those who accept traditional Christian teachings by making them feel unwanted in the mix of self-styled "prophetic" activism. This seems to be happening in some quarters of the United Methodist Church.

"Special-interest theologies" (a phrase that appeared in the 1976 United Methodist *Discipline*) must like all other views be held accountable to the established standards. The church must ask whether these new theologies inveigh against those standards or whether they deny that which those standards affirm.

What is meant by "special-interest theologies"? The 1980 *Discipline* mentioned not only "black theology, female liberation, political and ethnic theologies, third-world theology, and theologies of human rights," but also "neo-fundamentalism, new pentecostalism, new forms of Christian naturalism and secularity" (*Disc., 1980, 82, 83*). These theologies are invited to show how they can make their distinctive contributions from within the frame of reference of historic Wesleyan teaching. They are by no means exempted from accountability to the church's doctrinal standards. Views that are not contrary to our established standards may be preached and taught in United Methodist churches and schools; but insofar as they are contrary to these standards, they are potentially subject to admonition or trial.

Do 1972–84 Disciplines Textually Specify "Established Doctrinal Standards"?

All United Methodist *Disciplines* since the Plan of Union in 1968 plainly declare that Wesley's *Sermons* and *Notes*, along with the *Articles of Religion* and the E.U.B. *Confession* of 1962, are protected by the constitution from the establishment of contrary standards. This is seen in five different instances:

1. In case there should be a dispute as to how "our doctrinal standards" are to be interpreted, the *Discipline* specifically directs that "the Annual and General Conferences are the appropriate courts of appeal, under the guidance of the first two Restrictive Rules (which is to say, accordingly, the *Articles, Confession, Sermons,* and *Notes*)" (*Disc., 1984, 49*).

2. The 1972–84 *Disciplines* specifically hold that there is a dual norm operative in the "established standards of doctrine" referred to in the First Restrictive Rule: "The original distinction between the intended functions of the Articles on the one hand, and of the *Sermons* and *Notes* on the other, may be inferred from the double reference to them in the First Restrictive Rule (adopted in 1808 and unchanged ever since)" (*Disc., 1984, 45*). The *Discipline* further explains:

On the one hand, it [the constitution] forbids any further *alterations* of the Articles and, on the other, any further contrary *additions* "to our present existing, and established standards of doctrine" (i.e., the Minutes, *Sermons,* and *Notes*). (Ibid., 45).

The two-clause reading of the First Rule emphasizes the difference and complementarity between two sources—the *Articles* and other "established standards."

3. All *Disciplines* following the Plan of Union espouse as an official view the theory that the 1784 Conference accepted Wesley's *Sermons* and *Notes* as doctrinal standards:

> From their beginnings, the Methodists in America understood themselves as the dutiful heirs of Wesley and the Wesleyan tradition. In 1773 they affirmed their allegiance to the principles of the "Model Deed" and ratified this again in 1784, when they stipulated that "The London Minutes," including the doctrinal minutes of the early Conferences and the Model Deed, were accepted as their own doctrinal guidelines. In this way they established a threefold agency—the *Conference,* the *Sermons,* and the *Notes*—as their guides in matters of doctrine (Ibid., 44).

Unless amended, this interpretation must be considered the official United Methodist view of "established standards of doctrine."

4. The *Discipline* argues that "by plain historical inference," even if not by direct stipulation, Wesley's *Sermons* and *Notes* are constitutionally protected doctrinal standards. The following language was hammered out in connection with the Plan of Union between the Methodist Church and the Evangelical United Brethren in 1968:

> Wesley's *Sermons* and *Notes* were specifically included in our present and established standards of doc-

trine by plain historical inference (Ibid., 49).

5. Among "Foundation Documents" listed in the introduction to the section on "Foundation Documents" in the 1984 *Discipline* are "John Wesley's 'standard' Sermons" (Ibid., 54). The *Notes* are described as "Wesleyan Doctrinal Standards" and their function clarified in Paragraph 67 (Ibid., 41–44).

These five statements constitute both the historic consensus and the current official interpretation of United Methodist Doctrinal Standards.

Much of the discussion in our day hinges on whether the present *Discipline* is correct and well-grounded historically in drawing these conclusions. The purpose of Part One has been to make these historical references as precise as they reasonably can be and to show that the traditionally received view, currently under attack, is in fact well-grounded.

However clear or impressive the language of the present *Discipline* may be on these five points, it is regrettable that the preliminary Report of the Committee on Our Theological Task—a fine report in most other respects—has eliminated each and every one of the above five references. Thus, the Committee appointed by the 1984 General Conference to inquire into the "proper use of the so-called Methodist Quadrilateral" seems to have whittled away at the traditional standards, insofar as it omits precisely these five guarantees and specifications.

General Conferences of the future will serve the church well by retaining these passages or their equivalent in disciplinary revisions. If omitted by a particular General Conference, for the sake of clarity these provisions or their equivalent should be reinstated by a subsequent Conference.

Are Standards Enforceable?

What is to prevent clergy from inveighing against these standards? Are they only a paper tiger without plausible effectiveness—a private joke among clergy? Is there a will and way to sustain doctrinal integrity? Although disciplinary administration varies widely, the United Methodist *Discipline* itself states the following:

1. The *Discipline* concedes that the *Sermons, Notes, Articles,* and *Confession* are subject to continued historical interpretation. Reflection upon them will go through a process of development. Furthermore "there is no objection in principle to the continued development of still other doctrinal summaries and liturgical creeds that may gain acceptance and use in the church—without displacing those we already have" (*Disc., 1984,* 50).

2. The *Discipline* holds that theological inquiry in the United Methodist Church freely proceeds "within the boundaries defined by four main sources and guidelines for Christian theology: Scripture, tradition, experience, reason" (Ibid., 78). This is not to be construed as indifferentism or latitudinarianism. The *Discipline* specifically rejects the position of " 'theological indifferentism' — the notion that there are no essential doctrines" (Ibid., 73) preached in the Wesleyan tradition. "Serious concern for our 'doctrine and doctrinal standards' should inform, evaluate, and strengthen all

the forms of ministry by which we fulfill our calling" (Ibid., 85).

3. More importantly, these doctrinal standards have not only moral but also directive (sometimes called juridical or "legal," in the sense of "church law") power in the assessment of the work of the minister. For any pastor could be subject under the *Discipline* to admonition or trial on the charge of "dissemination of doctrines contrary to the established standards of doctrine of the Church." Standards protected by the constitution have been previously specified in a clear way by the *Discipline*: the *Articles, Confession, Sermons,* and *Notes* (Ibid., 44, 45, 49, 54). Hence one cannot claim that the doctrinal standards are wholly without definition and effective power.

4. The ordinal questions assume that those preparing for ordination will have studied carefully the historic Wesleyan "doctrines," be thoroughly examined on them, and in good conscience view them as scriptural teaching, and be willing to preach these doctrines and maintain them (*Disc., 1984,* 212). No candidate can be approved for conference membership without answering these questions. If candidates enter the United Methodist ministry without deliberately consenting to these standards, the fault lies both with the Conference Board of Ministry and the conscience of the ordinand.

The historic consensus has been fairly and concisely defined by Nolan B. Harmon in a way that reflects the post-Plan of Union situation: "United Methodist standards of doctrine are more definitely stated in Twenty-five Articles of Religion, The Confession of Faith, Fifty-Two Sermons of John Wesley, and Notes on the New Testament by John Wesley."[3]

How Is Binding Character to Be Defined?

It is best not to make an overly simple distinction between "legal standards of doctrine" and "the traditionally accepted doctrinal writings." Heitzenrater has proposed that the former should include only the *Articles of Religion,* which he calls "*the* standards of doctrine."[4] The latter category, having no binding status, would extend expansively to include not only Wesley's *Sermons* and *Notes* but "the broad range of Wesley's works" and "the writings of Fletcher"; yet all of these would function merely "in a supplemental and illustrative role," serving not as "doctrinal *standards*" but only "as exemplary illustrations of the Methodist doctrinal heritage."[5]

I have three principal objections to this proposed twofold distinction:

1. The proposed distinction needlessly adds to the corpus of "traditionally accepted doctrinal standards" materials that have never gained sufficient general consent to be given equal categorical status with Wesley's *Sermons* and *Notes* and that were never intended to be protected by the First Rule.

2. More seriously, the proposal takes away from the *Sermons* and *Notes* the long-accepted status of "standard sermons" or "established doctrinal standards" and reduces them to diffuse "statements" or "writings." In other words, this proposal neglects to distinguish the special place of the *Sermons* and *Notes* as normative doctrinal guides within the larger Wesleyan corpus. If the *Sermons* and *Notes* are thrown

into a more general secondary category of Wesleyan doctrinal writings—including Fletcher, Watson, and various catechisms—that would amount to a subtle demotion of the role of Wesley in United Methodist doctrinal standards and to the most significant amendment in doctrinal standards since 1808.

3. The proposed distinction has little precedent in the previous two centuries of consensual reception.

To avert these problems, a threefold distinction would seem more in accord with the facts of the received tradition. Such a threefold distinction would show that two types of doctrinal standards are protected by the constitution: (1) the concise standard that stands alone and separable from the others only in the case of the trial of preachers (i.e., the *Articles of Religion*) and (2) the broader "established standards of doctrine" that apply to preaching and interpretation (i.e., Wesley's *Sermons* and *Notes*). In addition to these constitutionally protected standards of doctrine, it is fitting to recognize a third category of (3) other writings of doctrinal instruction not included under the First Rule but received by wide usage and having high expository value. This third category includes the Six Tracts printed at various times in the *Disciplines* of 1788–1808, the remainder of Wesley's *Works,* the Wesley's hymns, the doctrine contained in the *Large Minutes,* and the catechisms approved by the General Conference of 1852.

Can Constitutional Protection of the Standards Continue?

Will the First Restrictive Rule die the death of a thousand qualifications? With few exceptions, the only portions of the *Discipline* of 1808 that have been retained without change are those protected by the Restrictive Rules. Almost everything else has been repeatedly tinkered with, some paragraphs almost every four years. The constitution writers of 1808 understood the force of a legislative version of Murphy's Law, that "anything that can be amended will be amended."

We can be grateful that they had sufficient sagacity to prevent our doctrinal experimentation and presumed "improvements" for eighteen decades. Their success is attested by the fact that "no amendment calling for doctrinal change has ever been proposed by any General Conference of any body of American Methodism" (Harmon, *EWM*, 702–93).

But a new situation has emerged in which the Rule may be circumvented, not by amendment, but by an imaginative reinterpretation of history. Now historians may succeed in what others have been unable legislatively or constitutionally to accomplish: to circumvent the First Restrictive Rule.

To counter this challenge, three specific statements should be retained in future *Disciplines* to prevent the implication that United Methodists are now rejecting historic Wesleyan doctrinal standards:

1. Current church law assumes that for the determination of otherwise irreconcilable doctrinal disputes, the Conference must stand "under the guidance of the first two Restrictive Rules (which is to say, the Articles and Confession, the *Sermons* and the *Notes*" (*Disc., 1984,* 49). This sentence clearly specifies that the *Sermons* and *Notes* are protected under the First Rule. Many

who are committed to Wesleyan roots will work against the exclusion of this statement. And if it is excluded, they would undertake a rigorous effort using every democratic means to seek its inclusion at the next General Conference.

2. The two-clause theory has long been the accepted, official interpretation of the First Rule:

The original distinction between the intended functions of the Articles on the one hand, and of the *Sermons* and *Notes* on the other, may be inferred from the double reference to them in the First Restrictive Rule (adopted in 1808 and unchanged ever since). (*Disc., 1984,* 45).

This statement should also be retained.

3. Finally, all *Disciplines* since the Plan of Union have contained a simple, descriptive paragraph that cannot easily be circumvented by subsequent General Conference action. Even if this paragraph is omitted, it belongs permanently and intrinsically to the Plan of Union. It is a statement of fact concerning what the 1968 Plan of Union decided and in fact enacted:

In the Plan of Union for the United Methodist Church, the Preface to the Methodist Articles of Religion and the Evangelical United Brethren Confession of Faith explains that both had been accepted as doctrinal standards for the new church. It was declared that "they are deemed congruent if not identical in their doctrinal perspectives, and not in conflict." Additionally, it was stipulated that although the language of the First Restrictive Rule has never been formally defined, Wesley's *Sermons* and *Notes* were specifically included in our present existing and established standards of doctrine by plain historical inference. (*Disc., 1984*, 49).

This paragraph is a crucial, straightforward, factual report describing the premise of the Plan of Union and its reasoning about doctrinal standards. Since the Plan of Union is a decisive event, it cannot be legislatively refashioned by a subsequent General Conference. The Plan of Union brought together the constitutions of two bodies so as to form a new church, and hence was itself a significant constitutional act, creating the United Methodist Church, which heretofore had not existed as a legal entity.

These eggs cannot be unscrambled. Even if this phrase of paragraph 67 were to be omitted by a later General Conference, that would not revise the terms of Union. If a subsequent General Conference should attempt substantively to revise the Plan of Union (which is highly unlikely), that action doubtlessly would set in motion or lead to a complex series of judicial challenges.

If any of the above three passages are preserved, the *Discipline* has sufficiently preserved its protection of the *Sermons* and *Notes* as doctrinal standards. Even if all three passages are omitted in a future *Discipline,* that would not necessarily constitute an outright rejection of the two-clause theory, unless that were clearly specified by a General Conference (since it has been affirmed by Judicial Council determinations). Regrettably, all three sentences were stricken in early drafts for a revised Discipline of the General Conference Committee on Our Theological Task.[6]

What If the "Worst Case" Occurs?

Let us suppose a more radically deteriorated situation, however, in which (a) a General Conference might publicly disavow one or more aspects of the *Articles, Sermons,* or *Notes,* (b) the Judicial Council affirms that disavowal, and (c) civil courts uphold that such a disavowal is legal and not a violation of the fiduciary duty of the Conference to the church. Would not that be a time for concerned Wesleyans to abandon the ship and separate from an apostate church? Although it is very hazardous to anticipate nuances of potential future situations, here are some questions and principles to be applied to such a reflection:

Only those who remain in the church are in a position to influence its possible reform. Those who abandon the church are by that action indicating their unwillingness to stay and reshape the church.

Would not abandonment simply turn over the vast properties of the United Methodist Church to those who care less about their Wesleyan roots? The real winners in a massive withdrawal of Wesleyans and Evangelicals from the United Methodist Church would be a few liberal elitists whose day otherwise may be shorter than many imagine. It is well to take a long view of the recovery of the church rather than a short-range view of immediate problems.

But is there not some point at which withdrawal becomes necessary? There must be—and one cannot at that time be the conscience for another. But we are more likely to be too quick to judge the unredeemability of the church and too hesitant in actually working on a long-term, realistic basis for its gradual, incremental reformation. Even if neo-Wesleyan United Methodists stand in tension with many aspects of present church leadership, mustn't we continue to pray for the church and be attentive to how the Holy Spirit is working quietly as leaven within it?

Perhaps Evangelicals can ultimately persuade the liberal wing of United Methodism to become more inclusive, in accordance with its own ideology of inclusivism, so as to be better included in the mix of pluralism. The Anglican Evangelicals provide a profound pattern for this situation. Taking the long view, patiently remaining in the Anglican church, they have come into considerably more influence than most thought possible some decades ago. This is an important pattern for Wesleyans languishing in the oppressive ethos of liberal elitism.

Do we not have in Wesley's own life a pattern of rigorous loyalty to one's own church, even when there remain outstanding differences? Wesley stood fast as an Anglican minister until his dying day, despite many differences with its leadership. Wesleyans don't split. They stay and work to heal.

Conclusions

In this chapter we have inquired into continuing issues that attend the discussion of Wesleyan doctrinal standards. Six conclusions may be derived:

1. While cultural pluralism is intrinsic to Christian community, and theological pluralism characterizes theological life in the academic community, doctrinal pluralism is problematic and at best proceeds under the guidance of the church's established doctrinal standards.

2. The current United Methodist *Discipline* adequately specifies textually the established doctrinal standards of Methodism.

3. The established standards are adequately warranted for enforcement in current church law.

4. Their binding character is best highlighted by not confusing the *Sermons, Notes,* and *Articles of Religion* with other materials not protected by the constitution.

5. The constitutional protection of the standards is best insured by a traditional consensual reading of the Restrictive Rules.

6. The "worst case" scenario still asks hard questions of those who would tend toward separation.

PART TWO:
Doctrinal Documents
of the Wesleyan Tradition

The main purpose of Part Two is to provide documentary resources for further study of doctrinal standards in the Wesleyan tradition. In Part One we traced the historic debate on doctrinal definition in the largest of the Wesleyan-rooted church bodies (the United Methodist Church and its predecessors) through its major phases to the present crisis. Now we broaden our range of study to include primary documentation of doctrinal definition from the scattered Wesleyan family of church bodies. This requires examination of selected documents on doctrinal standards from various international Wesleyan-rooted churches, revealing their similarities and differences.

A major need in the emergent pan-Wesleyan dialogue on doctrinal standards is to make pivotal documentation available so that comparative studies can in fact proceed. No single volume of this sort is currently available. Since these documents are scattered widely in numerous separable church bureaucracies and rather difficult to locate (even assuming good library facilities), we thought it best not to shift the burden of searching for these documents to the reader, but rather to provide them in convenient form. Hence, the last part of this book has been conceived essentially as an appendix of primary sources with a spare apparatus of commentary. We have reserved space only for the most crucial and representative forms of documents.

Accordingly, Chapter 6 explores (1) how the *Explanatory Notes upon the New Testament* function as doctrinal standards, with brief selections from the Preface to the *Notes* and from the commentary on the Beatitudes, (2) how the *Sermons* are to be viewed as doctrinal standards, with selections from the Preface to the *Sermons,* an outline summary covering major themes of Wesley's *Sermons on Several Occasions,* and the doctrinal core of Wesley's sermon on "The Catholic Spirit," and (3) the *Articles of Religion* as doctrinal standards, with a discussion of the nature and problems of assent to the *Articles* and a documentary analysis of the reduction of the (Anglican) Thirty-nine to (Wesleyan) Twenty-five *Articles.*

Chapter 7 presents a preliminary definition of the pan-Wesleyan family of churches, a collation of variants of phrases of *Articles of Religion* in the doctrinal statements of Wesleyan-rooted churches, a series of short documents about international statements of Wesleyan doctrinal standards (by church bodies that stem largely from international missions of Wesleyan-type churches), selections from the 1852 *Catechism No. 1* and from doctrinal traditions of the Evangelical Church and the United Brethren Church.

Chapter 8 presents a syllabus of a lay study course on the *Articles of Religion,* with annotations by Thomas Coke and Francis Asbury from the rare 1798 *Discipline.*

6.

The Textual Core of the Wesleyan Doctrinal Tradition

The foregoing "state of the family" review has made recurrent reference to Wesley's *Notes, Sermons,* and *Articles* as the textual core of the Methodist doctrinal tradition. Our purpose now is to show how these three types of doctrinal standards function in a complementary way to guide the contemporary Wesleyan family.

There are crucial clues embedded within these documents as to how they are best conceived and implemented as doctrinal standards. In this chapter we will search out some of those clues. Our first task is to set forth a sufficient introduction of the *Explanatory Notes upon the New Testament* that modern readers may understand them functionally as doctrinal standards.

I. The Notes As Doctrinal Standards

From late 1753 to early 1754, Wesley underwent a period of illness and enforced recuperation that prevented his usual schedule of heavy travel. In Bristol, he began to put together the *Explanatory Notes upon the New Testament,* which were published in 1755.

Wesley launched out on this task in response to "a loud call from God," aware that his life might be cut short. (He continued to live for almost four more decades—but at that time he felt that "my day is far spent" and "I must not delay any longer.")

The preface to the *Notes,* written on January 4, 1754, provides the most precise statement of Wesley's own view of their function and sources.[1] Wesley openly acknowledged his debt to Johann Albrecht Bengel (*Gnomon novi Testamenti,* 1742), Philip Doddridge (*The Family Expositor,* 1761, 1762), John Heylyn of Westminster (*Theological Lectures,* 2 vols., 1749–61), and John Guyse of Hartford (*Practical Expositor,* 3 vols., 1739–52).

Does the Translation Signal Openness to the Critical Spirit?

Wesley's distinctive translation of the New Testament is just as significant as his exegetical *Notes,* as George Croft Cell has pointed out (*JWNT*). It is quite impossible to separate Wesley's translation from his annotations, since his *Notes* comment upon his (not the Authorized) translation, based upon his own sentence-by-sentence analysis of the Greek text. In Wesley's version, for example, the word *charity* becomes *love,* as in most modern translations. Repetitions are steadily pruned by Wesley and inverted syntax straightened out for easier reading.

That Wesley was a "man of one book" (*homo unius libri*) does not indicate a "boundary of his reading" so much as "the center of gravity in his thinking" (Cell, *JWNT,* viii). Daily Scripture study for Wesley always meant study of the Greek text. He had studied it so diligently over a lifetime that he often quoted the Greek text spontaneously in conversations. Since Wesley argued for the *sensus literalis* of Scripture unless a metaphorical intent seemed to be present in the text, and since he rejected any doctrine that could not be established by Scripture, some have erroneously viewed him as a proto-fundamentalist or a rigid biblical literalist, dubiously projecting twentieth-century patterns of exegesis upon his century. Wesley was indeed a strong biblicist—but not a rigid anti-metaphorical literalist. This is seen in the spirit of his *Notes* and in the way in which he dealt with numerous technical problems.

At the time Wesley retranslated many parts of the King James Version, it was piously regarded in its precise 1611 English form. But Wesley returned to the Greek text as his norm, frequently supplying his own amended translation. Further, he did not hesitate to apply the best methods of textual criticism to seek to establish which text was the most ancient and reliable. As a former Oxford tutor in Greek, he had access to the best Greek texts and textual methods of his day—far better than the translators of 1611 had.

Wesley minutely examined every word of the Greek New Testament in order to make his translation for the *Notes.* Some of his changes were stylistic, but he specifically disavowed making unnecessary alterations: "I have never knowingly, so much as in one place, altered it for altering's sake." Wesley did not want to change the received text too much or too little, or frivolously, or for the sake of innovation. He highly valued the "solemn and venerable [version] in the old language" and was himself "unwilling to part with what we have been long accustomed to, and to love the very words by which God has often conveyed strength."

In the preface, Wesley set forth his procedure and criteria for revisions. He strongly commended the "common English translation" (KJV) as "in general, so far as I can judge, abundantly the best that I have seen. Yet I do not say it is incapable of being brought, in several places, nearer to the original." Nor was he willing to admit that the Greek manuscripts from which the 1611 translation was taken were "always the most correct; and therefore I shall take the liberty, as occasion may require, to make here and there a small alteration."

Small alteration? In 12,000 instances he decided to depart from the King James text and supply his own translation from the Greek! The outcome was a substantially revised translation that remarkably anticipates more recent efforts at New Testament translation. Professor Cell found that on average one half to three fourths of "Wesley's deviations from the Authorized Version have been adopted by the revisers of 1881 and in more recent private translations." In the first seven chapters of Matthew, for example, "113 of Wesley's alterations (out of a total of 231), agree wholly or partly with those in the 1881 Revision" (Cell, *JWNT,* xiii). Many of these alterations were based upon the fact that Wesley had a Greek text far superior in reliability to those available in 1611.

This is one of the most surprising aspects of the Wesleyan doctrinal standards—they included, not excluded, the best available resources of critical Scripture study. Critical scholarship was not defensively avoided or grudgingly tolerated, but happily and enthusiastically undertaken as an aspect of faith's historical honesty. This is what has made the *Notes* an unusual sort of doctrinal standard. In translating and interpreting text after text, Wesley repeatedly demonstrated that he was keenly aware of the relation of text and historical context. A monograph should be written on the ways in which both Wesley's *Notes* and translation anticipate in a rudimentary way many themes of subsequent modern New Testament scholarship. There is little reason to think that Wesley would have taken a defensive stance against the developments in critical scholarship in the century that followed his. Indeed, his own pattern of openness was followed largely by Methodist biblical interpreters that came after him.

Neither Wesley nor Wesleyans make the claim that this English translation should be viewed as a definitive translation, for Wesley himself admitted that his own translation would be improvable, and he invited its improvement—assuming

further inquiry would follow into problems of alternative Greek texts, language studies, and historical issues. The more salient fact is that the Wesleyan connection has a doctrinal standard that permits and invites critical Scripture study, and seeks to utilize for students the best available linguistic and historical scholarship to obtain the best biblical text and its most accurate interpretation.

The first edition of the *Notes* was published in 1755; the standard edition was published in 1760. So convinced was Wesley of the value of his translation that in 1790 he published a convenient *pocket edition* of his New Testament translation without the *Notes.* In the preface to this pocket edition, he wrote (after having made one more careful revision): "In this edition, the translation is brought as near as possible to the original; yet the alterations are few and seemingly small; but they may be of considerable importance." This revision of his New Testament translation was to be Wesley's last important publication.

How Do the Notes Function As Doctrinal Standards?

Amid the vast quantity of Wesley studies, dissertations, and monographs, the *Notes* have been relatively neglected. John Lawson has written an introduction and commentary on selected notes in *Selections From John Wesley's Notes on the New Testament.* John Deschner has touched upon the authority of the notes as doctrinal standards in *Wesley's Christology*[2] and in his article "Methodism's Thirteenth Article."[3]

In the British Methodist tradition, there is an obligatory requirement for preachers on trial to read the

Notes. There has been no such stated requirement in the American Methodist tradition, although the *Notes* are repeatedly cited as doctrinal standards, and ministers are generally expected to know these standards.

There are several ways in which the *Notes* may be understood to function as doctrinal standards:

1. Minimally, they are doctrinal standards in the historical sense that they have in fact been regarded by the Methodist tradition as being of central value to Scripture study.

2. They continue to be read for edification and as requisite to an understanding of the Scriptures as viewed in the Wesleyan tradition.

3. While not exegetical standards in the direct sense that each note is to be taken as the standard of interpretation of a given text, the *Notes* provide a pattern for biblical study in the Wesleyan tradition.

4. A closely related, yet more diffuse, view has been stated by John Lawson: "Our Methodist 'standard' of preaching and doctrine implied by the *Notes on the New Testament* is not the adoption of Wesley's New Testament scholarship as a fixed pattern. It is the general principle that one should turn constantly to the book of God and study it with all the grace and all the sense one has" (Lawson, *SWMN*, 113).

A case can be made for each of these four complementary hypotheses. All are to some degree valid. It is regrettable that there has been so little recent discussion concerning strengths and limits of the *Notes* and how the *Notes* may reasonably function as standards. With the publication of the Bicentennial scholarly edition of the *Notes*,[4] it is hoped that the final decade of this century may elicit such inquiries.

What were Wesley's controlling purposes in writing the *Notes*? These he ably expressed in his preface:

1. They were designed primarily for the unlettered lay person of the Methodist Societies for guidance in the daily study of Scripture. Hence it does not appear that they were originally written as a doctrinal guide for preaching, although in due time (by 1763) they came to have that role and status. The *Notes* were originally written for "serious persons, who have not the advantage of learning," for "plain, unlettered" persons "who understand only their mother-tongue."

2. The *Notes* reveal a foundational principle of Methodism: that Scripture is the authoritative norm of Christian teaching, and all interpretation has reference to its texts.

3. The *Notes* served another implied purpose that was related to the controversies in which Wesley was engaged with the views of other exegetes. Wesley was responding to Calvinist, Antinomian, formalist, and Roman exegetes, all of whom

claimed the support of Scripture for their views, and the claims had to be met. In his *Notes,* the essential purpose of Wesley is to overturn the exegesis of customary Calvinist and Antinomian "proof-texts," as well as to emphasize the importance and significance of other passages in the face of formalist neglect (Lawson, *SJWN,* 10).

The minister today may wonder: Why should I read Wesley's *Notes* when I have available much more up-to-date scholarship in contemporary commentaries? Some responses for consideration:

1. Wesley's *Notes* would not suggest that one should rule out inquiry

into succeeding biblical scholarship. So one need not put the question in terms of "either/or." Both Wesley's and contemporary commentaries can be read in a complementary way with profit.

2. If one limits one's reading to modern biblical scholarship, one may lose touch with earlier insights into Scripture and hence become captive to a narrow modernity that assumes the intrinsic superiority of whatever is current.

3. Those who invest serious time in Wesley's *Notes* seldom come away feeling that the exercise was merely one of routine historical inquiry into a quaint document. The commentary can still touch hearts and challenge contemporary ways of living. This can be tested only by personal reading.

The Preface to the Notes

In the following presentation of the preface, I have added headings to the sections in brackets and omitted the last four paragraphs.

*   *   *

PREFACE (SELECTIONS)

[A Work Long Conceived, Long Delayed]

1. For many years I have had a desire of setting down, and laying together, what has occurred to my mind, either in reading, thinking, or conversation, which might assist serious persons, who have not the advantage of learning, in understanding the New Testament. But I have been continually deterred from attempting anything of this kind by a deep sense of my own inability; of my want, not only of learning for such a work, but much more of

experience and wisdom. This has often occasioned my laying aside the thought. And when, by much importunity, I have been prevailed upon to resume it, still I determined to delay it as long as possible, that (if it should please God) I might finish my work and my life together.

2. But having lately had a loud call from God to arise and go hence, I am convinced that, if I attempt anything of this kind at all, I must not delay any longer. My day is far spent, and, even in a natural way, the shadows of the evening come on apace; and I am the rather induced to do what little I can in this way because I can do nothing else, being prevented by my present weakness from either traveling or preaching. But, blessed by God, I can still read and write and think. Oh that it may be to His glory!

3. It will be easily discerned, even from what I have said already, and much more from the notes themselves, that they were not principally designed for men of learning, who are provided with many other helps; and much less for men of long and deep experience in the ways and Word of God. I desire to sit at their feet, and to learn of them. But I write chiefly for plain, unlettered men, who understand only their mother-tongue, and yet reverence and love the Word of God, and have a desire to save their souls.

[Criteria for Amending the Authorized King James Version]

4. In order to assist these in such a measure as I am able, I design, first, to set down the text itself, for the most part, in the common English translation, which is, in general, so far as I can judge, abundantly the best that I have seen. Yet I do not

say it is incapable of being brought, in several places, nearer to the original. Neither will I affirm that the Greek copies from which this translation was made are always the most correct; and therefore I shall take the liberty, as occasion may require, to make here and there a small alteration.

5. I am very sensible this will be liable to objection; nay, to objections of quite opposite kinds. Some will probably think the text is altered too much, and others that it is altered too little. To the former I would observe, that I have never knowingly so much as in one place, altered it for altering's sake: but there and there only, where, first, the sense was made better, stronger, clearer, or more consistent with the context; secondly, where the sense being equally good, the phrase was better or nearer the original. To the latter, who think the alterations too few, and that the translation might have been nearer still, I answer, This is true; I acknowledge it might. But what valuable end would it have answered to multiply such trivial alterations as add neither clearness nor strength to the text? This I could not prevail upon myself to do; so much the less, because there is, to my apprehension, I know not what peculiarly solemn and venerable in the old language of our translation. And suppose this to be a mistaken apprehension, and an instance of human infirmity; yet is it not an excusable infirmity, to be unwilling to part with what we have been long accustomed to, and to love the very words by which God has often conveyed strength or comfort to our souls?

[The Intended Audience]

6. I have endeavoured to make the notes as short as possible, that the comment may not obscure or swallow up the text; and as plain as possible, in pursuance of my main design, to assist the unlearned reader. For this reason I have studiously avoided not only all curious and critical inquiries, and all use of the learned languages, but all such methods of reasoning and modes of expression as people in common life are unacquainted with. For the same reason as I rather endeavour to obviate than to propose and answer objections, so I purposely decline going deep into many difficulties, lest I should leave the ordinary reader behind me.

[Sources for Commentary and Method of Abridgment]

7. I once designed to write down barely what occurred to my own mind, consulting none but the inspired writers. But no sooner was I acquainted with that great light of the Christian world (lately gone to his reward) Bengelius, than I entirely changed my design, being thoroughly convinced it might be of more service to the cause of religion, were I barely to translate his *Gnomon Novi Testamenti,* than to write many volumes upon it. Many of his excellent notes I have therefore translated; many more I have abridged, omitting that part which was purely critical, and giving the substance of the rest. Those various readings, likewise, which he has showed to have a vast majority of ancient copies and translations on their side, I have without scruple incorporated with the text; which, after his manner, I have divided all along (though

not omitting the common division into chapters and verses, which is of use on various accounts) according to the matter it contains, making a larger or small pause, just as the sense requires. And even this is such a help, in many places, as one who has not tried it can scarcely conceive.

8. I am likewise indebted for some useful observations to Dr. Heylyn's *Theological Lectures;* and for many more to Dr. Guyse, and to *The Family Expositor* of the late pious and learned Dr. Doddridge. It was a doubt with me, for some time, whether I should not subjoin to every note I received from them the name of the author from whom it was taken, especially considering I had transcribed some, and abridged many more, almost in the words of the author. But upon further consideration I resolved to name none, that nothing might divert the mind of the reader from keeping close to the point in view, and receiving what was spoke, only according to its own intrinsic value.

9. I cannot flatter myself so far (to use the words of one of the above-named writers) as to imagine that I have fallen into no mistakes in a work of so great difficulty. But my own conscience acquits me of having designedly misrepresented any single passage of Scripture, or of having written one line with a purpose of inflaming the hearts of Christians against each other. . . .

* * *

The Beatitudes:
A Selection From the Notes

A brief example here of Wesley's translation and *Notes* may be useful to the reader unacquainted with them. Wesley's treatment of the Beatitudes shows how he anticipated modern translations and commented concisely upon the text. (Italics in the text indicate a deviation from the KJV, while an ellipsis indicates the omission of a word or words appearing in the KJV.)

* * *

Matthew. Chap. V. 2. And he opened his mouth and taught them, saying: *Happy* are the poor in spirit; for theirs is the kingdom of heaven. *Happy* are they that mourn; for they shall be comforted. *Happy* are the meek; for they shall inherit the earth. *Happy* are they *that* . . . hunger and thirst after righteousness; for they shall be *satisfied. Happy* are the merciful; for they shall obtain mercy. *Happy* are the pure in heart; for they shall see God. *Happy* are the peace makers; for they shall be called the children of God. *Happy* are they who are persecuted for righteousness' sake; for theirs is the kingdom of heaven. *Happy* are ye when men shall revile . . . and persecute you, and . . . say all manner of evil against you falsely for my sake: Rejoice and be exceeding glad; for great is your reward in heaven; for *so* persecuted they the prophets *who* were before you (Matt. 5:3–7, *JWNT,* 6).

2. *And he opened his mouth*—A phrase which always denotes a set and solemn discourse. *And taught them*—To bless men, to make men happy, was the great business for which our Lord came into the world. And accordingly He here pronounces eight blessings together, annexing them to so many steps in Christianity. Knowing that happiness is our common aim, and that an innate instinct continually urges us

to the pursuit of it. He in the kindest manner applies to that instinct, and directs it to its proper object.

Though all men desire, yet few attain, happiness, because they seek it where it is not to be found. Our Lord therefore begins His divine institution, which is the complete art of happiness, by laying down, before all that have ears to hear, the true, and only true, method of acquiring it.

Observe the benevolent condescension of our Lord. He seems, as it were, to lay aside His supreme authority as our Legislator, that he may the better act the part of our friend and Saviour. Instead of using the lofty style, in positive commands, He in a more gentle and engaging way, insinuates His will and our duty, by pronouncing those happy who comply with it.

3. *Happy are the poor*—In the following discourse there is, (1) a sweet invitation to true holiness and happiness (verses 3–12); (2) a persuasive to impart it to others (verses (13–16); (3) a description of true Christian holiness (verses 17–vii.12); in which it is easy to observe, the latter part exactly answers the former; (4) the conclusion, giving a sure mark of the true way, warning against false prophets, exhorting to follow after holiness. *The poor in spirit*—They who are unfeignedly penitent; they who are truly convinced of sin; who see and feel the state they are in by nature, being deeply sensible of their sinfulness, guiltiness, helplessness. *For theirs is the kingdom of heaven*—The present inward kingdom; righteousness and peace and joy in the Holy Ghost; as well as the eternal kingdom, if they endure to the end.

4. *They that mourn*—Either for their own sins, or for other men's, and are steadily and habitually serious. *They shall be comforted*—More solidly and deeply even in this world; and eternally, in heaven.

5. *Happy are the meek*—They that hold all their passions and affections evenly balanced. *They shall inherit the earth*—They shall have all things really necessary for life and godliness. They shall enjoy whatever portion God hath given them here, and shall hereafter possess the new earth, wherein dwelleth righteousness.

6. *They that hunger and thirst after righteousness*—After the holiness here described. *They shall be satisfied*—with it.

7. *The merciful* — The tenderhearted; they who love all men as themselves. *They shall obtain mercy*—Whatever mercy therefore we desire from God, the same let us show to our brethren. He will repay us a thousand-fold the love we bear to any for His sake.

8. *The pure in heart*—The sanctified; they who love God with all their hearts. *They shall see God*—In all things here; hereafter in glory.

9. *The peacemakers*—They that, out of love to God and man, do all possible good to all men. Peace, in the Scripture sense, implies all blessings, temporal and eternal. *They shall be called the children of God*—Shall be acknowledged such by God and men. One would imagine a person of this amiable temper and behavior would be the darling of mankind. But our Lord well knew it would not be so, as long as Satan was the prince of this world. He therefore warns them before of the treatment all were to expect who were determined thus to tread in His steps, by immediately subjoining,

Happy are *they who* are *persecuted for righteousness' sake.*

Through this whole discourse, we cannot but observe the most exact method that can possibly be conceived. Every paragraph, every sentence, is closely connected both with that which precedes and that which follows it. And is not this the pattern for every Christian preacher? If any then are able to follow it without any premeditation, well; if not, let them not dare to preach without it. No rhapsody, no incoherency, whether the things spoken be true or false, comes of the Spirit of Christ.

10. *For righteousness' sake*—That is, because they have, or follow after, the righteousness here described. He that is truly a righteous man, he that mourns, and he that is "pure in heart," yea, all "that will live godly in Christ Jesus, shall suffer persecution" (2 Tim. 3:12). The world will always say, "Away with such fellows from the earth!" "They are made to reprove our thoughts. They are grievous to us even to behold. Their lives are not like other men's; their ways are of another fashion" (Wisd. of Sol. 2:14–15).

11. *Revile*—When present. *Say all evil*—When you are absent.

12. *Your reward*—Even over and above the happiness that naturally and directly results from holiness.

*   *   *

While the above selections cannot substitute for a careful examination of the text of the *Notes*, they provide an introduction to the gist of the work and a preliminary view of how the *Notes* may be understood as a doctrinal standard.

II. Wesley's Sermons As Doctrinal Standards

Our limited purpose in this section is (1) to present a selection of texts and summary statements that reveal the general character of the "four volumes of Sermons" mentioned in Wesley's Model Deed and (2) to consider the role Wesley intended them to play as doctrinal standards. We will clarify the purpose of the *Sermons* by examining Wesley's 1746 preface to them, by tracking the deliberate sequence of themes of the *Sermons* through their own implicit organizational structure, and by identifying the doctrinal core of the "catholic spirit" that is concisely set forth in paragraphs 12–18 of Wesley's sermon by that title.

Wesley's Preface to the Sermons on Several Occasions

In 1746 Wesley wrote a moving preface to his *Sermons on Several Occasions,* and it was reprinted in every edition of the *Sermons* published in his lifetime. It set forth his interpretation of the role the *Sermons* were to play for Methodists.

He showed why the sermonic form was the most appropriate teaching format for Methodist doctrine, how this teaching was to be grounded in Scripture, and why he sought to speak "plain truth for plain people." The preface asked three questions: (1) Whence comes our teaching? (2) Whether we have changed our doctrine? and (3) In what spirit is the truth to be sought? The preface contained a series of memorable paired contrasting terms that have made it among the most-quoted of Wesley's writings:

all I have read . . . forgotten	sentiments of my heart . . . expressed
philosophical speculations	plain truth for plain people
perplexed reasonings	naked truths of the gospel
words not easily understood	words used in common life
bodies of divinity	follow the chain of my own thought
outside religion	heart religion
a show of learning	a man of one Book
elegant, oratorical dress	essentials of true religion
the inventions of men	scriptural experimental religion
the busy ways of men	the way to heaven
an arrow through the air	unchangeable eternity
beat me down	take me by the hand
give me hard names	point me out a better way
truth without love	love lacking complete knowledge
the smoke of anger	dimmed eyes searching for truth

It is fitting that Wesley's preface be included in this documentary part of our study as an indicator of the unique type of doctrinal standard found in the Wesleyan tradition.

*   *   *

PREFACE

1. The following sermons contain the substance of what I have been preaching for between eight and nine years last past. During that time I have frequently spoken in public on every subject in the ensuing collection: and I am not conscious that there is any one point of doctrine on which I am accustomed to speak in public which is not here—incidentally, if not professedly—laid before every Christian reader. Every serious man who peruses these will therefore see in the clearest manner what those doctrines are which I embrace and teach as the essentials of true religion.

2. But I am thoroughly sensible these are not proposed in such a manner as some may expect. Nothing here appears in an elaborate, elegant, or oratorical dress. If it had been my desire or design to write them, my leisure would not permit. But in truth I at present designed nothing less, for I now write (as I generally speak) *ad populum*—to the bulk of mankind—to those who neither relish nor understand the art of speaking, but who notwithstanding are competent judges of those truths which are necessary to present and future happiness. I mention this that curious readers may spare themselves the labour of seeking for what they will not find.

3. I design plain truth for plain

people. Therefore of set purpose I abstain from all nice and philosophical speculations, from all perplexed and intricate reasonings, and as far as possible from even the show of learning, unless in sometimes citing the original Scriptures. I labour to avoid all words which are not easy to be understood, all which are not used in common life; and in particular those kinds of technical terms that so frequently occur in bodies of divinity, those modes of speaking which men of reading are intimately acquainted with, but which to common people are an unknown tongue. Yet I am not assured that I do not sometimes slide into them unawares: it is so extremely natural to imagine that a word which is familiar to ourselves is so to all the world.

4. Nay, my design is in some sense to forget all that ever I have read in my life. I mean to speak, in the general, as if I had never read one author, ancient or modern (always excepting the inspired). I am persuaded that, on the one hand, this may be a means of enabling me more clearly to express the sentiments of my heart, while I simply follow the chain of my own thoughts, without entangling myself with those of other men; and that, on the other, I shall come with fewer weights upon my mind, with less of prejudice and prepossession, either to search for myself or to deliver to others the naked truths of the gospel.

5. To candid, reasonable men I am not afraid to lay open what have been the inmost thoughts of my heart. I have thought, I am a creature of a day, passing through life as an arrow through the air. I am a spirit come from God and returning to God; just hovering over the great gulf; till a few moments hence I am no more seen—I drop into an unchangeable eternity! I want to know one thing, the way to heaven—how to land safe on the happy shore. God himself has condescended to teach the way: for this very end he came from heaven. He hath written it down in a book. O give me that book! At any price give me the Book of God! I have it. Here is knowledge enough for me. Let me be *homo unius libri*. Here then I am, far from the busy ways of men. I sit down alone: only God is here. In his presence I open, I read his Book; for this end, to find the way to heaven. Is there a doubt concerning the meaning of what I read? Does anything appear dark or intricate? I lift up my heart to the Father of lights: "Lord, is it not thy Word, 'If any man lack wisdom, let him ask of God'? Thou 'givest liberally and upbraidest not.' Thou hast said, 'If any be willing to do thy will, he shall know.' I am willing to do, let me know, thy will." I then search after and consider parallel passages of Scripture, "comparing spiritual things with spiritual." I meditate thereon, with all the attention and earnestness of which my mind is capable. If any doubt still remains, I consult those who are experienced in the things of God, and then the writings whereby, being dead, they yet speak. And what I thus learn, that I teach.

6. I have accordingly set down in the following sermons what I find in the Bible concerning the way to heaven, with a view to distinguish this way of God from all those which are the inventions of men. I have endeavoured to describe the true, the scriptural, experimental

religion, so as to omit nothing which is a real part thereof, and to add nothing thereto which is not. And herein it is more especially my desire, first to guard those who are just setting their faces toward heaven (and who, having little acquaintance with the things of God, are the more liable to be turned out of the way) from formality, from mere outside religion, which has almost driven heart-religion out of the world; and secondly, to warn those who know the religion of the heart, the faith which worketh by love, lest any time they make void the law through faith, and fall back into the snares of the devil.

7. By the advice and at the request of some of my friends, I have prefixed to the other sermons contained in this volume three sermons of my own and one of my brother's preached before the University of Oxford. My design required some discourses on those heads. And I preferred these before any other, as being a stronger answer than any which can be drawn up now to those who have frequently asserted that we have changed our doctrine of late, and do not preach now what we did some years ago. Any man of understanding may now judge for himself, when he has compared the latter with the former sermons.

8. But some may say I have mistaken the way myself, although I take upon me to teach it to others. It is probable many will think this; and it is very possible that I have. But I trust, whereinsoever I have mistaken, my mind is open to conviction. I sincerely desire to be better informed. I say to God and man, "What I know not, teach thou me."

9. Are you persuaded you see more clearly than me? It is not unlikely that you may. Then treat me as you would desire to be treated yourself upon a change of circumstances. Point me out a better way than I have yet known. Show me it is so by plain proof of Scripture. And if I linger in the path I have been accustomed to tread, and am therefore unwilling to leave, labour with me a little, take me by the hand, and lead me as I am able to bear. But be not displeased if I entreat you not to beat me down in order to quicken my pace. I can go but feebly and slowly at best—then, I should not be able to go at all. May I not request of you, farther, not to give me hard names in order to bring me into the right way? Suppose I was ever so much in the wrong. I doubt this would not set me right. Rather it would make me run so much the farther from you— and so get more and more out of the way.

10. Nay, perhaps, if you are angry so shall I be too, and then there will be small hopes of finding the truth. If once anger arise, *heute kapnos* (as Homer somewhere expresses it), this smoke will so dim the eyes of my soul that I shall be able to see nothing clearly. For God's sake, if it be possible to avoid it let us not provoke one another to wrath. Let us not kindle in each other this fire of hell, much less blow it up into a flame. If we could discern truth by that dreadful light, would it not be loss rather than gain? For, how far is love, even with many wrong opinions, to be preferred before truth itself without love? We may die without the knowledge of many truths and yet be carried into Abraham's bosom. But if we die without love, what will knowledge avail?

Just as much as it avails the devil and his angels!

The God of love forbid we should ever make the trial! May he prepare us for the knowledge of all truth, by filling our hearts with all his love, and with all joy and peace in believing.

*   *   *

Sequential Organization of Themes of the Standard Sermons

The "four volumes of sermons" referred to in the Model Deed of 1763 were the *Sermons on Several Occasions,* originally published in 1746 (Sermons 1–12), 1748 (13–24), 1750 (25–37), and 1760 (currently numbered 38–44), totaling forty-three sermons.[5] In a second edition of the 1750 volume, a sermon was added ("Wandering Thoughts"), making a total of forty-four. When the collected *Works* were published in 1771 in 32 volumes, the first four contained these forty-four sermons plus nine others: "The Witness of the Spirit—Discourse 2" (1767); "On Sin in Believers" (1763); "The Repentance of Believers" (1767); "The Great Assize" (1758); "The Lord Our Righteousness" (1765); "The Scripture Way of Salvation" (1765); "The Good Steward" (1768); "The Reformation of Manners" (1763); and "On the Death of Mr. Whitefield" (1770). This brought the total to fifty-three sermons. Since the sermon on Whitefield is largely biographical, it is often not included in the numbering of the doctrinal series. Hence Burwash's version of *Wesley's Doctrinal Standards* contains fifty-two sermons

(Burwash, *WDS*; also the scheme followed by Harrison, *WS*).

The story of Wesley's sermons, however, gets more complicated:

After Wesley's death, during the years 1829–31, a third edition of Wesley's *"Works"* was issued. In his preface the editor made himself responsible for the statement that the first four volumes of the series contained the sermons referred to in Methodist trust-deeds. This statement had already been made by the same editor in the preface to a two-volume edition of the same sermons published in 1825. Such was the impression gradually made that it became assumed throughout Methodism that the Standard Sermons numbered fifty-three. However, Wesley had issued another, and a final, edition of all his printed sermons in 1787–8, in eight volumes. In this, nine of the ten sermons added to the first four volumes in the 1771 edition were omitted, the one remaining being that on "Wandering Thoughts." Thus the first four volumes of the eight-volume edition comprise forty-four sermons. There is evidence that Wesley regarded the eight-volume edition as the authoritative edition of his sermons.[6]

The British Methodist Conference sought a legal opinion in 1894 as to whether the Standard Sermons were to be numbered forty-three (argued by Richard Green, leaving out "Wandering Thoughts"),[7] or forty-four (including "Wandering Thoughts"), or fifty-two (including the second series except for the sermon on Whitefield), or fifty-three (including Whitefield). After obtaining this legal opinion, the British Conference of 1914 went on record stating that the natural sense and proper intention of the phrase "the first four volumes of sermons" of Clause 20 of the Chapel Model Deed of 1832 referred to the 1787–88 edition of Wesley's *Works* (forty-four sermons), and not to Wesley's collected works of 1771.[8] Hence the precise, full title of Edward H. Sugden's critical edition of the sermons is this:

> *Wesley's Standard Sermons Consisting of Forty-four Discourses, Published in Four Volumes, in 1746, 1748, 1750, and 1760 (Fourth Edition, 1787), to which are added Nine Additional Sermons Published in Vols. I to IV of Wesley's Collected Works, 1771.*[9]

Although some Wesley scholars still technically dispute the number of his Standard Sermons, there is general agreement that at least forty-four are indisputably doctrinal standards. British Methodists are more likely to say forty-four, while Americans (following the tradition of Burwash and Harrison) are more likely to say fifty-two. These sermons (minimally forty-four) have been generally referred to since the mid-nineteenth century as Wesley's "Standard Sermons." The titles and themes of these sermons (variously numbered in differing editions) fall into a distinct and intentional pattern of organization as the following schema shows. Our purpose is not to explicate these themes, but to present their skeletal structure and principal concerns, following the numbering system of Albert C. Outler's Bicentennial Edition of the *Sermons* (*WJWB*, vols. 1–2).

* * *

Titles and Themes of Wesley's Forty-four Sermons on Several Occasions

PART ONE:
THE FOUNDATION: JUSTIFICATION BY GRACE THROUGH FAITH

1. *Salvation by Faith*. Eph. 2:8, June 11, 1738. The nature of faith and of present salvation by grace. Christ given for us, and living in us, saving from the power of sin, from guilt and fear, for good works.

2. *The Almost Christian*. Acts 26:28, July 25, 1741. The almost Christian (having the form but not the power of godliness) and the altogether Christian (wholly loving God and the neighbor grounded in faith).

3. *Awake Thou that Sleepest*. Eph. 5:14, Charles Wesley, April 4, 1742. The spiritually asleep, and those dreadfully awakening to judgment, seeking an inward change, to whom Christ gives light.

4. *Scriptural Christianity*. Acts 4:31, Aug. 24, 1744. With small beginnings in repentance, faith, and love, the gospel spreads from one to another, covering the earth, facing persecution.

5. *Justification by Faith*. Rom. 4:5, 1746. Good works follow after justification; faith its only necessary condition. Justification teaches what God does for us through his Son; sanctification what God works in us by his Spirit.

PART TWO:
THE ASSURANCE OF THE SPIRIT: FAITH TAKING ROOT IN THE HEART

6. *The Righteousness of Faith*. Rom. 10:5–8, 1746. The righteousness of law demanding perfect obedience distinguished from the righteousness of faith, which proclaims the Son's obedience for us.

7. *The Way to the Kingdom*. Mark 1:15, 1746. True religion not exterior, but righteousness, peace, and joy.

8. *First Fruits of the Spirit*. Rom. 8:1, 1746. Marks of a Christian: walking by faith, freedom from the bondage of sin, lacking condemnation, exhibiting the Spirit's fruits; distinguishing sins past, present, inward, and sins of surprise, and infirmity.

9. *The Spirit of Bondage and of Adoption*. Rom. 8:15, 1746. Distinguishes natural humanity (false peace, assumed liberty), humanity under law (the disturbed conscience), and humanity under grace (no condemnation, liberty from guilt, fear, and sin).

10. *The Witness of the Spirit, Discourse I*. Rom. 8:16, 1746. Answering enthusiasts and rationalists. The witness of the Spirit defined and distinguished from presumption and delusion; conscience testifies that one has scriptural marks of the child of God; the Holy Spirit directly witnesses; true assurance distinguished from false by antecedent repentance and consequent accompanying fruits.

11. *The Witness of the Spirit, Discourse II*. Rom. 8:16, April 4, 1767. An inward impression on the soul whereby the Spirit of God immediately and directly witnesses to my spirit that I am a child of God. Why and how the witness is received, with accompanying fruits—a distinct calling of Methodist testimony.

12. *The Witness of Our Own Spirit*. 2 Cor. 1:12, 1746. A good conscience experiences joy. Continuing in one's conversation in the world by grace in simplicity and godly sincerity.

13. *On Sin in Believers*. 2 Cor. 5:17, Mar. 28, 1763. Regeneration does not mean permanent freedom from all sin; grace coexists with nature; warnings against antinomianism.

14. *The Repentance of Believers*. Mark 1:15, Apr. 24, 1767. Though sin does not reign in believers, it may remain. The call to repentance and belief that God is able to save from all the sin that still remains.

15. (See Part 5.)

16. *The Means of Grace*. Mal. 3:7, 1746. Nature of means; chief means: prayer, Scripture, and the Supper; how means are to be rightly used.

17. *The Circumcision of the Heart*. Rom. 2:29, Jan. 1, 1733. Holiness as a habitual disposition of the soul; humility removing pride, faith embracing the divine evidence, hope attesting providence; love of God and the neighbor.

18. *Marks of the New Birth*. John 3:8, 1748. Confident faith bearing fruit (power over sin, and serenity of soul); a living hope; joyful, obedient love.

19. *The Great Privilege of Those That are Born of God*. 1 John 3:9, 1748. Justification implies a change in the believer's relation with God; the new birth implies an actual embodiment of that change, wherein those that are born of God are freed from sin.

20. *The Lord Our Righteousness*. Jer. 23:6, Nov. 24, 1765. Imputation of Christ's righteousness to believer; yet not to be used as a cover for sinning.

PART THREE:
FAITH BEARING FRUIT
IN THE CHRISTIAN LIFE

21–25. *Sermon on the Mount, Discourses 1–5*. Matt. 5, 1748. The sum of all true religion. (Discourse 1)

Poverty of Spirit; the blessedness of those that mourn; (2) Of meekness; hungering and thirsting for righteousness; the merciful; (3) Of purity of heart; peacemaking; facing persecution; (4) Christianity is a social, not a solitary religion; (5) Complementary relation of law and gospel.

26. *Sermon on the Mount. Discourse 6.* Matt. 6:1–15, 1748. Purity of heart, almsgiving, and prayer.

27. *Sermon on the Mount. Discourse 7.* Matt. 6:16–18, 1748. Grounds, reasons, and ends of fasting, a means of grace. Instruction for fasting.

28. *Sermon on the Mount. Discourse 8.* Matt. 6:19–23, 1748. Service in worldly employment; lay not up treasure upon earth, but in heaven.

29. *Sermon on the Mount. Discourse 9.* Matt. 6:24–34, 1748. Worldliness and anxiety. You cannot serve God and mammon. On seeking first the kingdom of God.

30. *Sermon on the Mount. Discourse 10.* Matt. 7:1–12, 1750. Hindrances to true religion: judging others; giving what is holy to dogs; refusing to ask the Father in heaven.

31. *Sermon on the Mount. Discourse 11.* Matt. 7:13–14, 1750. The narrow way; enter by the straight gate; readiness for self-denial.

32. *Sermon on the Mount. Discourse 12.* Matt. 7:15–20, 1750. Beware of false prophets: who they are, the deceptions by which they come, knowing them by their fruits.

33. *Sermon on the Mount. Discourse 13.* Matt. 7:21–27, 1750. Building on sand and on rock.

34. *The Original, Nature, Property, and Use of the Law.* Rom. 7:12, 1750. The nature of moral obligation; the law is holy, just, and good, convicting the sinner, driving us to Christ, and keeping the believer alive. The law sends us to Christ, and following justification, Christ sends us to the law.

35. *The Law Established Through Faith, Discourse 1.* Rom. 3:31, 1750. How to make void the law; justification is without works of law, yet works are the immediate fruit of that faith by which we are justified.

36. *The Law Established Through Faith, Discourse 2.* Rom. 3:31, 1750. How to establish the law: by faith active in love; by preaching faith in Christ as not to supercede but produce holiness.

PART FOUR:
THE IRENIC SPIRIT

37. *The Nature of Enthusiasm.* Acts 26:24, 1750. Defined and typified.

38. *A Caution Against Bigotry.* Mark 9:38–39, 1750. Defined and warned against.

39. *Catholic Spirit.* 2 Kings 10:15, 1750. If your heart is as my heart, give me your hand.

40–42. (See Part 6.)

PART FIVE:
THE WAY OF SALVATION

43. *The Scripture Way of Salvation.* Eph. 2:8, 1765. The teaching of salvation.

44. *Original Sin.* Gen. 6:5, 1759. Its historical evidence, its remedy: Jesus Christ—God's way of healing (*therapeia psuches*) a soul diseased.

45. *The New Birth.* John 3:7, 1760. Regeneration, its nature and necessity, and relation to baptism; sanctification as growth after the new birth.

46. *The Wilderness State.* John 16:22, 1760. Its nature: loss of faith, joy, love, peace; its causes: sins of omission and commission and ignorance; its cure: understanding and removing the cause.

47. *Heaviness through Manifold*

Temptations. 1 Peter 1:6, 1760. Heaviness of soul, sorrow, grief; its causes: disease, poverty, calamity, death, eclipse of God; its purpose: testing, purification, holiness, gain.

48. *Self-Denial.* Luke 9:23, 1760. A requirement of the Christian life.

15. *The Great Assize.* Rom. 14:10, Mar. 10, 1758. Signs of the general judgment, wherein Christ is the judge to whom all give account.

PART SIX:
CHRISTIAN PERFECTION

40. *Christian Perfection.* Phil. 3:12, 1741. What it is not (an exemption from ignorance, mistake, infirmity, or temptation), and is (personal holiness enabled by grace, growing in grace, daily advancing in the knowledge and love of God).

41. *Wandering Thoughts.* 2 Cor. 10:5, 1762. The libidinal energies explored and related to sin.

42. *Satan's Devices.* 2 Cor. 2:12, 1750. The demonic sphere explored.

49. *The Cure of Evil-Speaking.* Matt. 18:15–17, 1760. Methods proposed.

50. *The Use of Money.* Luke 16:9, 1760. Gain all you can, yet not at the expense of life, health, or strength; save all you can, for gratification increases desire; and give away all you can.

51. *The Good Steward.* Luke 16:2, May 14, 1768. Responsibilities of Christians. All will be called to give account, for stewardship must come to an end.

52. *The Reformation of Manners.* Ps. 94:16, Jan. 30, 1763. How Christians seek social change.

53. *On the Death of George Whitefield.* Num. 23:10, Nov. 18, 1770. Eulogy to one who proclaimed "the grand doctrines."

*   *   *

Burwash provides perhaps the most accurate summary of the doctrinal teaching of the Standard Sermons:

1. The universality and impartiality of God's grace to man as manifested in the provisions of the atonement.

2. The freedom of the human will, and man's individual, probational responsibility to God.

3. The absolute necessity, in religion, of holiness in heart and life.

4. The natural impossibility of this to fallen human nature.

5. The perfect provision for this necessity and impossibility, as well as for the pardon of past sins, in the salvation offered by Christ.

6. The sole condition of this salvation—faith.

7. The conscious witness of the Spirit to this salvation.[10]

The Catholic Spirit

Some prematurely take Wesley's sermon on the catholic spirit to be a defense of doctrinal latitudinarianism or indifferentism. Those who do so may not have attended sufficiently to the heart of the sermon. Wesley distinctly rejects doctrinal latitudinarianism and sets out the doctrinal core assumed in the catholic spirit.

This is done by the unique means of a series of questions asked the hearer. It is to Wesley's credit that he states this doctrinal core not in the form of propositional statements but in candid, simple questions asked from the heart. Organized in a trinitarian frame, they are found in paragraphs 12–18 of the sermon. To show the triune structure of these questions, we have added bracketed topical headings and numbered the questions, but otherwise the sermon is quoted verbatim.

* * *

[THE DOCTRINAL CORE OF THE CATHOLIC SPIRIT]

My only question at present is this, "Is thine heart right, as my heart is with thy heart?"

But what is properly implied in the question? I do not mean what did Jehu imply therein, but what should a follower of Christ understand thereby when he proposes it to any of his brethren?

[GOD]

The First thing implied is this:
(1) Is thy heart right with God?

[GOD'S EXISTENCE AND ATTRIBUTES]

(2) Dost thou believe his being, and his perfections?
(3) His eternity, immensity, wisdom, power; his justice mercy, and truth?

[PROVIDENCE]

(4) Dost thou believe that he now "upholdeth all things by the word of his power"?
(5) And that he governs even the most minute, even the most noxious, to his own glory, and the good of them that love him? Hast thou a divine evidence, a supernatural conviction, of the things of God? Dost thou "walk by faith, not by sight"? "Looking not at temporal things, but things eternal"?

[CHRIST]

(6) Dost thou believe in the Lord Jesus Christ, "God over all, blessed for ever"?
(7) Is he "revealed in" thy soul?
(8) Dost thou "know Jesus Christ and him crucified"?

(9) Dost he "dwell in thee, and thou in him"?
(10) Is he "formed in thy heart by faith"?

[JUSTIFICATION BY GRACE THROUGH FAITH]

(11) Having absolutely disclaimed all thy own works, thy own righteousness, hast thou "submitted thyself unto the righteousness of God," "which is by faith in Christ Jesus"?
(12) Art thou "found in him, not having thy own righteousness, but the righteousness which is by faith"?
(13) And art thou, through him, "fighting the good fight of faith, and laying hold of eternal life"?

[THE HOLY SPIRIT AND THE CHRISTIAN LIFE]

(14) Is thy faith *energoumenē di agapēs*—filled with the energy of love?
(15) Dost thou love God? I do not say "above all things," for it is both an unscriptural and an ambiguous expression, but "with all thy heart, and with all thy mind, and with all thy soul, and with all thy strength"?
(16) Dost thou seek all thy happiness in him alone?
(17) And dost thou find what thou seekest?
(18) Does thy soul continually "magnify the Lord, and thy spirit rejoice in God thy Saviour"?
(19) Having learned "in everything to give thanks," dost thou find it is "a joyful and a pleasant thing to be thankful"?
(20) Is God the centre of thy soul?
(21) The sum of all thy desires?
(22) Art thou accordingly "laying up" thy "treasure in heaven," and "counting all things else dung and dross"?

(23) Hath the love of God cast the love of the world out of thy soul?

(24) Then thou are "crucified to the world." "Thou art dead" to all below, "and thy life is hid with Christ in God."[11]

. . . If thou art thus minded, may every Christian say—yea, if thou art but sincerely desirous of it, and following on till thou attain—then "thy heart is right, as my heart is with thy heart."

* * *

In the light of this, it cannot reasonably be claimed that Wesley's "catholic spirit" brushed doctrinal issues aside or circumvented key points of Christian orthodoxy. While these selections cannot substitute for a careful reading of Wesley's *Sermons,* they have sought to fulfill a more limited function of introducing in Wesley's own words the purpose of the sermons, setting forth key themes of the *Sermons* through their implicit organizational sequence, and presenting the doctrinal core of the catholic spirit that has been so often taken as the prototype of doctrinal pluralism. If this is pluralism, it is deeply rooted in the classical ecumenical consensus.

III. The Articles
As Doctrinal Standards

The remainder of this chapter focuses upon the *Articles of Religion,* their sources, meaning, and pedagogical significance. Our twofold purpose is to inquire into the nature of proper assent to the Twenty-five *Articles* and to show in precise detail how the Twenty-five were derived from the Anglican Thirty-nine Articles.

With the exception of one article ("Of the Rulers of the United States of America"), the Twenty-five *Articles of Religion* are older than Wesleyan theology by two centuries. These articles deliver to the Wesleyan traditions a theology infused with the ancient ecumenical council decisions and the distilled major confessional achievements of Protestantism. They put Wesleyan theology and preaching in direct touch with the Nicene and Athanasian creeds and with the spirit of the Augsburg Confession and other Reformed confessions that anteceded and informed the Anglican Thirty-nine Articles, from which the Twenty-five were taken. Methodism brought to the New World a tradition of Christian teaching that had guided the English Reformation since the sixteenth century and that had substantially guided ancient ecumenical Christianity. Yet, however traditional, the Wesleyan *Articles* are valid only insofar as they teach scriptural doctrine without deficit, according to their own testimony.

The Twenty-five *Articles* stand in the moderate center of the Protestant confessional tradition. A *confession* in the New Testament sense is a public attestation of the truth made known in Jesus Christ (see Rom. 10:9–10; 1 John 4:2ff.; 1 Tim. 6:13). In the sixteenth century, churches that rejected Roman medieval scholasticism defined their theological teaching by writing confessions. The purpose of the confession was to set forth precisely key points of biblical teaching and to distinguish true from false teaching. As a consequence, the *Articles,* rather than being merely negative statements, are crystallized declarations of religious truth forged out of centuries of debate, risk, and testimony. They are not obsolete. The *Articles* intend to preserve the unity of the body of Christ and guard the body against false, unscriptural teaching.

The Roots of the Twenty-five Articles in the Augsburg Confession

Primary roots of the *Articles* are found in the Augsburg Confession of 1530, some sections of which were significantly anticipated by the Schwabach Articles of 1529 and by drafts made by Martin Luther for the Torgau Articles of 1530. Luther's statements were subsequently redrafted and extended by Melanchthon to include the twenty-nine Augsburg articles (twenty-two of which stated positive Reformation teachings and seven of which protested papal abuses). This twofold purpose of the Augsburg Confession—to teach Reformation doctrine and resist certain unscriptural abuses—would eventually shape the language, form, and organization of the Twenty-five *Articles,* by way of the Anglican Articles from which they were revised.

The sixteenth-century Reformers in Germany, Switzerland, and England would have been rightly charged with schism if they had not been able to demonstrate that their faith stood in continuity with ancient Christianity, which itself had been abandoned in certain medieval scholastic abuses. The Augsburg Confession, attempting such a demonstration, was a united confession of faith agreed upon by the German Reformers and princes, then presented to Emperor Charles V at the Diet of Augsburg in 1530.

The Augsburg Confession appealed to ancient formulae and symbols of Christianity—those of the ecumenical councils. Far from attempting to create a new theology, the Reformers at Augsburg were simply trying to be accountable to ancient ecumenical orthodoxy and the apostolic witness, especially as it had become recently illumined by the rediscovery of the truth of justification by grace through faith. The Augsburg and Anglican articles sought wherever possible to ground Christian teaching in the most ancient and undisputed ecumenical formularies, rather than in new or untested language or speculative ideas.

The headings of the Augsburg articles, when compared with the Anglican Thirty-nine Articles, show how closely they correspond in structure and sequence and how indebted the Wesleyan tradition is to classical Reformation teaching.

The following schema shows that the core of the Thirty-nine and Twenty-five *Articles* was derived from the Augsburg Confession of 1530.

Augsburg	Anglican Thirty-nine	Wesleyan Revision to Twenty-five Articles

Key to third column: + retained, *slightly retranslated, **greatly revised

Part First:
Chief Articles of Faith

Augsburg	Anglican Thirty-nine	Wesleyan Revision to Twenty-five Articles
1. Of God	1. Of Faith in the Holy Trinity	1.*
2. Of Original Sin	9. Of Original or Birth Sin	7.**
3. Of the Son of God	2. Of the Word or Son of God	2.*
	3. Of the Going Down of Christ Into Hell	Omitted
	4. Of the Resurrection of Christ	3.*
	5. Of the Holy Ghost	4.+
	6. Of the Sufficiency of Scriptures for Salvation	5.*
	7. Of the Old Testament	6.*
	8. Of the Creeds	Omitted
4. Of Justification	11. Of Justification	9.*
5. Of the Ministry of the Church	23. Of Ministering in the Congregation	Omitted
6. Of New Obedience	14. Of Works of Supererogation	11.*
7. Of the Church	19. Of the Church	13.*
	21. Of the Authority of General Councils	Omitted
	22. Of Purgatory	14.*
	24. Of Speaking in the Congregation in Such a Tongue as the People Understandeth	15.*

Augsburg	Anglican Thirty-nine	Wesleyan Revision to Twenty-five Articles
8. What the Church Is	34. Of the Traditions of the Church	22. Rites and Ceremonies of Churches
9. Of Baptism	27. Of Baptism	17.*
10. Of the Lord's Supper	28. Of the Lord's Supper	18.*
	29. Of the Wicked Which Eat Not the Body of Christ in the Use of the Lord's Supper	Omitted
	31. Of the One Oblation of Christ Finished Upon the Cross	20.*
11. Of Confession		
12. Of Repentance	16. Of Sin After Baptism	12. Of Sin After Justification*
13. Of the Use of Sacraments	25. Of the Sacraments	26.*
14. Of Ecclesiastical Orders	26. Of the Unworthiness of Ministers	Omitted
15. Of Ecclesiastical Rites	20. Of the Authority of the Church	Omitted
16. Of Civil Affairs	37. Of the Power of Civil Magistrates	22. Of the Rulers of the United States of America
17. Of Christ's Return to Judgment		
18. Of Free Will	10. Of Free Will	8.*
19. Of the Cause of Sin		
20. Of Good Works	12. Of Good Works	10.*
	13. Of Works Before Justification	Omitted
	15. Of Christ Alone Without Sin	Omitted
	17. Of Predestination and Election	Omitted

Augsburg	Anglican Thirty-nine	Wesleyan Revision to Twenty-five Articles
	18. Of Obtaining Eternal Salvation Only by the Name of Christ	Omitted
21. Of the Worship of Saints		
22. Summary		
Part Second: Abuses Which Have Been Corrected		
1. Of Both Kinds	30. Of Both Kinds	19.*
	33. Of Excommunicate Persons, How Avoided	Omitted
	35. Of the Homilies	Omitted
2. Of the Marriage of Priests	32. Of the Marriage of Priests	21.*
3. Of the Mass		
4. Of Confession		
5. Of the Distinction of Meats, and of Traditions		
6. Of Monastic Vows		
7. Of Ecclesiastical Power	36. Of the Consecration of Bishops and Ministers	Omitted
	38. Of Christian Men's Goods	24.*
	39. Of a Christian Man's Oath	25.+

Early Anglican Sources of the Thirty-nine Articles

The first English formula appeared during the reign of Henry VIII—the Ten English Articles of 1536, five of which were on doctrine, five on church practice. In 1538 a group of Lutheran theologians were invited to England to confer with the English Reformers under the leadership of Archbishop Thomas Cranmer, seeking a correspondence of Anglican and Lutheran views. Their consultation resulted in the Thirteen Articles of 1538. They were more readily agreeable on questions of doctrine than church practice. These Articles were not published or formally approved, but they proved to be important historically, because they provided Cranmer with a model for the drafting of certain of the Forty-two Articles of 1553, from which the Anglican Thirty-nine and the Methodist Twenty-five were largely taken.

Edward VI became king in 1547. On June 19, 1553, under the reign of Edward, the Forty-two Articles were published and mandated for subscription from all clergy, schoolmasters, and members of universities on admission to degrees. These articles took a Catholic position against the extreme left wing of the Reformation (regarding certain tendencies toward Pelagianism, antitrinitarianism, christological errors, Antinomianism, anti-pedobaptism, communism, and certain forms of millenarianism) and a Protestant position against Rome (on the relation of Scripture and tradition, transubstantiation, grace *ex opere operato,* marriage of clergy, works of supererogation, fallibility of General Councils, use of Latin liturgy, etc.). Hence the Anglican pattern of theology, followed by Methodism, was called a middle way (*via media*) between Geneva and Rome.

In the reign succeeding Edward, Catholic Queen Mary repealed the Forty-two Articles and restored the papacy in England. The short-lived Protestant achievements of the Edwardian period were largely lost under the reign of Mary. Cranmer, Latimer, and Ridley were all burned at the stake.

In 1552 the state of Wurttemberg drew up a confession of faith that significantly influenced the Anglican model. It was presented to the Council of Trent at the very time the Anglicans were seriously searching for clarity of doctrinal definition; thus it became also a model for the later Anglican Articles.

Mary was succeeded in 1558 by Elizabeth, who in time restored many elements of Protestantism. In 1562 a revision of the Forty-two Articles was undertaken, which resulted in the Thirty-Eight Articles of 1562–63. These were not submitted in revised form to Parliament until 1571, when they were promulgated with the assent of Convocation and revised into the present form of the Thirty-nine Articles, sometimes called the Elizabethan Articles. The influence of Calvinists (e.g., Peter Martyr, Ochino, Martin Bucer, Henry Bullinger) was on the ascendancy at this time. Bishop John Jewel wrote to Peter Martyr in 1562 concerning the Thirty-nine Articles: "We have pared everything to the very quick, and do not differ from you by a nail's breadth" (Shaw, *DDS,* 14). The articles on Eucharist, predestination, and soteriology had a strong Calvinistic flavor (later somewhat modified by Wesley); but many aspects of Latin theology would remain in the *Articles* so as to sustain a genuine *via media.*

These articles were not the work of any one eminent theologian; were not devised by any Council, Conference, or Convocation. They were a growth, a development calculated to meet and resist errors that had arisen in the Church of Christ in different centuries. They mark the struggles of the Church to arrive at a clear and correct definition of truth, to emerge from error and guard herself against inroads of dangerous heresies. They bear the marks of many minds.[12]

Wesley's Omissions and Amendments

In 1784 Wesley abridged the Thirty-nine Articles to twenty-four and sent them by Coke to the Christmas Conference. To these the Conference added one article, "Of the Rulers of the United States of America." These Twenty-five *Articles of Religion* were published in the *Disciplines* of 1788 and following, and they were protected by the First Restrictive Rule following 1808.

Wesley omitted several complete articles from the Anglican Articles: (3) "Descent into Hell"; (8) "Of the Creeds"; (13) "Works Before Justification"; (15) "Christ Alone Without Sin" (17); "Predestination and Election"; (18) "Eternal Salvation only by the Name of Christ"; (20) "Authority of the Church"; (21) "Authority of General Councils"; (23) "Ministering in the Congregation"; (24) "Unworthiness of Ministers"; (29) "Of the Wicked which Eat not the Body of Christ in the use of the Lord's Supper"; (33) "Excommunication"; (35) "Homilies"; and (36) "Consecration of Bishops and Ministers." The most concise analysis of Wesley's reasoning concerning omissions was set forth by Edwin Lewis:

> The omissions do not mean in every case that Wesley was not in sympathy. In some cases, however, they do mean this. His omission of [Article] III may be ascribed to a lack of clear Scriptural support. The omission of VIII is characteristically Wesleyan. Wesley accepted for himself both the Nicene and Athanasian symbols, so far as their intent

was concerned, but he objected to their non-biblical terms, especially "Persons" and "Trinity," and he disapproved the damnatory clauses. The Apostles' Creed he certainly accepted, and it was included in the Order of Public Worship of the Methodist Episcopal Church (the Conference of 1786 omitting the clause on the Descent into Hades). Wesley believed in justification by faith alone, but he omitted XXIII, because it conflicted with Wesley's teaching on Christian perfection (although he never taught an absolute perfection). The omission of XVII sprang from Wesley's convinced Arminianism. He would regard the intent of XVIII as self-evident.

Wesley was a thoroughgoing churchman, but he recognized the rights of the individual; hence the omission of XX. He omitted XXI as not relevant to the situation in the United States of America. He omitted XIII not because he did not believe in "order," but because his own experience had convinced him that men not formally set aside by the Church could effectively preach. The omission of XXIV reflects Wesley's true churchmanship: the minister, good or bad, is always a possible organ of the Holy Ghost for conveying good to others. Wesley agreed with the sentiment of XXIX but omitted it none the less, perhaps because of its controversial origin. The omission of XXXIII was certainly wise: the article reflects a historical situation not likely ever to be duplicated in the United States. Of XXXV, Wheeler frankly says: "There is no place for this article in Methodism." XXXVI was rendered irrelevant to the new Communion by Wesley's own provision for the "consecration" and "ordination" of its ministry, even although this provision consisted of an abridgment of Anglican forms (Lewis, *DSMC*, 3–4).

A concise summary of Wesley's deletions, changes, and additions, in the *Articles* that he retained was also formulated by Lewis:

Wesley retained [Article] I entire, but the Conference of 1786 omitted "begotten from everlasting of the Father." Since, however, Methodism is officially committed to both the Trinity and the Eternal Sonship of Christ, the omission has no doctrinal significance. From IV, Wesley omitted "flesh and bones," perhaps as being too specific at a point where a *fact* (continued existence) was more agreed upon than a *mode*. Wesley omitted the Apocryphal Books from VI as not being canonical. He considerably shortened IX, thereby modifying its extreme Augustinianism. The reference to the Homily of Justification is omitted from XI. The title of XVI is changed from *Of Sin after Baptism* to *Of Sin after Justification*, and the change is maintained through the article; while the opening words, "not every deadly sin," are written by Wesley as "not every sin." The change of title suggests that Wesley was seeking to avoid giving support to the doctrine of regeneration by baptism; and "deadly" is omitted because the following word "willingly" describes the only "sin" which Wesley recognized as morally significant. The names of Churches that have "erred" in various ways are omitted from XIX. In the opening sentence of XXV, the description of Sacraments as "certain sure witnesses, and effectual signs of grace," is changed by Wesley to "certain signs of graces." The change registers Wesley's gradual emergence from a sacramentarian to an experiential emphasis. XXVII is considerably shortened to indicate that while baptism is a "sign" of regeneration, it is not itself a guarantee of it. There are purely verbal changes in XXXII, and there is an interesting omission, "ordained only by man's authority" in the closing sentence of XXXIV (the reference is to Church rites and ceremonies). The title of this same article (XXXIV) is changed by Wesley from *Of the Traditions of the Church* to *Of the Rites and Ceremonies of Churches*, and throughout the Article Wesley substitutes "rites" for "traditions." The article also omits, "hurteth the authority of the Magistrate" (a phrase implying a close relation of Church and State). XXXVII, *Of the Civil Magistrates*, is substituted by XXIII in the Methodist Articles (Ibid., 4–5).[13]

The classical orthodoxy of Methodism is grounded textually in the *Articles of Religion*:

The theology of American Methodism is essentially that of the Anglican Church in all things which according to that Church and the general consent of Christianity are necessary to theological orthodoxy or the doctrines of grace, unless the entire omission of the historically equivocal Seventeenth Article on "Predestination and Election" be considered an exception.[14]

The polemical elements of the *Articles* must be viewed in the historical context of the debates following the Council of Trent. The United Methodist General Conference of 1970 responded to petitions requesting removal of "derogatory references to the Roman Catholic Church" in the *Articles* by adopting a "Resolution of Intent," which declared that henceforth we shall "interpret all our Articles, Confession, and other 'standards of doctrine' in consonance with our best ecumenical insights and judgment." This resolution referred especially to Articles 14, 15, 16, 18, 19, 20, and 21.[15]

How the Anglican Tradition of Pastoral Subscription Became Transmuted in the Wesleyan Tradition

It has been common among Protestant communions to require clergy to consent or subscribe to their confession upon ordination. A mutated form of assent, although without a formal signature of subscription, has been assumed of ordinands in the Methodist church (*Disc., 1984,* 25, 212), based on their primary model—the Anglican tradition. As the Thirty-nine Articles were printed in every *Book of Common Prayer,* so the Twenty-five *Articles of Religion* became printed in every Methodist *Discipline.* As the Thirty-nine are the stated doctrine of the Church of England, sometimes called the title-deeds of Anglican theology, so have the Twenty-five *Articles* become for Methodism. They seek to articulate the most central doctrines of Christianity and resist perennial errors.

In the Church of England even to this day, every ordained person assents to the doctrine of the Thirty-nine Articles of Religion. On the first Sunday in which a pastor assumes a new parish, it is by tradition required that the pastor read the Articles aloud to the congregation and confirm assent to them. The English tradition of clerical subscription goes back to 1571, as set forth in an Act of Parliament "for

Ministers of the Church to be of sound religion." The language of the Clerical Subscription Act of 1865 formalized the assent in this straightforward language: "I assent to the Thirty-nine Articles and to the Book of Common Prayer and of the ordering of bishops, priests, and deacons. I believe the doctrine of the Church of England as therein set forth to be agreeable to the Word of God." The 1968 Anglican Archbishop's Commission on Christian Doctrine changed the Form of Assent to read: "I, A.B., profess my firm and sincere belief in the faith set forth in the Scriptures and in the catholic creeds, and my allegiance to the doctrine of the Church of England," doctrine which is attested in "the Thirty-nine Articles of Religion."[16]

By tradition it is expected that the assent be sincere, heartfelt, "from the soul" *(ex animo),* and made in reference to the plain, historical sense *(sensus literalis)* of the Articles as understood by the English Reformers. The *ex animo* language came from Canon 36 of 1604, which prescribed a form of assent in which "I do willingly and *ex animo* subscribe" to "all things that are contained" in the Articles. Others argue that the assent must be sincere and from the heart but is subject to interpretations other than that given by their compilers, the sixteenth-century English Reformers (J. H. Newman, *Tract 90*). In modern times, many Anglican ministers have simply ignored the Articles or argued that assent does not mean sincere assent from the heart. The prevailing Anglican modernist interpretation was stated by E. J. Bicknell, that "we are not called to assent to every phrase or detail of the

Articles but only to their general sense."[17]

The Nature and Problems of Assent to the Twenty-five Articles

In giving assent to Methodism's Twenty-five *Articles of Religion,* it is well to keep in mind at least five principles of assent: (1) that the *Articles* have a history and thus deserve to be studied as historical documents, utilizing the best methods of historical research into their context and original intent; (2) that all *Articles* seek to be nothing more or less than a fitting statement of scriptural teaching and hence are to be viewed under the authority of Scripture; they must not be viewed as being autonomously authoritative; (3) that the *Articles* are not merely an antiquated historical statement of what was once believed, but remain as a doctrinal standard exercising determinative authority here and now, according to the First Restrictive Rule of the United Methodist Church and its correlates in other Wesleyan bodies; (4) that the *Articles* are to be taken, not in isolation from other authoritative teachings of Scripture, tradition, and other Wesleyan doctrinal standards, but in relation to them—particularly to Wesley's *Standard Sermons* and *Explanatory Notes upon the New Testament*; and (5) that the affirmation of the *Articles* must leave open the possibility that the Holy Spirit is able to awaken profound insight into the faith once for all delivered to the saints, hence the *Articles* invite fresh ways of stating and applying Christian teaching that complement affirmations of Scripture and the *Articles,* so long as they do not contradict Scripture or the *Articles.*

Assent to the *Articles* has traditionally implied that one has carefully studied them, has sincerely and thoughtfully measured them by Scripture, and has found them agreeable to the Word of God, It implies that one affirms their truth without serious mental reservation, voluntarily binds oneself to follow them, and seeks to appropriate them in one's behavior and teaching. It implies finally that one publicly attests one's resolve to preach the gospel they declare and to resist the unscriptural teachings they resist.

The church has a right to expect from its clergy sincere assent to the *Articles of Religion*. It is the church's way of showing that its representative ministers teach key points of biblical truth and do not subvert them. The Articles provide the basis for a minimal level of doctrinal trust between laity and clergy. Assent therefore must not be deceptive but should imply a genuine commitment to teach these doctrines and embody them in one's life. A local church has a right to inquire and redress by due process if clergy consent proves insincere.

All this is based upon an assumed duty of the church "to contend for the faith that was once for all entrusted to the saints" (Jude 3) and seek to be "God's household, the church of the living God, the pillar and foundation of the truth" (1 Tim. 3:15).

There are at least two basic positions in the Wesleyan traditions with respect to the *Articles*: *Evangelicals,* believing that Scripture is the revelation of God, generally have held that the *Articles* are a reliable statement of biblical doctrine and hence should be taken seriously and rigorously as church teaching unless shown contrary to Scripture. *Liberals* (who exercise far greater influence in the United Methodist Church than in other Wesleyan branches) wish to maximize intellectual freedom to explore and develop various new theological positions more amenable to emergent culture. Many other ministers are somewhere between these two positions. Any serious debate about the role of the *Articles* quickly turns into a debate about the mission of the church and the historic task of the Wesleyan tradition, as viewed from varying points of this theological spectrum.[18]

The Challenge of the Articles Today

A part of the problem is that many modern heirs of Wesley are not fully agreed on the basic premise of the *Articles*: that *Scripture is the norm of Christian teaching*. Those who understand Scripture as the trustworthy revelation of God have little difficulty receiving the *Articles* as a reliable summary of biblical teaching. Those who resist this premise may wish to resist, ignore, or circumvent the *Articles*.

The present-day challenge is to increase awareness among laity of the usefulness, vitality, and relevance of these doctrinal standards. It is a major task for doctrinal reformation and the deepening of the Wesleyan tradition in our time. (This is why an "Outline for a Local Church Study on the *Articles*" has been provided at the conclusion of this book.)

Some may contend that the *Articles* are currently affirmed only by a minority of persons in our churches.

To this, three crucial counter-questions may be posed:

1. How is it known that only a minority affirm the *Articles*? Is that an informed judgment based upon accurate data-gathering?

2. Does majority rule determine Christian truth? If only a minority of a congregation affirmed the truth of Paul's Letter to the Galatians, for example, would that make it any less valid as Christian teaching?

3. If few laypersons are aware of the contents of the *Articles*—that Methodist doctrinal standard most clearly defined and protected by the church constitution—does that not place an obligation upon clergy and church leadership to teach them ever more diligently?

Usual objections to the *Articles* were summarized and answered some eight decades ago by Henry Wheeler:

> that they infringe Christian liberty, and supercede the Scriptures by substituting in their place a number of humanly formed propositions; that to exhibit the Christian faith in any limited number of statements is virtually to declare that all besides is superfluous; that such Articles nourish hypocrisy and hinder advancement in divine knowledge. Against this view it is contended that the design of such Articles is not to sum up the whole of Christianity, but merely to set forth the belief of a given Church upon the leading truths of religion, as well as touching those matters that have been subjects of heretical corruption or controversy, and respecting which it is necessary that there be, for the sake of peace, agreement among members of the same Church (*H&E*, 12–13).

The seemingly simple option of abolishing the *Articles* as doctrinal standards is virtually impossible constitutionally. Another alternative would seek to leave them quietly in the *Discipline,* yet practically neglect them and in effect seek to set them aside as if without force or meaning as doctrinal standards. This alternative tends, however, to leave the remaining church body without doctrinal moorings for ecumenical dialogue. Regrettably, this could also have the unintended effect of pushing certain persons farther away from the churches and clergy to whom these doctrinal standards have been entrusted. If the *Articles* should be reduced to the status of a pitiful historical relic, without moral or normative power, many Methodists would interpret that to be an act of abandonment of the evangelical heart of the Wesleyan heritage. Some would argue that such a body has forfeited its legitimate claim to view itself as standing in connection with Wesley.

Another alternative would be to seek to revise the words and symbols of the *Articles* to make them more easily acceptable or adaptable to certain modern audiences and certain supposed modes of modern consciousness. It is probable, however, that there would be even less agreement on proposed revisions than there is on the received language. This would be a bit like proposing a chic revision of the Chalcedonian Creed or of the baptismal formula. It is better to supplement the *Articles* with further clarifications than to attempt to touch up their language for accommodation to certain supposed modern and secularized audiences (who would be prone to ignore these modifica-

tions anyway). Furthermore, even if this were attempted, in many Wesleyan-related church bodies revisions would be virtually impossible, since constitutional protections given to specific terms of these *Articles* are rigorous.

Considerable numbers of United Methodist clergy do not understand their ordination to require positive commitment to the *Articles,* but it is doubtful that this view can be held with complete consistency and integrity. Ideally, those who have mental reservations about the *Articles* have a duty to the church to state them before ordination or, if their commitment changes after ordination, to state that plainly. Moreover, those who serve on ordinal examining committees have a duty to inquire to what extent the commitment of prospective ordinands is sincere and *ex animo* (from the soul). One who assents to the *Articles* upon ordination yet teaches things contrary to the *Articles* after ordination not only is subject to the charge of disingeniousness but also could become liable to admonition or trial.

The *Articles* are best studied and reappropriated not only as a matter of historical interest, but as they were intended to be understood—as doctrinal standards. Hence an active pedagogical effort is needed, utilizing the *Articles* as the basis for instruction in Christian faith. Serious study of the *Articles* will deepen theological vision, enlarge catholic Christian sympathy, serve to resist faddism and excess in theology, and put modern worshipers vitally in touch with the doctrinal cohesion of the patristic, Protestant, and Wesleyan traditions. It will show that Christian teaching can proceed with a minimum of dogmatic pretension and maximum accountability to the central themes of Scripture and Christian tradition.[19]

What more can be done to emphasize the central importance of the *Articles of Religion*? Several ideas may be helpful. For example, nothing prevents local congregations from petitioning their judicatories to ask that the *Articles* be regarded rigorously as requisite to ordination. Nothing prevents clergy from preaching a series of sermons on the *Articles of Religion* or from taking one article each year as a theme of preaching.

The Systematic Structure of the Twenty-five Articles

There is a deliberate ordering principle in the Twenty-five *Articles of Religion*:

Articles 1–4: Faith in the Triune God

God the Father, God the Son, the Incarnation, atoning death, and resurrection of Jesus Christ, and the Holy Spirit

Articles 5–6: Holy Writ

Canonical Scripture as the norm of Christian teaching, the sufficient rule of faith for salvation

Articles 7–12: Sin and Salvation

The human predicament, freedom fallen in sin, yet met by divine grace that reconciles the sinner to God

through justifying faith in Christ, eliciting good works out of gratitude for the divine mercy

Articles 13–22: Church and Sacraments

Issues of the nature, authority, right ordering, ministry, sacraments, and worship of the church

Articles 23–25: The Christian in Society

The Christian community in relation to civil authority and property.

Our remaining task is to inquire into the specific manner in which the Twenty-five *Articles* were derived from the Anglican Thirty-nine.

How the Thirty-nine Articles Were Amended to Twenty-five

The texts below show precisely how the Twenty-five *Articles of Religion* were derived by Wesley by amendment, deletion, and retranslation from the Latin form of the Anglican Articles. It is intriguing and illuminating to analyze these differences. The following analysis of Wesley's recension of the *Articles* has been adapted from H. M. DuBose, *The Symbol of Methodism* (Nashville: Smith and Lamar, 1907), and P. A. Peterson, *The History of the Revisions of the Discipline* (Nashville: Smith and Lamar, 1889).[20]

THE THIRTY-NINE ANGLICAN ARTICLES

Showing the Wesleyan recension, which served as the basis for the Twenty-five Articles of Methodism, with subsequent variations. The changes and omissions made by Mr. Wesley are indicated by the letter "W" in brackets. Changes made subsequently are put in brackets, with the dates. Asterisk (*) indicates phrase unchanged. Standard numbering of Twenty-five Articles in parentheses.

Anglican Articles	Wesleyan Articles
I. Of Faith in the Holy Trinity.	*
There is but one living and true God,	*
everlasting,	*
without body, parts, or passions;	[W] body or parts
of infinite power, wisdom, and	*
goodness; the maker and preserver of all things	*
visible and invisible.	[1820] both visible and invisible.
And in unity of this godhead,	*
there be	[W] there are
three persons of one substance, power, and	*
eternity—the Father, the Son, and the Holy	*
Ghost.	*
II. Of the Word, or Son of God,	*
which was made very Man.	[W] *who was made very Man.*
The Son, which	[W] The Son, who
is the Word of the Father,	*
begotten from everlasting of the Father,	[1786] *Omitted*
the very and eternal God, of one substance with	*
the Father, took man's nature in the womb of	*
the blessed Virgin,	*
of her substance	[W] *Omitted*
so that two whole and perfect natures—that is	*
to say, the Godhead and manhood—were joined	*
together in one person, never to be divided,	*
whereof is one Christ, very God and very man,	*
who truly suffered, was crucified, dead, and	*
buried, to reconcile his Father to us, and to be	*
a sacrifice, not only for original guilt,	*
but also for actual sins of men.	*
III. Of the Going Down of Christ into Hell.	[W] *Article omitted*
As Christ died for us and was buried, so also is it to be believed that he went down into hell.	
(III.) Of the Resurrection of Christ.	*
Christ did truly rise again from	*
death	[W] the dead

Anglican Articles	Wesleyan Articles
and took again his body, with	*
flesh, bones, and	[W] *Omitted*
all things appertaining to the perfection of man's	*
nature, wherewith he ascended into heaven, and	*
there sitteth until he return to judge all men at	*
the last day.	*
(IV.) Of the Holy Ghost.	*
	*
The Holy Ghost, proceeding from the Father	*
and the Son, is of one substance, majesty, and	*
glory with the Father and the Son, very and	*
eternal God.	*
VI. (V.) Of the Sufficiency of the Holy Scriptures	*
for Salvation.	*
Holy Scripture containeth	[1816] The Holy Scrip-
all things necessary to salvation; so that	* tures contain
whatsoever is not read therein nor may be	*
proved thereby, is not to be required of any	*
man, that it should be believed as an article of	*
the faith,	[1789] faith,
or be thought requisite or necessary to salvation.	*
In the name of the Holy	*
Scripture,	[1816] Scriptures,
we do understand those canonical books of the	*
Old and New Testaments, of whose authority	*
was never any doubt in the Church.	*
Of the Names	[1790] *The Names*
and Number	[W] *Omitted*
of the Canonical Books.	*
Genesis, Exodus, Leviticus, Numbers, Deutero-	*
omy, Joshua, Judges, Ruth, The First Book of	*
Samuel, The Second Book of Samuel, The First	*
Book of Kings, The Second Book of Kings, the	*
First Book of Chronicles, The Second Book of	*
Chronicles,	*
The First Book of Esdras,	[W] The Book of Ezra,
The Second Book of Esdras,	[W] The Book of
The Book of Esther, The Book of Job, The	* Nehemiah,
Psalms, The Proverbs, Ecclesiastes, or the	*
Preacher, Cantica or Song of Solomon, Four	*
Prophets the Greater, Twelve Prophets the Less.	*
All the other books (as Hierome[21] saith) the	[W] *Section omitted*
Church doth read for example of life and	
instruction of manners; but yet doth it not	
apply them to establish any doctrine. Such are	

Anglican Articles	Wesleyan Articles
the following:	
The Third Book of Esdras, The Fourth Book of Esdras, The Book of Tobias, The Book of Judith, The Rest of The Book of Esther, The Book of Wisdom, Jesus, the Son of Sirach, Baruch the Prophet, The Song of the Three Children, The Story of Susanna, Of Bel and the Dragon, The Prayer of Manasses, The First Book of Maccabees, The Second Book of Maccabees.	[W] *Section omitted*
All the books of the New Testament, as they are commonly received, we do receive and account them canonical.	* * [W] account canonical.
VII. (VI.) Of the Old Testament. The Old Testament is not contrary to the New; for both in the Old and New Testament everlasting life is offered to mankind by Christ, who is the only Mediator between God and man, being God and man. Wherefore* they are not to be heard which feign that the old fathers did look only for transitory promises. Although the law given from God by Moses, as touching ceremonies and rites[22] do not bind Christian men,	* * * [1882] Old and New * Testaments * * * [W] who feign * * * [W] doth not bind Christians,
nor the civil precepts thereof ought of necessity to be received in any Commonwealth; yet, notwithstanding, no Christian man whatsoever is free from the obedience of the commandments which are called moral.	[W] nor ought the civil * precepts thereof * [W] no Christian * *
VIII. Of the Three Creeds. The three Creeds—Nicene Creed, Athanasius' Creed, and that which is commonly called the Apostles' Creed—ought thoroughly to be received and believed: for they may be proved by most certain warrants of Holy Scripture.	[W] *Article omitted*
(VII.) Of Original or Birth Sin. Original sin standeth not in the following of Adam (as the Pelagians do vainly talk), but it is the fault and corruption of the nature of every man, that naturally is	* * * [W] corruption *

Anglican Articles	Wesleyan Articles
engendered of the offspring of Adam, whereby	*
man is very far gone from original	*
righteousness,	*
and is of his own nature	[W] and of his own
inclined to evil	* nature
so that the flesh lusteth always	[W] Omitted
contrary to the spirit,	[W] Omitted
and that continually.	*

And therefore in every person born into this world, it deserveth God's wrath and condemnation. And this infection of nature doth remain; yea, in them that are regenerated, whereby the lust of the flesh, called in Greek, *phronema sarkos,* which some do expound the wisdom, some sensuality, some the affection, some the desire of the flesh, is not subject to the law of God. And although there is no condemnation for them that believe and are baptized, yet the apostle doth confess that concupiscence and lust hath of itself the nature of sin.	[W] Section omitted

X. (VIII.) Of Free Will.

The condition of man after the fall of Adam is	*
such that he cannot turn and prepare himself,	*
by his own natural strength	*
and good works,	*
to faith, and calling upon God; wherefore we	[W] and works,
have no power to do good works, pleasant and	*
acceptable to God, without the grace of God by	*
Christ preventing us, that we may have a good	*
will, and working with us, when we have that	*
good will.	*
	*

XI. (IX.) Of the Justification of Man.

We are accounted righteous before God, only	*
for the merit of our Lord and Saviour Jesus	*
Christ, by faith, and not for our own works or	*
deservings: wherefore, that we are justified by	*
faith only, is a most wholesome doctrine,	*
and very full of comfort	*
as more largely expressed in	[W] Omitted
the Homily of Justification.	[W] Omitted

XII. (X.) Of Good Works.

Albeit that good works,	[W] Although good
which are the fruits of faith, and follow after	* works,
justification, cannot put away our sins, and	*

Anglican Articles	Wesleyan Articles
endure the severity of God's judgment; yet are	*
they pleasing and acceptable to God in Christ,	*
and spring out necessarily of	[W] and spring out of
a true and lively faith, insomuch that by them a	*
lively faith may be as evidently known as a tree	*
discerned	[1812] is discerned
by the fruit.	[W] by its fruit.

XIII. Of Works before Justification.   [W] *Article omitted*

Works done before the grace of Christ, and the
inspiration of his Spirit, are not pleasant to God;
forasmuch as they spring not of faith in Jesus
Christ, neither do they make men meet to
receive grace, or (as the school authors say),
deserve grace of congruity; yea, rather, for that
they are not done as God hath willed and
commanded them to be done, we doubt not but
they have the nature of sin.

XIV. (XI.) Of Works of Supererogation.	*
Voluntary works, besides over and above God's	*
commandments, which are called works of	*
supererogation, cannot be taught without	*
arrogance and impiety. For by them men do	*
declare that they do not only render unto God	*
as much as they are bound to do, but that they	*
do more for his sake than of bounden duty is	*
required: whereas Christ saith plainly, When	*
ye have done	*
all that are commanded to you,	[W] all that is com-
say, We are unprofitable servants.	* manded you

XV. Of Christ Alone Without Sin.   [W] *Article omitted*

Christ in the truth of our nature was made like
unto us in all things, sin only except, from
which he was clearly void, both in his flesh and
in his spirit. He came to be the Lamb without
spot, who, by sacrifice of himself once made,
should take away the sins of the world; and sin,
as St. John saith, was not in him. But all the
rest, although baptized, and born again in
Christ, yet offend in many things; and if we
say we have no sin, we deceive ourselves, and
the truth is not in us.

XVI. (XII.) Of Sin after Baptism.	[W] *Of Sin after*
	Justification
Not every deadly sin	[W] Not every sin

Anglican Articles	Wesleyan Articles
willingly committed	*
after baptism is the	[W] after justification is
sin against the Holy Ghost, and unpardonable.	*
Wherefore, the grant of repentance is not to be	*
denied to such as fall into sin	*
after baptism:	[W] after justification:
after we have received the Holy Ghost, we may	*
depart from grace given, and fall into sin, and,	*
by the grace of God rise again and amend our	*
lives. And, therefore, they are to be condemned	*
who say they can no more sin as long as they	*
live here, or deny the place of forgiveness	*
to such as truly repent.	*

XVII. Of Predestination and Election.

[W] *Article omitted*

Predestination to life is the everlasting purpose
of God, whereby (before the foundations of the
world were laid) he hath constantly decreed by
his counsel, secret to us, to deliver from curse
and damnation those whom he hath chosen in
Christ out of mankind, and to bring them by
Christ to everlasting salvation, as vessels made
to honour. Wherefore they which be endued
with so excellent a benefit of God, be called
according to God's purpose by his Spirit working in due season: they through grace obey the
calling, they be justified freely: they be made
sons of God by adoption: they be made like the
image of his only begotten Son Jesus Christ:
they walk religiously in good works, and, at
length, by God's mercy, they attain to everlasting felicity.

As the godly consideration of predestination and
our election in Christ is full of sweet, pleasant,
and unspeakable comfort to godly persons, and
such as feel in themselves the working of the
Spirit of Christ, mortifying the works of the
flesh and their earthly members, and drawing up
their mind to high and heavenly things; as well
because it doth greatly establish and confirm
their faith of eternal salvation, to be enjoyed
through Christ, as because it doth fervently
kindle their love towards God: so for curious
and carnal persons, lacking the Spirit of Christ,
to have continually before their eyes the
sentence of God's predestination, is a most
dangerous downfall, whereby the devil dost
thrust them either into desperation, or into

recklessness of most unclean living, no less perilous than desperation.

Furthermore, we must receive God's promises in such wise as they be generally set forth to us in Holy Scripture: and in our doings that will of God is to be followed which we have expressly declared unto us in the word of God.

XVIII. Of Obtaining Eternal Salvation Only by the Name of Christ.	[W] *Article omitted*

They also are to be had accursed that presume to say that every man shall be saved by the law or sect which he professeth, so that he be diligent to frame his life according to that law, and the light of nature. For Holy Scripture doth set out unto us only the name of Jesus Christ, whereby men must be saved.

XIX. (XIII.) Of the Church.	*
The visible Church of Christ is a congregation	*
of faithful men, in which the pure word of God	*
is preached, and the sacraments duly	*
ministered,	[W] administered
according to Christ's ordinance, in all those	*
things that of necessity are requisite to the	*
same.	

As the Church of Jerusalem, Alexandria, and Antioch have erred, so also the Church of Rome hath erred, not only in their living and manner of ceremonies, but also in matters of faith.	[W] *Section omitted*

XX. Of the Authority of the Church.	[W] *Article omitted*

The Church hath power to decree rites or ceremonies, and authority in controversies of faith; and yet it is not lawful for the Church to ordain anything that is contrary to God's word written; neither may it expound one place of Scripture, that it be repugnant to another. Wherefore, although the Church be a witness and a keeper of holy writ, yet as it ought not to decree any thing against the same, so, besides the same ought it not to enforce any thing to be believed for necessity of salvation.

XXI. Of the Authority of General Councils.	[W] *Article omitted*

Anglican Articles	Wesleyan Articles
General Councils may not be gathered together without the commandment and will or princes. And when they be gathered together (forasmuch as they be an assembly of men, whereof all be not governed with the Spirit and word of God), they may err, and sometimes have erred, even in things pertaining unto God. Wherefore things ordained by them as necessary to salvation have neither strength nor authority, unless it may be declared that they be taken out of Holy Scripture.	

Anglican Articles	Wesleyan Articles
XXII. (XIV.) Of Purgatory.	*
The Romish doctrine concerning purgatory,	*
pardons, worshiping, and adoration, as well as	*
images as of relics, and also invocation of	*
saints, is a fond thing, vainly invented, and	*
grounded upon no	*
warranty	[W] warrant
of Scripture,	*
but rather repugnant	[W] but repugnant
to the word of God.	*

Anglican Articles	Wesleyan Articles
XXIII. Of Ministering in the Congregation.	[W] *Article omitted*
It is not lawful for any man to take upon him the office of public preaching, or ministering the sacraments in the congregation, before he be lawfully called and sent to execute the same. And those we ought to judge who have public authority given unto them in the congregation, to call and send ministers into the Lord's vineyard.	

Anglican Articles	Wesleyan Articles
XXIV. (XV.) Of Speaking in the Congregation in Such a Tongue as the People Understand.	*
	*
It is a thing plainly repugnant to the word of	*
God, and the custom of the Primitive Church,	*
to have public prayer in the church, or to	*
minister the sacraments, in a tongue	*
not understanded of	[W] not understood by
the people.	*

Anglican Articles	Wesleyan Articles
XXV. (XVI.) Of the Sacraments.	*
Sacraments, ordained of Christ, are not only	*
badges or tokens of Christian men's profession,	*
but rather they are certain	*
sure witnesses and effectual	[W] *Omitted*
signs of grace and God's good-will toward us,	*

Anglican Articles	Wesleyan Articles
by the which he doth work invisibly in us, and doth not only quicken, but also strengthen and confirm our faith in him.	* *
There are two sacraments ordained of Christ our Lord in the gospel—that is to say, Baptism and the Supper of the Lord.	* *
Those five, commonly called sacraments—that is to say, Confirmation, Penance, Orders, Matrimony, and Extreme Unction—are not to be counted for sacraments of the gospel, being such as have grown partly out of the corrupt following of the apostles, and partly are states of life allowed in the Scriptures, but yet have not like nature of sacraments with Baptism and the Lord's Supper, because they have not any visible sign or ceremony ordained of God.	* * * * * * * [W] the like nature of * baptism *
The sacraments were not ordained of Christ to be gazed upon, or to be carried about, but that we should duly use them. And in such only as worthily receive the same they have a wholesome effect or operation; but they that receive them unworthily purchase to themselves damnation as St. Paul saith.	* * * * * * [W] condemnation *
XXVI. Of the Unworthiness of the Ministers, Which Hinders Not the Effect of the Sacrament. Although in the visible Church the evil be ever mingled with the good, and sometimes the evil have chief authority in the ministration of the word and sacraments: yet forasmuch as they do not the same in their own name, but in Christ's, and do minister by his commission and authority, we may use their ministry, both in hearing the word of God and in the receiving of the sacraments. Neither is the effect of Christ's ordinance taken away by their wickedness, nor the grace of God's gifts diminished from such as by faith and rightly do receive the sacraments ministered unto them, which be effectual because of Christ's institution and promise, although they be ministered by evil men.	[W] *Article omitted*
Nevertheless, it appertaineth to the discipline of the Church that inquiry be made of evil ministers, and that they be accused by those	

Anglican Articles	Wesleyan Articles
that have knowledge of their offenses: and finally, being found guilty, by just judgment be deposed.	

XXVII. (XVII.) Of Baptism.

Anglican Articles	Wesleyan Articles
Baptism is not only a sign of profession, and	*
mark of difference, whereby	*
Christian men are discerned	[W] Christians are
from others that are not	* distinguished
christened,	[W] baptized,
but it is also a sign of regeneration or	*
new birth	[W] the new birth
whereby, as by an instrument,	[W] Omitted
they that receive baptism rightly	[W] Omitted
are grafted into the Church:	[W] Omitted
the promises of the forgiveness of sin,	[W] Omitted
and of our adoption to be the sons of God	[W] Omitted
by the Holy Ghost, are visibly signed	[W] Omitted
and sealed: faith is confirmed and grace	[W] Omitted
increased by virtue of prayer unto God.	[W] Omitted
The baptism of young children is	*
in any wise	[W] Omitted
to be retained in the Church	*
as most agreeable with the institution of Christ.	[W] Omitted

XXVIII. (XVIII.) Of the Lord's Supper.

Anglican Articles	Wesleyan Articles
The Supper of the Lord is not only a sign of the love[23] that Christians ought to have among themselves one to another, but rather is a sacrament of our redemption by Christ's death: insomuch that to such as rightly, worthily, and with faith receive the same, the bread which we break is a partaking of the body of Christ; and likewise the cup of blessing is a partaking of the blood of Christ.	* * * * * * * * *
Transubstantiation, or the change of the substance of bread and wine in the Supper of the Lord, cannot be proved by Holy Writ, but is repugnant to the plain words of Scripture, overthroweth the nature of a sacrament, and hath given occasion to many superstitions.	* * * * * *
The body of Christ is given, taken, and eaten in the Supper only after a heavenly and spiritual[24] manner. And the means whereby the body of Christ is received and eaten, in the Supper, is faith.	* * * * *
The sacrament of the Lord's Supper was not by	*

Anglican Articles	Wesleyan Articles
Christ's ordinance reserved, carried about, lifted up, or worshiped.	* *
XXIX. Of the Wicked which Eat Not the Body of Christ in the Use of the Lord's Supper.	[W] *Article omitted*
The wicked, and such as be void of a lively faith, although they do carnally and visibly press with their teeth (as St. Augustine saith) the sacrament of the body and blood of Christ; yet in no wise are they partakers of Christ, but rather to their condemnation do eat and drink the sign or sacrament of so great a thing.	
XXX. (XIX.) Of Both Kinds.	*
The cup of the Lord is not to be denied to the lay people; for both the parts of	* *
the Lord's Sacrament	[W] the Lord's Supper
by Christ's ordinance and commandment, ought	*
to be ministered	[W] to be administered
to all Christian men alike.	[W] to all Christians alike.
XXXI. (XX.) Of the One Oblation of Christ Finished upon the Cross.	* *
The offering of Christ, once made, is that perfect redemption, propitiation, and satisfaction for all the sins of the whole world, both original and actual; and there is none other satisfaction for sin but that alone. Wherefore the sacrifice of masses,	* * * * * *
in which it was	[W] in which it is
commonly said that the priest doth offer Christ for the quick and the dead, to have remission of pain or guilt,	* * *
were blasphemous fables and dangerous deceits.	[W] is a blasphemous fable and dangerous deceit.
XXXII. (XXI.) Of the Marriage of Priests.	* [W] *Ministers*
Bishops, priests, and deacons	[W] The ministers of
are not commanded by God's law either to vow the estate of single life, or to abstain from marriage; therefore it is lawful for them, as for all other	* Christ * * *
Christian men,	[W] Christians
to marry at their own discretion, as they shall judge the same	* *
to serve better	[W] to serve best
to godliness.	*

Anglican Articles	Wesleyan Articles
XXXIII. Of Excommunicate Persons, How They Are to be Avoided.	[W] *Article omitted*
That person which, by open denunciation of the Church, is rightly cut off from the unity of the Church and excommunicated, ought to be taken of the whole multitude of the faithful as an heathen and publican, until he be openly reconciled by penance, and received into the Church by a judge that hath authority thereunto.	
XXXIV. (XXII.) Of the Traditions of the Church.	[W] *Of the Rites and Ceremonies of Churches.*
	*
It is not necessary that traditions and ceremonies	[W] rites and ceremonies
be in all places	[W] should in all places be
one or utterly alike;	[W] the same, or exactly alike;
for at all times they have been diverse,	[W] for they have been always different,
and may be changed according to the diversity	*
of countries, times, and men's manners, so that	*
nothing be ordained against God's word.	*
Whosoever, through his private judgment,	*
willingly and purposely, both openly break	*
the traditions	[W] the rites
and ceremonies of the Church,	*
	[W] to which he belongs,
which are repugnant to the word of God, and	*
are ordained and approved by common	*
authority, ought to be rebuked openly, that	*
others may fear to do the like,	*
as he that offendeth	[W] as one that
against the common order of the Church	* offendeth
and hurteth the authority of the magistrate	[W] *Omitted*
and woundeth the consciences of	*
the weak brethren.	[W] weak brethren.
Every particular or national Church	[W] Every particular Church
hath authority to ordain, change,	[W] may ordain, change,
and abolish ceremonies or rites	[W] or abolish [W] rites and ceremonies
of the Church,	[W] *Omitted*

Anglican Articles	**Wesleyan Articles**
ordained only by man's authority, so that all things be done	[W] *Omitted*
	*
to edifying.	[W] to edification.

XXXV. Of the Homilies.

[W] *Article omitted*

The second Book of Homilies, the several titles whereof we have joined under this article, doth contain a goodly and wholesome doctrine, and necessary for these times, as doth the former Book of Homilies, which were set forth in the time of Edward the Sixth, and therefore we judge them to be read in Churches by the ministers diligently and distinctly, that they may be understood by the people.

OF THE NAMES OF THE HOMILIES.

1. Of the Right Use of the Church. 2. Against Peril of Idolatry. 3. Of Repairing and Keeping Clean of Churches. 4. Of Good Works: First of Fasting. 5. Against Gluttony and Drunkenness. 6. Against Excess of Apparel. 7. Of Prayer. 8. Of the Place and Time of Prayer. 9. That Common Prayers and Sacraments Ought to be Ministered in a Known Tongue. 10. Of the reverend Estimation of God's Word. 11. Of Almsgiving. 12. Of the Nativity of Christ. 13. Of the Passion of Christ. 14. Of the Resurrection of Christ. 15. Of the Worthy Receiving of the Sacrament of the Body and Blood of Christ. 16. Of the Gifts of the Holy Ghost. 17. For the Rogation-days. 18. Of the State of Marriage. 19. Of Repentance. 20. Against Idleness. 21. Against Rebellion.

XXXVI. Of Consecration of Bishops and Ministers.

[W] *Article omitted*

The Book of Consecration of Archbishops and Bishops, and ordering of Priests and Deacons, lately set forth in the time of Edward the Sixth, and confirmed at the same time by authority of Parliament, doth contain all things necessary to such consecration and ordering; neither hath it any thing that of itself is superstitious and ungodly. And, therefore, whosoever are consecrated or ordered according to the rites of that book, since the second year of the forenamed King Edward, unto this time or hereafter, shall be consecrated or ordered according to the same

Anglican Articles	Wesleyan Articles
rites, we decree all such to be rightly, orderly, and lawfully consecrated and ordered.	

Anglican Articles

rites, we decree all such to be rightly, orderly, and lawfully consecrated and ordered.

XXXVII. Of the Civil Magistrates.
The king's majesty hath the chief power in this realm of England, and his other dominions, unto whom the chief government of all estates of this realm, whether they be ecclesiastical or civil, in all causes doth appertain, and is not, nor ought to be, subject to any foreign jurisdiction.

Where we attribute to the king's majesty the chief government, by which titles we understand the minds of some slanderous folks to be offended; we give not to our princes the ministering whether of God's word, or of the sacraments, to which things the injunctions also lately set forth by Elizabeth our queen do most plainly testify; but that only prerogative, which we see to have been given always to all godly princes in Holy Scriptures by God Himself; that is, that they should rule all estates and degrees committed to this charge by God, whether they be ecclesiastical or temporal, and restrain with the civil sword the stubborn and evil doers.

The Bishop of Rome hath no jurisdiction in this realm of England.

The laws of the realm may punish Christian men with death for heinous and grievous offenses.

It is lawful for Christian men, at the commandment of the magistrate, to wear weapons and serve in wars.

Wesleyan Articles

[W] *Article omitted*

[W] *(XXIII.)*[25] *Of the Rulers of the United States of America*
[1790] The President, [1784] the Congress, the General Assemblies, the Governors, and the councils of state, as the delegates of the people, are the rulers of the United States of America, according to the division of power made to them by the general act of confederation ([1804] Constitution of the

Anglican Articles	Wesleyan Articles
	United States), and by the Constitutions of their respective States. And the said States ([1804] are a sovereign and independent nation, and) ought not to be subject to any foreign jurisdiction.
	[1820] Note.—As far as it respects civil affairs, we believe it the duty of Christians, and especially all Christian ministers, to be subject to the supreme authority of the country where they may reside, and to use all laudable means to enjoin obedience to the powers that be; and, therefore, it is expected that all our preachers and people who may be under the British or any other ([1854] any foreign) government, will behave themselves as peaceable and orderly subjects.[26]

XXXVIII. (XXIV.)[27] *Of Christian Men's Goods Which Are Not Common.*
    * [W] *Omitted*

The riches and goods of Christians are not
common, as touching the right, title, and
possession of the same,
as certain Anabaptists
do falsely boast. Notwithstanding, every man
ought, of such things as he possesseth, liberally
to give alms to the poor according to his
ability.
    *
    *
    *
[W] as some
    *
    *
    *
    *

XXXIX. (XXV.)[28] *Of a Christian Man's Oath.*
    *

As we confess that vain and rash swearing is
forbidden Christian men by our Lord Jesus
Christ and James his apostle, so we judge that
the Christian religion doth not prohibit, but that
a man may swear when the magistrate
requireth, in a cause of faith and charity,
so it be done according to the prophet's
teaching, in justice, judgment, and truth.
    *
    *
    *
    *
    *
    *
    *
    *
    *

7.

Doctrinal Inheritance
of the Wesleyan Family of Churches

The comparative study of Wesleyan-based churches' official doctrinal standards is an ecumenical inquiry in its infancy. This study seeks to resource, enable, and encourage further comparative doctrinal inquiry among international Wesleyan bodies.

It is ironic that United Methodists have spent enormous amounts of energy on ecumenical affairs in the last century, but most of that energy has been directed toward conversations with persons and institutions in Reformed, Lutheran, Eastern Orthodox, Roman Catholic, and other traditions. Meanwhile, there as been precious little attempt made to reach out for our nearest neighbors in the ecumenical village: our own Wesleyan-rooted family of churches.

Wesleyan-based churches that have been most consistently and substantively involved in ecumenical dialogue with United Methodists are the black Methodist traditions (A.M.E., A.M.E. Zion, C.M.E.), the former Evangelical United Brethren Church, and the Salvation Army. But it has been much rarer to find liberal United Methodists earnestly searching out ecumenical dialogue with those of other more conservative Wesleyan traditions—such as the Wesleyan Church or Free Methodists—or with those of Holiness or Pentecostal traditions that obviously stem from nineteenth-century Methodist, holiness, and sanctificationist revivalism. Largely apart from United Methodist circles, a significant pan-Wesleyan dialogue has been proceeding through such organizations as the Christian Holiness Association, the Wesleyan Theological Society, the Evangelical Theological Society, some Wesleyan colleges and seminaries, certain journals, and various dialogues between judicatories.

Our limited objective at this stage is to allow the official doctrinal documents of these churches to speak for themselves without extensive secondary interpretation. Since primary official church documentation rather than secondary individual commentary is our main interest, the reader is left to reflect upon affinities and differences within these documents. At some future stage of discussion, it is hoped that further attention will be given to applying more detailed textual analysis and critical-historical study to these documents and their comparison.

I. Toward a Definition of International Pan-Wesleyan Doctrine

The phrase "pan-Wesleyan" refers to those varied church bodies that are rooted in Wesleyan theology, discipline, ethos, practice, and usage. The prefix, from the Greek *pan* ("all"), suggests an overarching inclusion that embraces the entirety of a diversified group. There is, for example, in the various ethnic traditions of Eastern Orthodoxy an emerging consciousness of a "pan-Orthodox" reality or possibility. So there is emerging among the various strains of Wesleyan-rooted churches a sense of the possibility of a "pan-Wesleyan" communion or constellation of churches, movements, and missions. Rather than being counter-ecumenical, this is an expression of deepening ecumenical awareness.

Defining the Family

It is fitting to be as descriptive as possible when using phrases such as "the Wesleyan family of churches" or "churches of Wesleyan origin" or "Wesleyan tradition churches." What do such phrases mean? What churches do they embrace? The *Yearbook of American and Canadian Churches*[1] arranges the Wesleyan-rooted churches in the United States into these categories:

METHODIST BODIES

African Methodist Episcopal Church; African Methodist Episcopal Zion Church; Bible Protestant Church; Christian Methodist Episcopal Church; Evangelical Methodist Church; Free Methodist Church of North America; Fundamental Methodist Church, Inc.; Primitive Methodist Church, U.S.A.; Reformed Methodist Union Episcopal Church; Reformed Zion Union Apostolic Church; Southern Methodist Church; The United Methodist Church; The Wesleyan Church

CHURCHES OF GOD

Church of God (Anderson, Ind.); Church of God (Huntsville, Ala.); Churches of God, General Conference (Oregon, Ill.)

SALVATION ARMY

CHURCH OF THE NAZARENE

AFFILIATED ORGANIZATIONS OF THE CHRISTIAN HOLINESS ASSOCIATION

(Includes some listed above)

Bible Holiness Movement; Brethren in Christ Church; Churches of Christ in Christian Union; Evangelical Christian Church; Evangelical Church of North America; Evangelical Friends Alliance; Evangelical Methodist Church; Free Methodist Church of North America; The Canadian Holiness Federation; United Brethren in Christ Church (Sandusky Conference); Japan Immanuel Church; Christ Alive, Inc.; The Church of the Nazarene; Salvation Army; The Wesleyan Church; and cooperating organizations: Primitive Methodist Church; Congregational Methodist Church; Church of God (Anderson, Ind.); Methodist Protestant Church; and the Missionary Church.

To these may be added certain Wesleyan-rooted Pentecostal Holiness denominations, especially The Apostolic Faith; the Church of God; Church of God (Cleveland, Tenn.); The Church of God in Christ; The Church of God of Prophecy; Congregational Holiness Church; the

International Pentecostal Holiness Church; and Pentecostal Fire-Baptized Holiness Church.[2]

This list is not exhaustive.[3] Our present purpose is not to determine a denomination's degree of affinity with Wesley or to survey the theology of these groups. Rather it is to select from the documents of some of these groups representative statements that indicate official doctrinal standards and to ask how far they are similar, both in language and intent, to the established standards of Mr. Wesley's connection two centuries ago.

We should note that some of these Wesleyan-influenced international churches are among the fastest growing in the world. The world missions of these churches have established congregations in Africa, Asia, Australasia and the Pacific Islands, Europe, North America, and Latin America. For example, the Salvation Army has a worldwide membership of an estimated two million. Combined membership of the A.M.E., A.M.E. Zion, and C.M.E. churches is currently listed at over five million with about fifteen thousand congregations. The Church of the Nazarene grew from 165,532 members in 1940 to about five hundred thousand currently in the United States (706,000 worldwide). The Church of God (Cleveland, Tenn.) grew from 63,216 members in 1940 to 456,797 in 1981 in the United States. The largest of these church bodies, the United Methodist Church, peaked at eleven million members in 1965 and now has about nine-and-a-half million members in the United States.

A Chronology of the American Forms of the Wesleyan Family of Churches

Which groups may reasonably be included under the rubric of the "Wesleyan family of churches"? Some would define the family so as to include—and others to exclude—various Pentecostal denominations, while yet others would draw the boundaries by other criteria.

It may be helpful to study the following chronology of movements that grew out of the Wesleyan tradition. The list includes holiness denominations of the late nineteenth century and Pentecostal denominations of the twentieth (yet excluding those Pentecostal groups that deny the Trinity and those that do not stress other Wesleyan theological themes):

1784   The Methodist Episcopal Church
1787   African Methodist Episcopal Church
1792   Republican Methodists (the James O'Kelley movement, later uniting with the Congregational Church)
1796   African Methodist Episcopal Zion Church
1800   United Brethren Christ (later the E.U.B.)
1803   The Evangelical Church (became the Evangelical Association in 1816, later the E.U.B.)
1805   The Union African Methodist Episcopal Church
1814   Reformed Methodist Church (anti-episcopal)
1829   Primitive Methodist Church, U.S.A. (from the British "camp-meeting" Methodists)

1830	Methodist Protestant Church (lay representation; reentered the Methodist Church in 1939)
1843	The Wesleyan Methodist Church of America (abolitionist and anti-episcopal)
1844	Methodist Episcopal Church, South (result of the North/South struggle; reentered the Methodist Church in 1939)
1850	Union American Methodist Episcopal Church
1852	The Congregational Methodist Church
1860	Free Methodist Church of North America (abolitionist, free pews)
1864	United Christian Church (withdrawing from the United Brethren in Christ)
1867	National Holiness Movement (emerging from various camp-meeting associations; later the Christian Holiness Association)
1869	Reformed Zion Union Apostolic Church
1870	Colored Methodist Episcopal Church (later the Christian Methodist Episcopal Church)
1880	The Salvation Army (founded in London, 1865)
1880	Church of God (Anderson, Ind.)
1880	The Holiness Church
1885	Reformed Methodist Union Episcopal Church (withdrawing from the A.M.E. Church)
1886	The Church of God (Cleveland, ·Tenn.)
1889	United Brethren in Christ (Old Constitution; stemming from the United Brethren)
1890	The Fire-Baptized Holiness Church (Wesleyan)
1894	United Evangelical Church (perfectionists withdrawing from the Evangelical Association)
1890–95	Pentecostal Holiness Church, International
1897	Pilgrim Holiness Church
1898	The Pentecostal Alliance (later united with the Church of the Nazarene)
1900	The Apostolic Faith Mission
1901	Pillar of Fire (withdrawing from the Methodist Church)
1903	The Church of God (Huntsville, Ala.)
1903	The Church of God of Prophecy
1906	Independent Assemblies of God, International
1906	The Church of God in Christ
1907	International Pentecostal Assemblies
1907	The Apostolic Faith
1908	The Church of the Nazarene
1914	Assemblies of God
1917	Pentecostal Church of Christ (later united with the International Pentecostal Assemblies to form the International Pentecostal Church of Christ)
1918	Pentecostal Fire-Baptized Holiness Church
1920	Holiness Church of God, Inc.
1939	The Methodist Church (a unification of the Methodist Episcopal Church; the Methodist Episcopal Church, South; and the Methodist Protestant Church)

1939 Southern Methodist Church (declined unification with the Methodist Church)
1942 Fundamental Methodist Church, Inc.
1946 Evangelical United Brethren (a unification of the Church of the United Brethren in Christ and the Evangelical Church)
1946 Evangelical Methodist Church
1959 Wesleyan Holiness Association of Churches
1968 The Wesleyan Church (a unification of the Pilgrim Holiness Church and the Wesleyan Methodist Church of America)
1968 United Methodist Church (a unification of the Methodist Church and the Evangelical United Brethren)
1968 Evangelical Church of North America (a unification of some congregations of the Evangelical United Brethren, which declined unification with the United Methodist Church, with the Holiness Methodist Church)
1969 Missionary Church (a unification of the Missionary Church Association and the United Missionary Church)

The various branches of Methodism in Great Britain may be summarized in these groups and periods: The Methodist New Connection (1797–1907); The Primitive Methodist Conference (1820–1932); The United Methodist Conference (1907–1932); the United Methodist Free Churches (1857–1907); the Bible Christians (1815–1907); Wesleyan Protestant Methodist Association (1829–1907); Wesleyan Methodist Association (1836–1856); and The Wesleyan Methodist Conference (1791–1932). Several of these united in 1932 to form the Methodist Conference. Other existing Methodist groups in the United Kingdom include the Irish Methodist Conference (1868–present) and the Welsh Methodist Assembly (1899–present).

Such a list is astonishing, even if historians disagree about the precise degree to which Wesleyan doctrine has influenced each of these groups. The total worldwide membership of such Wesleyan-related groups is difficult to estimate. *The Encyclopedia of World Methodism* listed the membership of "World Methodism" in 1970 as 20,430,885; but that figure did not include many of the church bodies listed above. A current estimate of well over thirty million is not improbable.

No one would contend that these churches agree on matters of doctrine in all details. However, as one carefully examines the doctrinal statements of these groups, one is struck by the recurring phrases that show significant affinity and continuity with the early Wesleyan teaching. Some of these statements are collected here for the first time and presented without comment, so that pastors, laypersons, and scholars from various branches of the Wesleyan family might compare and study them, reflecting on the affinities and differences of their respective groups.

II. Variants of Articles
Collation and Variants of the Articles of Religion of Representative Wesleyan-rooted Church Bodies

This section is the heart of the chapter. It seeks to correlate the variant wordings of articles of faith and confessional statements of Wesleyan communions, showing the ways in which the Methodist *Articles of Religion* (whose wording is printed in italics in accord with the received United Methodist text) have been received and amended by various Wesleyan churches' doctrinal standards. It also shows the pre-1563 sources of the Anglican Articles. Where a substantial new article has been written or revised by a modern Wesleyan church body, that will appear indented in a separate paragraph. The 1563 Latin form of the Anglican Thirty-nine Articles is included in some paragraphs.[4] (Minor variants of spelling, grammar, or syntax will not be noted.) This coding system is used to track the variants.

Italics = *Twenty-five Articles of Religion*

   A = African Methodist Episcopal *Articles of Religion*
   C = Christian Methodist Episcopal *Articles of Religion*
 EUB = *Confession of Faith* (1962) of the former Evangelical United Brethren Church
   F = Free Methodist Church of North America *Basic Principles* (1969)[5]
   N = The Church of the Nazarene *Articles of Faith*[6]
   W = The Wesleyan Church *Articles of Religion*
 WTS = Wesleyan Theological Society *Doctrinal Position*
   Z = African Methodist Episcopal Zion *Articles of Religion*

I. Of Faith in the Holy Trinity

There is but one living and true God,	ACFWZ
[Unus est vivus et verus Deus]	
everlasting, [aeterus]	ACFWZ
without body or parts,	ACFZ
[incorporeus, impartibilis]	
of infinite power, wisdom, and goodness;	ACFWZ
[immensae potentiae, sapientiae ac bonitatis]	
the maker (Creator)	ACFZ
Maker	W
and preserver of all things,	ACFZ
[et conservator omnium]	
Preserver	W
both	AC
visible and invisible	ACFWZ
[tum visibilium tum invisibilium].	
And in unity of this Godhead	ACFW
in the unity	Z
there are three persons,	ACFWZ
of one substance, power, and eternity—	ACFWZ
the Father, the Son,	ACFWZ
(the Word),	W
and the Holy Ghost.	ACFWZ

Sources of Anglican Article 1 on God: Nicene Creed, Athanasian Creed, the Augsburg Confession,[7] Article 13 of 1538, Article 1 of the Forty-two Articles of Edward VI in 1553, and Chapter 2 of *Reformatio Legum Ecclesiasticarum*. Exclusions: pantheism and various forms of anti-Trinitarianism (such as Arianism, Tritheism, Sabellianism, Modalism, and Unitarianism).

E.U.B. CONFESSION OF 1962:

[God] We believe in the one living and true God, Eternal Spirit, who is Creator, Sovereign and preserver of all things visible and invisible. He is infinite in power, wisdom, justice, goodness and love, and rules with gracious regard for the well-being and salvation of men, to the glory of his name. We believe the one God reveals himself as the Trinity: Father, Son, and Holy Spirit, distinct but inseparable, eternally one in essence and power.

FREE METHODIST, 1972:

[The Holy Trinity] We believe in the one true and living God, the maker and preserver of all things. And in the unity of this Godhead there are three persons: the Father,

the Son and the Holy Spirit. These three are one in eternity, deity, and purpose; everlasting, of infinite power, wisdom, and goodness.

[The Father] We believe that the Father is the cause of all that exists whether of matter or spirit. He with the Son and the Holy Spirit made man to bear His image. By intention He relates to man as Father, thereby forever declaring His good-will toward man. He is, according to the New Testament, the one who both seeks and receives penitent sinners.

NAZARENE ARTICLES OF FAITH:

We believe in one eternally existent, infinite God, Sovereign of the universe; that He only is God, creative and administrative, holy in nature, attributes, and purpose; that He, as God, is Triune in essential being, revealed as Father, Son, and Holy Spirit.

WESLEYAN THEOLOGICAL SOCIETY DOCTRINAL POSITION:

We believe that there is one God, eternally existent in the Holy Trinity of Father, Son, and Holy Spirit, each with personality and deity.

II. *Of the Word, or Son of God, Who Was Made Very Man*	ACFZ
The Son of God	W
The Son, who is the Word of the Father,	ACFZ
[Filius, qui est verbum Patris]	
the very and eternal God,	ACFZ
[verus et aeternus Deus]	
of one substance with the Father,	ACFZ
[ac Patri constustantialis]	
took man's nature	ACFZ
[naturam humanam assumpsit]	
in the womb of the blessed Virgin;	ACFZ
[in utero beatae virginis]	
so that two whole and perfect natures,	ACFZ

[ita ut duae naturae]	
that is to say, the Godhead and Manhood,	
manhood,	ACFZ
[divina et humana]	
were joined together in one person,	ACFZ
[integre atque perfecte in unitate personae]	
never to be divided;	ACFZ
[fuerint inseparabiliter conjunctae]	
whereof is one Christ,	ACFZ
[ex quibus est unus Christus]	
very God and very Man,	
man,	ACFZ
[verus Deus et verus homo]	
who truly suffered,	ACFZ
[qui vere passus est]	
was crucified, dead, and buried,	ACFZ
[crufixus, mortuus et sepultus]	
to reconcile his Father to us,	ACFZ
[ut Patrem nobis reconciliaret]	
and to be a sacrifice,	ACZ
[essetque hostia]	
to be the one mediator between God and man	F
by the sacrifice of Himself	F
not only for original guilt,	ACZ
[non tantum pro culpa originis]	
both for original sin	F
but also for the actual sins of men.	ACZ
[verum etiam pro omnibus actualibus hominem peccatis].	
and for the actual transgressions of men.	F

Sources of Anglican Article 2 on the Son: the Nicene Creed,[8] Athanasian Creed, Chalcedonian Creed, and the Augsburg Confession (Article 3). Clauses on eternal generation and consubstantiality from the Wurttemberg Articles of 1552 and Article 2 of 1553.

E.U.B. CONFESSION OF FAITH:

[Jesus Christ] We believe in Jesus Christ, truly God and truly man, in whom the divine and human natures are perfectly and inseparably united. He is the eternal Word made flesh, the only begotten Son of the Father, born of the Virgin Mary by the power of the Holy Spirit. As ministering Servant he lived, suffered and died on the cross. He was buried. . . .

FREE METHODIST, 1972:

[The Son] We believe God was himself in Jesus Christ to reconcile man to God. Conceived by the Holy Spirit, born of the Virgin Mary, He joined together the deity of God and the humanity of man. Jesus of Nazareth was God in human flesh, truly God and man. He came to save us. For us the Son of God suffered, was crucified, dead and buried. He poured out His life as a blameless sacrifice for our sin and transgressions. We gratefully acknowledge that He is our Savior, the one perfect mediator between God and man.

WESLEYAN CHURCH ARTICLES
OF RELIGION:

[The Son of God] Jesus Christ, the only begotten Son of God, was conceived by the Holy Ghost, born of the Virgin Mary, very God and very Man, suffered under Pontius Pilate, was crucified, dead and buried—to be a sacrifice, not only for original guilt, but also for the actual sins of men, and to reconcile us to God.

NAZARENE ARTICLES OF FAITH:

[Jesus Christ] We believe in Jesus Christ, the Second Person of the Triune Godhead; that He was eter-nally one with the Father; that He became incarnate by the Holy Spirit and was born of the Virgin Mary, so that two whole and perfect natures, that is to say the Godhead and manhood, are thus united in one Person, very God and very man, the God-man.

WESLEYAN THEOLOGICAL SOCIETY
DOCTRINAL POSITION:

We believe that the Son, our Lord Jesus Christ, was manifested in the flesh through the Virgin Birth, and died on Calvary for the redemption of the human family, all of whom may be saved from sin through faith in Him.

III. *Of the Resurrection of Christ*	ACFZ
The Resurrection of Christ	W
Christ did truly rise again from the dead,	ACFZ
and took again	ACFZ
taking	W
his body,	ACFZ
His body	W
with all things appertaining to	ACFWZ
the perfection of man's nature,	ACFWZ
wherewith he ascended into heaven,	ACFWZ
He	W
and there sitteth until he return	
returns	Z
He shall return	AC
He returns	FW
to judge all men at the last day.	ACFWZ

Sources of Anglican Article 4 on the Resurrection: the Athanasian and Nicene Creeds, Apostles' Creed, Augsburg Confession (Article 3), Thirteen Articles of 1538; largely unchanged since Article 4 of 1553. *Contra* Docetism.

E.U.B. CONFESSION:

. . . rose from the dead and ascended into heaven to be with the Father, from whence he shall re-turn. He is eternal Savior and Mediator, who intercedes for us, and by him all men will be judged.

FREE METHODIST, 1972:

[His Resurrection and Exaltation] We believe Jesus Christ is risen victorious from the dead. His resurrection body became more glorious, not hindered by ordinary human limitations. Thus He ascended into heaven. There He sits as our

INHERITANCE OF THE WESLEYAN FAMILY OF CHURCHES **135**

exalted Lord at the right hand of God the Father, where He intercedes for us until all His enemies shall be brought into complete subjection. He will return to judge all men. Every knee will bow and every tongue confess Jesus Christ is Lord, to the glory of God the Father.

. . . and that He truly arose from the dead and took again His body, together with all things appertaining to the perfection of man's nature, wherewith He ascended into heaven and is there engaged in intercession for us.

IV. *Of the Holy Ghost*	ACFZ
The Holy Ghost	W
The Holy Ghost,	ACFWZ
proceeding from the Father and the Son,	ACFWZ
is of one substance, majesty, and glory	ACFWZ
with the Father and the Son,	ACFWZ
very and eternal God.	ACFWZ

Sources of Anglican Article 5 on the Holy Spirit: Council of Constantinople, A.D. 381, attested faith "in the Holy Ghost, the Lord and Giver of Life who proceeds from the Father." Wurttemberg Confession's article on the Holy Spirit is almost identical to the Anglican. Article 5 of 1563. *Reformatio Legum Ecclesiasticarum, de Haeresibus,* ch. 6.

E.U.B. CONFESSION:

[The Holy Spirit] We believe in the Holy Spirit who proceeds from and is one in being with the Father and the Son. He convinces the world of sin, of righteousness and of judgment. He leads men through faithful response to the gospel into the fellowship of the Church. He comforts, sustains and empowers the faithful and guides them into all truth.

FREE METHODIST, 1972:

[The Holy Spirit, His Person] We believe the Holy Spirit is the third person of the Trinity. Proceeding from the Father and the Son, He is

one with them, the eternal Godhead; equal in deity, majesty, and power. He is God effective in Creation, in life, and in the church. The Incarnation and ministry of Jesus Christ were accomplished by the Holy Spirit. He continues to reveal, interpret, and glorify the Son.

[His Work in Salvation] We believe the Holy Spirit is the administrator of the salvation planned by the Father and provided by the Son's death, Resurrection, and Ascension. He is the effective agent in our conviction, regeneration, sanctification, and glorification. He is our Lord's ever-present self, indwelling, assuring, and enabling the believer.

[His Relation to the Church] We believe the Holy Spirit is poured out upon the church by the Father and the Son. He is the church's life and witnessing power. He bestows the love of God and makes real the lordship of Jesus Christ in the believer so that both His gifts of words and service may achieve the common good, and build and increase the church. In relation to the world He is the Spirit of truth, and His instrument is the Word of God.

NAZARENE ARTICLES OF FAITH:

[The Holy Spirit] We believe in the Holy Spirit, the Third Person of the Triune Godhead, that He is ever present and efficiently active in and with the Church of Christ, convincing the world of sin, regenerating those who repent and believe, sanctifying believers, and guiding them into all truth as it is in Jesus.

V. *Of the Sufficiency of the Holy Scriptures for Salvation*	ACFWZ
The Sufficiency of the Holy Scripture for Salvation	Z
Scriptures	CF
The Sufficiency and Full Authority of the Holy	W
Scriptures for Salvation	W
The Holy Scripture containeth	AC
contain	FWZ
all things necessary to salvation;	ACFWZ
so that whatsoever is not read therein,	ACFWZ
nor may be proved thereby,	ACFWZ
is not to be required of any man,	ACFWZ
that it should be believed as an article of faith,	ACFWZ
or be thought requisite or necessary to salvation.	ACFWZ
In the name of the	ACZ
Holy Scripture we do understand	AC
Holy Scriptures we do understand	Z
By the term Holy Scriptures we understand	F
those canonical books of the Old and New Testament	ACFZ
Testaments	F
of whose authority was never any doubt in the Church.	ACFZ
We do understand the books of the Old and New Testaments to constitute the Holy Scriptures.	W
	W

E.U.B. CONFESSION:

[The Holy Bible] We believe the Holy Bible, Old and New Testaments, reveals the Word of God so far as it is necessary for our salvation. It is to be received through the Holy Spirit as the true rule and guide for faith and practice. Whatever is not revealed in or established by the Holy Scriptures is not to be made an article of faith nor is to be taught as essential to salvation.

FREE METHODIST, 1972:

[The Scriptures. Sufficiency] We believe the Holy Scriptures are God's record, uniquely inspired by the Holy Spirit. They have been given without error faithfully recorded by holy men of God as moved by the Holy Spirit, and subsequently transmitted without corruption of any essential doctrine. They are the authoritative record of the revelation of God's acts in Creation, in history, in our salvation, and especially in His Son, Jesus Christ.

We believe this written Word fully reveals the will of God concerning man in all things necessary to salvation and Christian living; so that whatever is not found therein, nor can be proved thereby, is not to be required of one as an article of faith or as necessary to salvation.

WESLEYAN CHURCH ARTICLES OF RELIGION:

These Scriptures we hold to be the inspired and infallibly written Word of God, fully inerrant in their original manuscripts and superior to all human authority.

NAZARENE ARTICLES OF FAITH:

[The Holy Scriptures] We believe in the plenary inspiration of the Holy Scriptures, by which we understand the 66 books of the Old and New Testaments, given by divine inspiration, inerrantly revealing the will of God concerning us in all things necessary to our salvation, so that whatever is not contained therein is not to be enjoined as an article of faith.

WESLEYAN THEOLOGICAL SOCIETY DOCTRINAL POSITION:

We believe in the plenary-dynamic and unique inspiration of the Bible as the divine Word of God, the only infallible, sufficient, and authoritative rule of faith and practice.

The names of the canonical books are:	ACFZ
The canonical books of the Old Testament are:	W
Genesis, Exodus, Leviticus, Numbers, Deuteronomy,	ACFWZ
Joshua, Judges, Ruth, The First Book of Samuel, The Second Book	ACFWZ
of Samuel, The First Book of Kings, The Second Book of Kings,	ACFWZ
The First Book of Chronicles, The Second Book of Chronicles, The	ACFWZ
Book of Ezra, The Book of Nehemiah, The Book of Esther, The	ACFWZ
Book of Job, The Psalms, The Proverbs, Ecclesiastes or the	ACFWZ
Preacher, Cantica or Songs of Solomon, Four Prophets the Greater,	ACFWZ
Isaiah, Jeremiah, Lamentations, Ezekiel, Daniel,	FW
Twelve Prophets the Less,	ACFZ
Hosea, Joel, Amos, Obadiah, Jonah, Micah, Nahum,	FW
Habakkuk, Zephaniah, Haggai, Zechariah, Malachi.	FW
All the books of the New Testament, as they are commonly	ACFZ
received, we do receive and account canonical.	ACFZ
The canonical books of the New Testament are:	W
Matthew, Mark, Luke, John, Acts, Romans, I and II	FW
Corinthians, Galatians, Ephesians, Philippians, Colossians, I and	FW
II Thessalonians, I and II Timothy, Titus, Philemon, Hebrews,	FW
James, I and II Peter, I, II, and III John, Jude, Revelation.	FW

Source of Anglican Article 6 (Of the Sufficiency of Scripture): Article 5 of 1553 (first part) and Article 6 of 1563 (canonical list, the list of Apocrypha omitting "The rest of the Book of Esther," "Baruch," "The Song of the Three Children," "Bel and the Dragon," and "The Prayer of Manasses"). Apocryphal books were in the Anglican list not "to establish any doctrine" but to be "read for example of life and instruction of manners." Wurttemberg Confession (1552), omitting the list of Apocrypha, read: "The name of Holy Scriptures applies to those canonical books of the Old and New Testament of whose authority there was never doubt in the Church." *Contra* Council of Trent, which made tradition an independent source of doctrine, and Anabaptists who claimed authority for the Spirit so as to deny the authority of Scripture.

VI. *Of the Old Testament*	ACFZ
The Old Testament	W
The Old Testament is not contrary to the New; for both in	ACFWZ
the Old and New Testament everlasting life is offered to mankind	ACFWZ
by Christ, who is the only Mediator between God and man,	ACFWZ
being both God and Man.	ACFWZ
Wherefore they are not to be heard, who feign that the	ACFWZ
old fathers did look only for transitory promises.	ACFWZ
Although the law given from God by Moses	FZ
to	ACW
as touching ceremonies and rites doth not bind	ACFWZ
Christians, nor ought the civil precepts thereof of necessity	ACFWZ
be received in any commonwealth yet notwithstanding,	ACFWZ
no Christian whatsoever is free from obedience	ACFWZ
of the commandments which are called moral.	ACFWZ

Source of Anglican Article 7: Derived from two separate articles (6 and 19 of the Edwardian series). *Contra* Anabaptists who set aside the Old Testament as unnecessary.

FREE METHODIST, 1972:

[Authority of the Old Testament] We believe the Old Testament is not contrary to the New. Both Testaments bear witness to God's salvation in Christ; both speak of God's will for His people. The ancient laws for ceremonies and rites, and the civil precepts for the nation Israel are not necessarily binding on Christians today. But, on the example of Jesus we are obligated to obey the moral commandments of the Old Testament. [New Testament] We believe the New Testament fulfills and interprets the Old Testament. It is the record of the revelation of God in Jesus Christ and the Holy Spirit. It is God's final word regarding man, his sin, and his salvation, the world, and destiny.

VII. *Of Original or Birth Sin*	ACFZ
Original or Birth Sin	W
Original sin standeth not in the following of Adam	ACFWZ
(as the Pelagians do vainly talk),	ACFW
say,	Z
but it is the corruption of the nature of every man,	ACFWZ
that naturally is engendered of the offspring of Adam,	ACFWZ
whereby man is very far gone from original righteousness,	ACFWZ
and of his own nature inclined to evil,	ACFWZ
and that continually.	ACFWZ

Sources of Anglican Article 9: Augsburg Confession, Article 2; Article 8 of Forty-two Articles (1553); Article 9 of 1563. *Contra* Pelagianism and Anabaptists.

E.U.B. CONFESSION:

[Sin and Free Will] We believe man is fallen from righteousness and, apart from the grace of our Lord Jesus Christ, is destitute of holiness and inclined to evil. Except a man be born again, he cannot see the Kingdom of God. In his own strength, without divine grace, man cannot do good works pleasing and acceptable to God. . . .

NAZARENE ARTICLES OF FAITH:

Sin, Original and Personal [Original Sin, or Depravity] We believe that sin came into the world through the disobedience of our first parents, and death by sin. We believe that sin is of two kinds: original sin or depravity, and actual or personal sin. . . .

WESLEYAN THEOLOGICAL SOCIETY DOCTRINAL POSITION:

We believe that man, although created by God in His own image and likeness, fell into sin through disobedience and "so death passed upon all men, for that all have sinned" (Rom. 5:12).

VIII. *Of Free Will*	ACFZ
The condition of man after the fall of Adam is such [Ea est hominis post lapsum Adae contitio]	ACFZ
that he cannot turn and prepare himself,	ACFZ
by his own natural strength and good works, [ut sese naturalibus suis viribus, et bonis operibus]	ACFZ
to faith, and calling upon God; [ad fidem et invocationem Dei ac convertere praeparare non possit]	ACF
to faith, and to calling upon God;	Z
wherefore we have no power to do good works,	ACFZ
pleasant and acceptable to God, [quae Deo grata sunt et accepta]	ACFZ
without the grace of God by Christ [Quare absque gratia Dei] [(quae per Christum est)]	ACFZ
preventing us, [nos praeveniente]	AC
assisting us,	Z
enabling us,	F
that we may have a good will, and working with us, [ut velimus, et cooperante]	ACFZ
when we have that good will. [dum volumus].	ACFZ

Sources of Anglican Article 10: Wurttemberg Articles (partly verbatim from Augustine, "On Grace and Free Will," xvii), Article 9 of 1553, Article 10 of 1563. *Contra* Pelagian and Anabaptist denial of absolute need of grace.

E.U.B. CONFESSION:

... We believe, however, man influenced and empowered by the Holy Spirit is responsible in freedom to exercise his will for good.

FREE METHODIST, 1972:

[Man. A Free Moral Person] We believe God created man in His own image, innocent, morally free and responsible to choose between good and evil, right and wrong. By the sin of Adam, man as the offspring of Adam is corrupted in his very nature so that from birth he is inclined to sin. He is unable by his own strength and work to restore himself in right relationship with God and to merit eternal salvation. God, the Omnipotent, provides all the resources of the Trinity to make it possible for man to respond to His grace through faith in Jesus Christ as Savior and Lord. By God's grace and help man is enabled to do good works with a free will.

WESLEYAN CHURCH ARTICLES OF RELIGION:

[Free Will] Man's creation in Godlikeness included ability to choose between right and wrong. Thus man was made morally responsible for his choices. The condition of man since the fall of Adam is such that he cannot turn and prepare himself, by his own natural strength and good works, to faith and calling upon God. Wherefore we have no power to do good works pleasant and acceptable to God without the grace of God by Christ working in

us, that we may have a good will, and working with us when we have that good will. That the grace of God through Jesus Christ is bestowed upon all men, enabling all who will to turn and be saved is clearly taught in both the Old and New Testaments. It is possible that one who is in possession of the highest experience of grace may fall from grace, for there is no such height or strength of holiness from which it is impossible to fall. But by the grace of God one who has fallen into sin may by true repentance and faith find forgiveness and restoration.

NAZARENE ARTICLES OF FAITH:

[Free Agency] We believe that man's creation in Godlikeness included ability to choose between right and wrong, and that thus he was made morally responsible; that through the fall of Adam he became depraved so that he cannot now turn and prepare himself by his own natural strength and works to faith and calling upon God. But we also believe that the grace of God through Jesus Christ is freely bestowed upon all men, enabling all who will to turn from sin to righteousness, believe on Jesus Christ for pardon and cleansing from sin, and follow good works pleasing and acceptable in His sight.

We believe that man, though in the possession of the experience of regeneration and entire sanctification, may fall from grace and apostatize and, unless he repent of his sin, be hopelessly and eternally lost.

[Repentance] We believe that repentance, which is a sincere and thorough change of the mind in regard to sin, involving a sense of personal guilt and a voluntary turning away from sin, is demanded of all who have by act or purpose become sinners against God. The Spirit of God gives to all who will repent the gracious help of penitence of heart and hope of mercy, that they may believe unto pardon and spiritual life.

| IX. *Of the Justification of Man* | ACWZ |
| Of the Justification and Regeneration of Man | F |

We are accounted righteous before God,	ACFWZ
only for the merit of our Lord and Savior Jesus Christ,	ACFWZ
by faith, and not for our own works or deservings:	ACFWZ
wherefore, that we are justified by faith only,	ACFWZ
is a most wholesome doctrine, and very full of comfort.	ACFWZ
Concurrently with justification we are regenerated by the Holy	F
Spirit, who imparts spiritual life and renews us after the image	F
of Him who created us.	F

Sources of Anglican Article 11: Augsburg Confession, Article 4; Article 5 of 1536; Article 4 of 1538; Article 11 of 1553; Article 11 of 1563; Wurttemberg Confession.

E.U.B. CONFESSION:

[Reconciliation Through Christ] We believe God was in Christ reconciling the world to himself. The offering Christ freely made on the cross is the perfect and sufficient sacrifice for the sins of the whole world, redeeming man from all sin, so that no other satisfaction is required.

FREE METHODIST, 1972:

[Salvation. Christ's Sacrifice] We believe Christ offered once and for all the one perfect sacrifice for the sins of the whole world. No other satisfaction for sin is necessary; none other can atone.

[The New Life in Christ] We believe a new life and a right relationship with God are made possible through the redemptive acts of God in Jesus Christ. God, by His Spirit, acts to impart new life and put us into a relationship with himself as we repent and our faith responds to His grace. Justification, regeneration, and adoption speak significantly to entrance into and continuance in the new life.

[Justification] Justification is a legal term that emphasizes that by our new relationship in Jesus Christ we are in fact accounted righteousness, being freed from both the guilt and the penalty of our sins.

[Regeneration] Regeneration is a biological term which illustrates that by our new relationship in Christ we do in fact have a new life and a new spiritual nature capable of faith, love, and obedience to Christ Jesus as Lord. The believer is born again. He is a new creation. The old life is past; a new life is begun.

[Adoption] Adoption is a filial term full of warmth, love, and acceptance. It denotes that by our new relationship in Christ we have become His wanted children freed from the mastery of both sin and Satan. The believer has the witness of the Spirit that he is a child of God.

WESLEYAN CHURCH ARTICLES
OF RELIGION:

[The Atonement] The offering of Christ, once made, through His sufferings and meritorious death on the cross, is that perfect redemption and propitiation for the sins of the whole world, both original and actual. There is none other ground of salvation from sin but that alone. This atonement is sufficient for every individual of Adam's race, and is graciously efficacious to the salvation of the irresponsible from birth, or to the righteous who have become irresponsible, and to the children in innocency, but is efficacious to the salvation of those who reach the age of responsibility only when they repent and believe.

NAZARENE ARTICLES OF FAITH:

[Atonement] We believe that Jesus Christ, by His sufferings, by the shedding of His own blood, and by His meritorious death on the Cross, made a full Atonement for all human sin, and that this Atonement is the only ground of salvation, and that it is sufficient for every individual of Adam's race. The Atonement is graciously efficacious for the salvation of the irresponsible and for the children in innocency, but is efficacious for the salvation of those who reach the age of responsibility only when they repent and believe.

WESLEYAN CHURCH ARTICLES
OF RELIGION:

[Regeneration] Regeneration is that work of the Holy Spirit by which the pardoned sinner becomes a child of God; this work is received through faith in Jesus Christ, whereby the regenerate are delivered from the power of sin which reigns over all the unregenerate, so that they love God and through grace serve Him with the will and affections of the heart—receiving "the Spirit of adoption, whereby we cry, Abba, Father."

E.U.B. CONFESSION:

[Justification and Regeneration] We believe we are never accounted righteous before God through our works or merit, but that penitent sinners are justified or accounted righteous before God only by faith in our Lord Jesus Christ.

We believe regeneration is the renewal of man in righteousness through Jesus Christ, by the power of the Holy Spirit, whereby we are made partakers of the divine nature and experience newness of life. By this new birth the believer becomes reconciled to God and is enabled to serve him with the will and the affections.

We believe, although we have experienced regeneration, it is possible to depart from grace and fall into sin; and we may even then, by the grace of God, be renewed in righteousness.

NAZARENE ARTICLES OF FAITH:

[Justification, Regeneration, and Adoption] We believe that justification is the gracious and judicial act of God by which He grants full pardon of all guilt and complete release from the penalty of sins committed, and acceptance as righteous, to all who believe on Jesus Christ and receive Him as Lord and Savior.

We believe that regeneration, or the new birth, is that gracious work of God whereby the moral nature of the repentant believer is spiritually quickened and given a distinctively spiritual life, capable of faith, love, and obedience.

We believe that adoption is that gracious act of God by which the justified and regenerated believer is constituted a son of God.

We believe that justification, regeneration, and adoption are simultaneous in the experience of seekers after God and are obtained upon the condition of faith, preceded by repentance; and that to this work and state of grace the Holy Spirit bears witness.

WESLEYAN THEOLOGICAL SOCIETY

DOCTRINAL POSITION:

We believe in the salvation of the human soul, including the new birth; and in a subsequent work of God in the soul, a crisis, wrought by faith, whereby the heart is cleansed from all sin and filled with the Holy Spirit; this gracious experience is retained by faith as expressed in a constant obedience to God's revealed will, thus giving perfect cleansing moment by moment (1 John 1:7–9), as taught by John Wesley.

X. *Of Good Works*	ACFZ
Good Works	W
Although good works, which are the fruits of faith,	ACFZ
fruit	W
[Bona opera, quae sunt fructus fidei]	
and follow after justification, cannot put away our sins,	ACFWZ
[et justificatos sequuntur,[9] quanquam peccata nostra expiare]	
and endure the severity of God's judgment;	ACW
judgments	FZ
[et divini judicii severitatem ferre non possunt];	
yet are they pleasing and acceptable to God in Christ,	AC
they are	FWZ
[Deo tamen grata sunt, et accepta in Christo]	
and spring out of a true and lively faith,	ACFWZ
[atque ex vera et viva fide necessario profluunt]	
insomuch that by them a lively faith may be	ACFWZ
[ut plane ex illis, aeque fides viva]	
as evidently known as a tree is discerned by its fruit.	AFWZ
[cognosci possit atque arbor ex fructu indicare].	
known, as a tree discerned by its fruit.	C

Sources of Anglican Article 12: Wurttemberg Confession; Articles of 1538; Article 12 of 1563. *Contra* solifidianism (that we are saved by a bare faith) and antinomianism (that the Christian is free from the moral law). Compare Council of Trent, Session 6.

E.U.B. CONFESSION:

[Good Works] We believe good works are the necessary fruits of

faith and follow regeneration but they do not have the virtue to remove our sins or to avert divine judgment. We believe good works, pleasing and acceptable to God in Christ, spring from a true and living faith, for through and by them faith is made evident.

FREE METHODIST, 1972:

[Good Works] We believe good works are the fruit of faith in Jesus

Christ, but works cannot save us from our sins nor from God's judgment. As expressions of Christian faith and love, our good works performed with reverence and humility are both acceptable and pleasing to God. However, good works do not earn God's grace.

XI. *Of Works of Supererogation*	ACFZ
Voluntary works—besides over and above God's	ACFZ
commandments—which they call works of supererogation,	ACFZ
cannot be taught without arrogance and impiety. For by them men do	ACFZ
declare that they do not only render unto God as much as they are	ACFZ
bound to do, but that they do more for his sake than the bounden	ACFZ
duty is required: whereas Christ saith plainly, When	ACFZ
ye have done all that is commanded you, say, We are	ACFZ
unprofitable servants.	ACFZ

Sources of Anglican Article 14: Article 11 of 1553 (slightly revised in the Elizabethan revision of 1563). *Contra* medieval scholastic view of supererogation. See *Reformatio Legum Ecclesiasticarum, de Haeresibus,* ch. 8.

XII. *Of Sin after Justification*	ACFZ
Sin After Justification	W
Not every sin willingly committed after justification	ACFWZ
is the sin against the Holy Ghost, and unpardonable.	ACF
is a sin	Z
and unpardonable (Matt. 12:31–32)	W
Wherefore, the grant of repentance is not to be denied	ACFWZ
to such as fall into sin after justification.	ACFWZ
After we have received the Holy Ghost, we may depart	ACFWZ
from grace given,· and fall into sin, and,	ACFZ
therefrom	W
by the grace of God, rise again and amend our lives.	ACFWZ
And, therefore, they are to be condemned who say	ACZ
Therefore,	FW
they can no more sin as long as they live here,	ACFWZ
or deny the place of forgiveness to such as truly repent.	ACZ
or who deny	F
repent (Mal. 3:7; Matt. 18:21–22; 1 John 1:9; 2:1)	W

Sources of Anglican Article 16 on sin after baptism: Augsburg Confession, Article 12; Article 15 of 1553; Article 16 of 1563. See *Reformatio Legum Ecclesiasticarum, de Haeresibus,* ch. 9, and Second Helvetic Confession on repentance. *Contra* Anabaptist errors.

FREE METHODIST, 1972:

[Restoration] We believe the Christian may be sustained in a growing relationship with Jesus as Savior and Lord. However, he may grieve the Holy Spirit in the relationships of life without returning to the dominion of sin. When he does, he must humbly accept the correction of the Holy Spirit, trust in the advocacy of Jesus, and mend his relationships.

The Christian can sin willfully and sever his relationship with Christ. Even so by repentance before God, forgiveness is granted and the relationship with Christ restored, for not every sin is the sin against the Holy Spirit and unpardonable. God's grace is sufficient for those who truly repent and, by His enabling, amend their lives. However, forgiveness does not give the believer liberty to sin and escape the consequences of sinning.

God has given responsibility and power to the church to restore a penitent believer through loving reproof, counsel, and acceptance.

WESLEYAN CHURCH ARTICLES OF RELIGION:

[Christian Liberty] Christ, through His death on the cross, has freed His followers from sin and from bondage to the law. The Christian is "called unto liberty" (Gal. 5:13), and is not under the law as a means of salvation. He is rather exhorted, "Stand fast therefore in the liberty wherewith Christ hath made us free, and be not entangled again with the yoke of bondage" (Gal. 5:1).

This liberty, however, is not to be construed as license (Gal. 5:13). Rather, love for Christ constrains the Christian to live righteously and holily as God demands. By the Spirit of God, His laws are written on the heart (Heb. 8:10). So the Christian resists evil and cleaves to the good, not in order to be saved, but because he has been saved.

Within the bounds of Christian liberty, there will be differences of opinion. In such cases, the believer seeks to avoid offending his brother. The stronger brother is mindful of the opinions of the one with the weaker conscience (1 Cor. 8 and 10), and is careful not to put a stumbling block in his brother's way (1 Cor. 10:24; Gal. 5:13). On the other hand, the weak does not criticize the strong (1 Cor. 10:29–30), for the conscience of the weak may need instruction.

The recognition and exercise of that liberty which Christ affords will glorify God and promote the unity of the Church.

[Relative Duties] Those two great commandments which require us to love the Lord our God with all the heart, and our neighbors as ourselves, contain the sum of the divine law as it is revealed in the Scriptures: they are the measure and perfect rule of human duty, as well for the ordering and directing of families and nations, and all other social bodies, as for individual acts, by which we are required to acknowledge God as our only Supreme Ruler, and all men as created by Him, equal in all natural rights. Wherefore all men are bound so to order all their individual and social and political acts as to render to God entire and absolute obedience, and to secure to all men the enjoyment of every natural right, as well as to promote the greatest happiness of each in the possession and exercise of such rights.

[The Gifts of the Spirit] The Gift of the Spirit is the Holy Spirit himself. He is to be desired more than the gifts of the Spirit, or the supernatural endowments which the Spirit in His wise counsel bestows upon individual members of the Church and enable them properly to fulfill their function as members of the body of Christ. The gifts of the Spirit, although different from natural endowments, function through them for the edification of the whole Church. These gifts are to be exercised in love under the administration of the Lord of the Church, not through human volition. The relative value of the gifts of the Spirit is to be tested by their usefulness in the Church and not by the ecstasy produced in the ones receiving them.

XIII. *Of the Church*	ACFZ
The visible Church of Christ	ACFZ
[Ecclesia Christi visibilis]	
is a congregation of faithful men,	ACFZ
[est coetus fidelium]	
in which the pure Word of God is preached,	ACFZ
[in quo verbum Dei purum praedicatur]	
and the Sacraments duly administered,	ACFZ
according to Christ's ordinance, in all those things	ACFZ
that of necessity are requisite to the same.	ACF
[et sacramenta, quoad ea quae necessario exiguntur, juxta Christi institutum recte administrantur.]	
of necessity required of the same.	Z

Sources of Anglican Article 19: Augsburg Confession, Article 7; Article 5 of 1538; Article 20 of 1553. See Article 3 of 1559; *Reformatio Legum Ecclesiasticarum, de Haeresibus,* ch. 21. *Contra* the Roman Catholic claim that Rome is the only church and the Anabaptist view of the church.

E.U.B. CONFESSION:

[The Church] We believe the Christian Church is the community of all true believers under the Lordship of Christ. We believe it is one, holy, apostolic and catholic. It is the redemptive fellowship in which the Word of God is preached by men divinely called, and the sacraments are duly administered according to Christ's own appointment. Under the discipline of the Holy Spirit the Church exists for the maintenance of worship, the edification of believers and the redemption of the world.

FREE METHODIST, 1972:

We believe the church is created by God; it is the people of God. Christ Jesus is its Lord and Head; the Holy Spirit is its life and power. It is both divine and human, heavenly and earthly, ideal and imperfect. It is an organism, not an unchanging institution. It exists to fulfill the purposes of God in Christ. It redemptively ministers to persons. Christ loved the church and gave himself for it that it should be holy and without blemish. The church is a fellowship of the redeemed and the redeeming, preaching the Word of God and administering the sacraments according to Christ's instruction. The Free Methodist Church purposes to be representative of what the church of Jesus Christ should be on earth. It therefore requires specific commitment regarding the faith and life of its members. In its requirements it seeks to honor Christ and obey the written Word of God.

WESLEYAN CHURCH ARTICLES OF RELIGION:

[The Church] The Christian Church is the entire body of believers in Jesus Christ. The Founder and only Head of the Church is Christ. It is composed of all faithful believers in Christ, some of whom have gone to be with the Lord and others of whom remain on the earth, having renounced the world, the flesh, and the devil and are dedicated to the work which Christ committed unto His Church till He come. The Church is to preach the pure Word of God and duly administer the Sacraments according to Christ's ordinance, in all those things that are of necessity requisite to the same.

A local church is a body of believers formally organized on gospel principles meeting regularly for the purposes of worship, edification, instruction, and evangelism.

The Wesleyan Church is a denomination consisting of those members within district conferences and local churches who as members of the Body of Christ hold the faith set forth in these Articles and acknowledge the ecclesiastical authority of its governing body.

WESLEYAN THEOLOGICAL SOCIETY DOCTRINAL POSITION:

We believe that the Church is the body of Christ; that all who are united by faith to Christ are members of the Church, and that, having thus become members one of another, it is our solemn and covenant duty to fellowship with one another in peace, and to love one another with pure and fervent hearts.

XIV. *Of Purgatory*	ACZ
The Romish doctrine concerning purgatory, pardons, worshiping, and	ACZ
adoration, as well of images as of relics, and also invocation of	ACZ
saints, is a fond thing, vainly invented, and grounded upon no	ACZ
warrant of Scripture, but repugnant to the word of God.	ACZ

Sources of Anglican Article 22: Luther; Article 23 of 1553 (unaltered except for addition in 1563 of "The Romish doctrine"); cf. Eleven Articles of 1559. *Contra* medieval scholasticism.

XV. *Of Speaking in the Congregation in Such a Tongue as the People Understand*		ACFZ
It is a thing plainly repugnant to the word of God, and the custom		ACFZ
of the Primitive Church, to have public prayer		ACF
	church	Z
in the church, or to minister the Sacraments,		ACF
	sacraments	Z
Church	sacraments	AC
church	sacrament	F
in a tongue not understood by the people.		AZCF

Sources of Anglican Article 24: Article 25 of 1553; Principal Heads of Religion, 1559, rewritten by Archbishop Parker; Article 24 of 1563.[10]

FREE METHODIST, 1972:

[The Language of Worship] We believe that according to the Word of God and the custom of the early church, public worship and prayer and the administration of the sacraments should be in a language understood by the people. The Reformation applied this principle to provide for the use of the common language of the people. It is likewise clear that the Apostle Paul places the strongest emphasis upon rational and intelligible utterance in worship. We cannot endorse practices which plainly violate these scriptural principles.

WESLEYAN CHURCH ARTICLES OF RELIGION:

[Language and Worship] Only a language readily understood by the congregation is to be used in public worship. Moreover, to teach that speaking in an unknown tongue or that the gift of tongues is the necessary proof of the baptism with the Holy Spirit, or of that entire sanctification which the baptism accomplishes, is contrary to the explicit teaching of the word of God as understood by the Wesleyan Church.

XVI. *Of the Sacraments*	ACFZ
The Sacraments	W
Sacraments ordained of Christ are not only	ACFWZ
badges or tokens of Christian men's profession,	ACFZ
tokens of Christian profession	W
but rather they are certain signs of grace	ACZ
but they are also	F
but they are	W
and God's good will toward us, by which he doth work	ACFWZ
invisibly in us, and doth not only quicken,	ACFWZ
but also strengthen and confirm our faith in him.	ACF
Him	WZ
There are two Sacraments ordained of Christ our Lord	ACW
of Jesus Christ our Lord	Z
in the Gospel; that is to say,	ACW
Baptism and the Supper of the Lord.	ACW
Lord's Supper.	Z
Those five commonly called sacraments—that is to say,	ACZ
confirmation, penance, orders, matrimony, and extreme unction—	ACZ
are not to be counted for Sacraments of the Gospel,	ACZ
being such as have grown partly out of the corrupt following	ACZ
of the apostles, and partly are states of life allowed	ACZ
in the Scriptures, but yet have not the like nature of Baptism	ACZ
and the Lord's Supper, because they have not any visible sign	ACZ
or ceremony ordained of God.	ACZ
The Sacraments were not ordained of Christ to be gazed upon,	ACZ
or to be carried about, but that we should duly use them.	ACZ
And in such only as worthily receive the same they have a	ACZ

wholesome effect or operation; but they that receive them   ACZ
unworthily purchase to themselves condemnation as St. Paul saith.
                   as St. Paul saith. I Cor. 11:29.   ACZ

Sources of Anglican Article 25: Augsburg Confession, Article 13; Article 9 of 1538; Principal Heads of Religion, 1559; important alterations made in Article 25 of 1563.[11] *Contra* Zwinglian and Anabaptist view of sacraments.

E.U.B. CONFESSION:

[The Sacraments] We believe the sacraments, ordained by Christ are symbols and pledges of the Christian's profession and of God's love toward us. They are means of grace by which God works invisibly in us, quickening, strengthening and confirming our faith in him. Two sacraments are ordained by Christ our Lord, namely Baptism and the Lord's Supper.

FREE METHODIST, 1972:

We believe water baptism and the Lord's Supper are the sacraments of the church commanded by Christ. They are means of grace through faith, tokens of our profession of Christian faith, and signs of God's gracious ministry toward us. By them, He works within us to quicken, strengthen, and confirm our faith.

METHODIST PROTESTANT:

[Of the Ordinances] Ordinances of Christ are not only badges or tokens of Christian men's profession; but rather they are certain signs of grace and God's good-will towards us, by which he doeth work invisibly in us, and doth not only quicken, but also strengthen and confirm our faith in him. There are two ordinances of Christ our Lord in the gospel; that is to say, Baptism and the Supper of our Lord.

XVII. *Of Baptism*   ACFZ
     Baptism   W

Baptism is not only a sign of profession, and mark of difference,   ACFWZ
whereby Christians are distinguished from others that are not   ACFWZ
baptized, but it is also a sign of regeneration or the new birth.   ACFWZ
All persons to be baptized shall have the choice of baptism   W
by immersion, sprinkling, or pouring.   W
The baptism of young children is to be retained in the church.   ACFZ

Sources of Anglican Article 27: Article 2 of 1536; Article 6 of 1538; Article 28 of 1553; Article 27 of 1563. *Contra* the Zwinglian and Anabaptist view of baptism, and the denial of infant baptism (cf. Augsburg Confession, Article 9).

FREE METHODIST, 1972:

[Baptism] We believe water baptism is a sacrament of the church, commanded by our Lord, signifying acceptance of the benefits of the atonement of Jesus Christ to be administered to believers, as declaration to their faith in Jesus Christ as Savior.

Baptism is a symbol of the new covenant of grace as circumcision was the symbol of the old covenant; and since infants are recognized as being included in the atonement, we hold that they may be baptized upon the request of parents or guardians who shall give assurance for them of necessary Christian training. They shall be required to affirm the vow for themselves before being accepted into church membership.

WESLEYAN CHURCH ARTICLES OF RELIGION:

[Baptism] Since children are born into this world with natures inclined to sin, and yet the prevenient grace of God provides for their redemption during that period before reaching the age of accountability, the parents of small children may testify to their faith in God's provision by presenting them for baptism. Parents who would prefer to emphasize baptism as a testimony by the individual believer to his own act of faith may present their children for dedication.

E.U.B. CONFESSION:

We believe Baptism signifies entrance into the household of faith, and is a symbol of repentance and inner cleansing from sin, a representation of the new birth in Christ Jesus and a mark of Christian discipleship.

We believe children are under the atonement of Christ and as heirs of the Kingdom of God are acceptable subjects for Christian baptism. Children of believing parents through baptism become the special responsibility of the Church. They should be nurtured and led to personal acceptance of Christ, and by profession of faith confirm their baptism.

NAZARENE ARTICLES OF FAITH:

[Baptism] We believe that Christian baptism, commanded by our Lord, is a sacrament signifying acceptance of the benefits of the atonement of Jesus Christ, to be administered to believers and (as) declarative of their faith in Jesus Christ as their Savior, and full purpose of obedience in holiness and righteousness.

Baptism being a symbol of the new covenant (New Testament), young children may be baptized, upon request of parents or guardians who shall give assurance for them of necessary Christian training.

Baptism may be administered by sprinkling, pouring, or immersion, according to the choice of the applicant.

XVIII. *Of the Lord's Supper*	ACFZ
The Lord's Supper	W
The Supper of the Lord is not only a sign of the love	ACFZ
of love	W
that Christians ought to have among themselves one to another,	ACFWZ
but rather is a sacrament of our redemption by Christ's death:	ACFZ
but it is also a Sacrament	W
insomuch that to such as rightly, worthily, and with faith	ACFWZ
receive the same, the bread which we break is a partaking	ACFZ
of the body of Christ; and likewise the cup of blessing is a	ACFZ
partaking of the blood of Christ.	ACFZ

receive the same, it is made a medium through which W
God doth communicate grace to the heart. W
Transubstantiation, or the change of the substance of bread ACFZ
and wine in the Supper of our Lord, cannot be proved ACFZ
by Holy Writ, but is repugnant to the plain words of Scripture, ACFZ
overthroweth the nature of a sacrament, and hath given occasion to ACFZ
many superstitions. The body of Christ is given, taken, and eaten ACFZ
in the Supper, only after a heavenly and spiritual manner. ACZF
And the means whereby the body of Christ is received and eaten, ACFZ
in the Supper, is faith. The sacrament of the Lord's Supper ACFZ
was not by Christ's ordinance reserved, carried about, lifted up, ACFZ
or worshiped. ACFZ

Sources of Anglican Article 28: Ten Articles of 1536; Article 29 of 1553 (significantly amended in 1563). *Contra* the Anabaptist view that the Lord's Supper is essentially a love feast, the Zwinglian view that it is a mere memorial of Christ's death, and the Roman Catholic teaching of transubstantiation (cf. *Reformatio Legum Ecclesiasticarum, de Haeresibus,* ch. 19).

E.U.B. CONFESSION:

We believe the Lord's Supper is a representation of our redemption, a memorial of the sufferings and death of Christ, and a token of love and union which Christians have with Christ and with one another. Those who rightly, worthily and in faith eat the broken bread and drink the blessed cup partake of the body and blood of Christ in a spiritual manner until he comes.

FREE METHODIST, 1972:

[The Lord's Supper] We believe the Lord's Supper is a sacrament of our redemption by Christ's death. To those who rightly, worthily, and with faith receive it, the bread which we break is a partaking of the body of Christ; and likewise the cup of blessing is a partaking of the blood of Christ. The supper is also a sign of the love and unity that Christians have among themselves.

Christ, according to his promise, is really present in the sacrament. But His body is given, taken, and eaten only after a heavenly and spiritual manner. No change is effected in the element; the bread and wine are not literally the body and blood of Christ. Nor is the body and blood of Christ literally present with the elements. The elements are never to be considered objects of worship. The body of Christ is received and eaten in faith.

NAZARENE ARTICLES OF FAITH:

[The Lord's Supper] We believe that the Memorial and Communion Supper instituted by our Lord and Savior Jesus Christ is essentially a New Testament sacrament, declarative of His sacrificial death, through the merits of which believers have life and salvation and promise of all spiritual blessings in Christ. It is distinctively for those who are prepared for reverent appreciation of its significance, and by it they show forth the Lord's death till He come again. It being the Communion feast, only those who have faith in Christ and love for the saints should be called to participate therein.

XIX. *Of Both Kinds*	ACZ

The cup of the Lord is not to be denied to the lay people;	ACZ
for both the parts of the Lord's Supper by Christ's ordinance and	ACZ
commandment, ought to be administered to all Christians alike.	ACZ

Sources of Anglican Article 30: Composed by Archbishop Parker in 1563; cf. Article 10 of 1559. *Contra* Council of Trent, 1562, Session 21.

XX. *Of the One Oblation of Christ Finished upon the Cross*	ACFZ

The offering of Christ, once made, is that perfect	AC
a	ZF
redemption, propitiation, and satisfaction for all the sins	ACFZ
of the whole world, both original and actual;	ACFZ
and there is none other satisfaction for sin but that alone.	ACFZ
Wherefore the sacrifice of masses,	ACZ
the masses	F
in which it is commonly said	ACZ
that the priest doth offer Christ for the quick and the dead,	ACFZ
to have remission of pain or guilt, is a blasphemous fable	ACFZ
and dangerous deceit.	ACFZ

Sources of Anglican Article 31: Augsburg Confession, Part 2, Article 3; only slightly amended from the Article 30 of 1553. *Contra* the medieval scholastic view that regarded each Mass as a sacrifice independent of or additional to the sacrifice of the Cross.

XXI. *Of the Marriage of Ministers*	ACZ

The ministers of Christ are not commanded by God's law	ACZ
either to vow the estate of single life, or to abstain from marriage;	ACZ
therefore it is lawful for them, as for all other Christians, to marry	ACZ
at their own discretion, as they shall judge the same to serve best	ACZ
to godliness.	ACZ

Sources of Anglican Article 32: Augsburg Confession, Part 2, Article 2; Article 3 of 1539; Article 31 of 1553; Principal Heads of Religion, 1559; rewritten by Archbishop Parker in 1563. *Contra* the medieval scholastic view that celibacy is required for clergy by Scripture.

XXII. *Of the Rites and Ceremonies of Churches*	ACFZ

It is not necessary that rites and ceremonies should in all places be	ACFZ
the same, or exactly alike; for they have been always different, and	ACFZ
may be changed according to the diversity of countries, times,	ACFZ

and men's manners, so that nothing be ordained against God's Word.	ACFZ
Whosoever, through his private judgment, willingly and purposely,	ACFZ
doth openly break the rites	ACFZ
and ceremonies of the church to which he belongs,	ACFZ
which are not repugnant to the Word of God, and are ordained	CF
are repugnant and are not ordained	Z
are repugnant and are ordained	A
and approved by common authority, ought to be rebuked openly,	ACFZ
that others may fear to do the like, as one that offendeth	ACFZ
against the common order of the church, and woundeth	ACFZ
the consciences of weak brethren.	CFZ
the conscience	A
Every particular church may ordain, change, or abolish	ACFZ
We recognize the right of every denomination to ordain,	F
change, or abolish	F
rites and ceremonies, so that all things may be done to edification.	ACFZ

Sources of Anglican Article 34: Article 5 of 1538; Article 33 of 1553; Article 3 of 1559; largely unaltered since 1553, except last sentence added in 1563. *Contra* Roman hegemony, Zwinglian Articles, 11.

WESLEYAN CHURCH ARTICLES OF RELIGION:

[Christian Worship and Fellowship—Rites and Ceremonies of Churches] True religion does not consist in any ritual observances such as forms or ceremonies, even of the most excellent kind, be they ever so decent and significant, ever so expressive of inward things. The religion of Christ rises infinitely higher and lies infinitely deeper than all these. Let no man conceive that rites and ceremonies have any intrinsic worth, or that true worship cannot subsist without them. Therefore, it is not necessary that rites and ceremonies should in all places be the same or exactly alike, for they have always been different and may be changed according to the diversities of countries, times, and customs, provided that nothing be ordained against God's Word.

E.U.B. CONFESSION:

[Public worship] We believe divine worship is the duty and privilege of man who, in the presence of God, bows in adoration, humility and dedication. We believe divine worship is essential to the life of the Church, and that the assembling of the people of God for such worship is necessary to Christian fellowship and spiritual growth.

We believe the order of public worship need not be the same in all places but may be modified by the Church according to circumstances and the needs of men. It should be in a language and form understood by the people, consistent with the Holy Scriptures to the edification of all, and in accordance with the order and Discipline of the Church.

E.U.B. CONFESSION:

[The Lord's Day] We believe the Lord's Day is divinely ordained for private and public worship, for rest from unnecessary work, and should be devoted to spiritual improvement, Christian fellowship and service. It is commemorative of our Lord's resurrection and is an emblem of our eternal rest. It is essential to the permanence and growth of the Christian Church, and important to the welfare of the civil community.

Added Articles:

WESLEYAN CHURCH ARTICLES OF RELIGION:

[Healing] The truth that Jesus is both able and willing to heal the bodies as well as the souls of men, whenever such healing is for His glory, is clearly set forth in God's Word and attested by the experience of many of His people at the present day. Prayer for healing according to the pattern set forth in the Scriptures shall be encouraged.

NAZARENE ARTICLES OF FAITH:

[Divine Healing] We believe in the Bible doctrine of divine healing and urge our people to seek to offer the prayer of faith for the sick. Providential means and agencies when deemed necessary should not be refused.

XXIII. *Of the Rulers of the United States of America*	ACZ
The President, the Congress, the general assemblies,	ACZ
the governors, and the councils of state,	ACZ
as the delegates of the people,	ACZ
are the rulers of the United States of America,	ACZ
according to the division of power made to them	AZC
by the Constitution of the United States,	ACZ
and by the constitution of their respective states.	ACZ
And the said states are a sovereign and independent nation,	ACZ
and ought not to be subject to any foreign jurisdiction.	ACZ

A paragraph entitled "Of the Duty of Christians to the Civil Authority" was appended to the Twenty-five *Articles of Religion* in the United Methodist *Discipline* (*Disc., 1984,* 62, 63), with this annotation: "The following provision was adopted by the Uniting Conference. This statement seeks to interpret to our churches in foreign lands Article XXIII of the Articles of Religion. It is a legislative enactment but it is not a part of the Constitution. (See Judicial Council Decision 41, 176, and Decision 6, Interim Judicial Council.)":

Of the Duty of Christians to the Civil Authority

It is the duty

As far as it respects civil affairs, we believe it is the duty	ACZ
of all Christians, and especially of all Christian ministers,	ACZ
to observe and obey the laws and commands of the governing or to be subject to the	ACZ
supreme authority of the country where they may reside, and to use	ACZ
all laudable means to enjoin obedience to the powers that be;	ACZ
and, therefore, it is expected that all our preachers and people	ACZ
who may be under any foreign government,	
will behave themselves as peaceable and orderly subjects.	ACZ

Source of Anglican Article 37: Article 34 of 1553; Articles of 1559, modified in 1563 so as to condemn Anabaptist attacks on the authority of the state and repudiate papal jurisdiction.

E.U.B. CONFESSION:

[Civil Government] We believe civil government derives its just powers from the sovereign God. As Christians we recognize the governments under whose protection we reside and believe such governments should be based on, and be responsible for, the recognition of human rights under God. We believe war and bloodshed are contrary to the gospel and spirit of Christ. We believe it is the duty of Christian citizens to give moral strength and purpose to their respective governments through sober, righteous and godly living.

FREE METHODIST, 1972:

[Law of Life and Love] We believe God's law for all human life, personal and social, is expressed in two divine commands: Love the Lord God with all your heart, and love your neighbor as yourself. These commands reveal what is best for man in his relationship with God, persons, and society. They set forth the principles of human duty in both individual and social action. They recognize God as the only Sovereign. All men as created by Him and in His image have the same inherent rights regardless of sex, race, or color. Men should therefore give God absolute obedience in their individual, social, and political acts. They should strive to secure to everyone respect for his person, his rights, and his greatest happiness in the possession and

exercise of the right within the moral law.

Of Sanctification:

METHODIST PROTESTANT CHURCH:

[Sanctification[12]] Sanctification is that renewal of our fallen nature by the Holy Ghost, received through faith in Jesus Christ, whose blood of atonement cleanseth from all sin; whereby we are not only delivered from the guilt of sin, but are washed from its pollution, saved from its power, and are enabled, through grace, to love God with all our hearts and to walk in his holy commandments blameless.

EVANGELICAL METHODIST CHURCH ARTICLES OF RELIGION:

[Perfect Love] Perfect Love is that renewal of our fallen nature by the Holy Spirit, received through faith in Jesus Christ, whose blood of atonement cleanseth from all sin; whereby we are not only delivered from the guilt of sin, but are washed from its pollution, saved from its power, and are enabled, through grace, to love God with all our hearts and to walk in His holy commandments blameless.

FREE METHODIST CHURCH:

[Of Entire Sanctification] Entire sanctification is that work of the Holy Spirit, subsequent to regeneration, by which the fully consecrated believer, upon exercise of faith in the atoning blood of Christ, is cleansed in that moment from all inward sin and empowered for service. The resulting relationship is attested by the witness of the Holy Spirit and is maintained by obedience and faith. Entire sanctification enables the believer to love God with all his heart, soul, strength, and mind, and his neighbor as himself, and prepares him for greater growth in grace.

[Sanctification and Christian Perfection] We believe sanctification is the work of God's grace through the Word and the Spirit, by which those who have been born again are cleansed from sin in their thoughts, words and acts, and are enabled to live in accordance with God's will, and to strive for holiness without which no one will see the Lord.

Entire sanctification is a state of perfect love, righteousness and true holiness which every regenerate believer may obtain by being delivered from the power of sin, by loving God with all the heart, soul, mind and strength, and by loving one's neighbor as one's self. Through faith in Jesus Christ this gracious gift may be received in this life both gradually and instantaneously, and should be sought earnestly by every child of God.

We believe this experience does not deliver us from the infirmities, ignorance, and mistakes common to man, nor from the possibilities of further sin. The Christian must continue on guard against spiritual pride and seek to gain victory over every temptation to sin. He must respond wholly to the will of God so that sin will lose its power over him; and the world, the flesh, and the devil are put under his feet. Thus he rules over these enemies with watchfulness through the power of the Holy Spirit.

FREE METHODIST, 1972:

[Entire Sanctification] We believe entire sanctification to be that work of the Holy Spirit, subsequent to regeneration, by which the fully consecrated believer, upon exercise of faith in the atoning blood of Christ is cleansed in that moment from all inward sin and empowered for service. The resulting relationship is attested by the witness of the Holy Spirit and is maintained by faith and obedience. Entire sanctification enables the believer to love God with all his heart, soul, strength, and mind, and his neighbor as himself, and it prepares him for greater growth in grace.

WESLEYAN CHURCH ARTICLES OF RELIGION:

[Entire Sanctification] Inward sanctification begins the moment one is justified. From that moment until a believer is entirely sanctified, he grows daily in grace and gradually dies to sin. Entire sanctification is effected by the Baptism of the Holy Spirit which cleanses the heart of the child of God from all inbred sin through faith in Jesus Christ. It is subsequent to regeneration and is wrought instantaneously when the believer presents himself a living sacrifice, holy and acceptable to God, and is thus enabled through His grace to love God with all the heart and to walk in all His holy commandments blameless. The crisis of cleansing is preceded and followed by growth in grace and the knowledge of our Lord and Savior Jesus Christ. When man is fully cleansed from all sin he is endued with the power of the Holy Spirit for the accomplishment of all to which he is called. The ensuing life of holiness is maintained by a continuing faith in the sanctifying blood of Christ, and is evidenced by an obedient life.

NAZARENE ARTICLES OF FAITH:

[Entire Sanctification] We believe that entire sanctification is that act of God, subsequent to regeneration, by which believers are made free from original sin, or depravity, and brought into a state of entire devotement to God, and the holy obedience of love made perfect.

It is wrought by the baptism with the Holy Spirit, and comprehends in one experience the cleansing of the heart from sin and the abiding, indwelling presence of the Holy Spirit, empowering the believer for life and service.

Entire sanctification is provided by the blood of Jesus, is wrought instantaneously by faith, preceded by entire consecration; and to this work and state of grace the Holy Spirit bears witness.

This experience is also known by various terms representing its different phases, such as "Christian perfection," "perfect love," "heart purity," "the baptism with the Holy Spirit," "the fullness of the blessing," and "Christian holiness."

We believe that there is a marked distinction between a pure heart and a mature character. The former is obtained in an instant, the result of entire sanctification; the latter is the result of growth in grace.

We believe that the grace of entire sanctification includes the impulse to grow in grace. However, this impulse must be consciously nurtured, and careful attention given to the requisites and processes of spiritual development and improvement in Christlikeness of character, and personality. Without such purposeful endeavor one's witness may be impaired and the grace itself frustrated and ultimately lost.

CONGREGATIONAL METHODIST CHURCH:

[Sanctification] Entire sanctification is that second definite work of grace, subsequent to regeneration, whereby the heart of a justified person is cleansed from the original or Adamic nature, and is filled with the Holy Ghost.

XXIV. *Of Christian Men's Goods*	ACFZ
The riches and goods of Christians are not common, as touching the	ACFZ
right, title, and possession of the same, as some do falsely boast.	ACFZ
Notwithstanding, every man ought, of such things as he possesseth,	ACFZ
liberally to give alms to the poor according to his ability.	ACFZ

Sources of Anglican Article 38: Articles of 1553. *Contra* Anabaptist communism.

E.U.B. CONFESSION:

[The Christian and Property] We believe God is the owner of all things and that the individual holding of property is lawful and is a sacred trust under God. Private property is to be used for the manifestation of Christian love and liberality, and to support the Church's mission in the world. All forms of property, whether private, corporate or public, are to be held in solemn trust and used responsibly for human good under the sovereignty of God.

XXV. *Of a Christian Man's Oath*	ACF
Of Christian Men's Oaths	Z
As we confess that vain and rash swearing is forbidden	ACFZ
Christian men by our Lord Jesus Christ and James his apostle,	ACZ
the Apostle	F
so we judge that the Christian religion doth not prohibit,	ACZ
hold	F
but that a man may swear when the magistrate requireth,	ACFZ
in a cause of faith and charity, so it be done according	ACZ
case	F
to the prophet's teaching, in justice, judgment, and truth.	ACFZ

Sources of Anglican Article 39: Articles of 1553; cf. *Reformatio Legum Ecclesiasticarum, de Haeresibus,* ch. 15. *Contra* Anabaptist objections to swearing before civil authorities.

FREE METHODIST:

[Note] This article shall not deprive of membership in our church those who have conscientious scruples against taking an oath.

WESLEYAN CHURCH ARTICLES OF RELIGION:

[Judicial Oaths] The Wesleyan Church reserves for its members the right to affirm the truth in testimony before the civil and criminal courts rather than to engage in a judicial oath.

On Eschatology:

METHODIST PROTESTANT:

[Of the Resurrection of the Dead] There will be a general resurrection of the dead, both of the just and the unjust, at which time the souls and bodies of men will be reunited, to receive together a just retribution for the deeds done in the body of this life.

[Of the General Judgment] There will be a General Judgment at the end of the world, when God will judge all men by Jesus Christ, and receive the righteous unto his heavenly kingdom, where they shall be forever secure and happy; and adjudge the wicked to everlasting punishment suited to the demerit of their sins.

FREE METHODIST, 1972:

[Last Things. The Kingdom of God] We believe that the kingdom of God is a prominent Bible theme providing the Christian with both his task and hope. Jesus announced its presence. The kingdom is realized now as God's reign is established in the hearts and lives of believers.

The church, by its prayers, example, and proclamation of the gospel, is the appointed and appropriate instrument of God in building His kingdom.

But the kingdom is also future and is related to the return of Christ when judgment will fall upon the present order. The enemies of Christ will be subdued; the reign of God will be established; a total cosmic renewal which is both material and moral shall occur; and the hope of the redeemed will be fully realized.

[The Return of Christ] We believe the return of Christ is certain and may occur at any moment. It is not given us to know the hour. At

His return He will fulfill all prophecies concerning His final triumph over all evil. The believer's response is joyous expectation, watchfulness, readiness, and diligence.

[Resurrection] We believe in the bodily resurrection from the dead of both the just and the unjust, they that have done good unto the resurrection of life; they that have done evil unto the resurrection of damnation. The resurrected body will be a spiritual body, but the person will be whole and identifiable. The resurrection of Christ is the guarantee of resurrection unto life to those who are in Him.

[Judgment] We believe God has appointed a day in which He will judge the world in righteousness in accordance with the gospel and men's deeds in this life.

[Final Destiny] We believe the eternal destiny of man is determined by God's grace and man's response, not by arbitrary decrees of God. For those who trust Him and obediently follow Jesus as Savior and Lord, there is a heaven and eternal glory and the blessedness of Christ's presence. But for the finally impenitent there is a hell of eternal suffering and of separation from God.

WESLEYAN CHURCH ARTICLES
OF RELIGION:

[The Second Coming of Christ] The doctrine of the second coming of Christ is a precious truth and a glorious hope to the people of God. The certainty of the personal and imminent return of Christ is a powerful inspiration to holy living and zealous effort for the evangelization of the world. We believe the Scriptures teach that at His return He will cause the fulfillment of all prophecies made concerning His final and complete triumph over all evil.

[The Resurrection of the Dead] We hold the Scriptural statements concerning the resurrection of the dead to be true and worthy of universal acceptance. We believe the bodily resurrection of Jesus Christ was a fact of history and a miracle of supreme importance. We understand the manner of the resurrection of mankind to be the resurrection of the righteous dead, at Christ's second coming, and the resurrection of the wicked at a later time. Resurrection will be the reuniting the soul and body preparatory to final reward or punishment.

[The Judgment of Mankind] The Scriptures reveal God as the judge of all mankind and the acts of His judgment to be based on His omniscience and eternal justice. His administration of judgment will culminate in the final meeting of mankind before His throne of great majesty and power, where records will be examined and final rewards and punishments will be administered.

[Destiny] The Scriptures clearly teach that there is a conscious, personal existence after the death of the body. The eternal destiny of man is determined by God's grace and man's response, evidenced inevitably by his moral character which results from his personal and volitional choices and not from any arbitrary decree of God. Heaven with its eternal glory and blessedness of Christ's presence is the final abode of those who choose the salvation which God provides through Jesus Christ. Hell with its eternal misery and separation from God is the final abode of those who neglect this great salvation.

NAZARENE ARTICLES OF FAITH:

[Second Coming of Christ] We believe that the Lord Jesus Christ will come again; that we who are alive at His coming shall not precede them that are asleep in Christ Jesus; but that, if we are abiding in Him, we shall be caught up with the risen saints to meet the Lord in the air, so that we shall ever be with the Lord.

[Resurrection, Judgment, and Destiny] We believe in the resurrection of the dead, that the bodies of the just and of the unjust shall be raised to life and united with their spirits—"they that have done good, unto the resurrection of life; and they that have done evil, unto the resurrection of damnation."

We believe in the future judgment in which every man shall appear before God to be judged according to his deeds in this life.

We believe that glorious and everlasting life is assured to all who savingly believe in, and obediently follow, Jesus Christ our Lord; and that the finally impenitent shall suffer eternally in hell.

E.U.B. CONFESSION:

We believe all men stand under the righteous judgment of Jesus Christ, both now and in the last day. We believe in the resurrection of the dead; the righteous to life eternal and the wicked to endless condemnation.

WESLEYAN THEOLOGICAL SOCIETY DOCTRINAL POSITION:

We believe that our Lord Jesus in His literal resurrection from the dead is the living guarantee of the resurrection of all human beings, the believing saved to conscious eternal joy, and the unbelieving lost to conscious eternal punishment.

We believe that our Lord Jesus Christ, in fulfillment of His own promise, both angelically and apostolically attested, will personally return in power and great glory.

FREE METHODIST, 1972:

[Concluding Paragraph] The doctrines of the Free Methodist Church are based upon the Holy Scriptures and are derived from their total biblical context. The references below are appropriate passages related to the given articles. They are listed in their biblical sequence and are not intended to be exhaustive. [Here follow scriptural references on themes of God, the Scriptures, Man, Salvation, the Church, Last Things.]

METHODIST PROTESTANT:

[Concluding Paragraph] These Articles of Religion set forth the doctrinal teachings of the Methodist Protestant Church, and those who enter the ministry thereof thereby avow their acceptance of the teachings thus formulated; and good faith towards the Church forbids any teaching on their part which is at variance with them.

III. Selected Documents

International Statements of Methodist Doctrinal Standards

The Wesleyan family is not lacking in a long-standing, generally recognized tradition of textual definition of those documents regarded in much of the worldwide Wesleyan tradition as doctrinal standards. Here are statements from a wide variety of international sources of both early and late vintage that demonstrate the familiar consensual textual definition:

The Doctrines of the Methodist Church are declared to be those contained in the twenty-five Articles of Religion, and those taught by the Rev. John Wesley, M.A., in his Notes on the New Testament, and in the first fifty-two Sermons of the first series of his discourses, published during his lifetime.

JAPAN[14]

The Nippon Methodist Kyokwai shall be permanently founded on the fundamental doctrine of the Holy Scripture, as unfolded by Christ and his apostles, formally stated in the Articles of Religion embodied in the plan of organization, and expounded in Mr. Wesley's Notes on the New Testament and the first fifty-two sermons published by him during his lifetime.

CARIBBEAN[15]

Doctrinal Standards. — (1) The doctrinal standards of the Church, as of the Parent Church, are:

The Methodist Church claims and cherishes its place in the Holy Catholic Church which is the body of Christ. It rejoices in the inheritance of the Apostolic Faith and loyally accepts the fundamental principles of the historic creeds and of the Protestant Reformation. It ever remembers that in the Providence of God Methodism was raised up to spread Scriptural Holiness through the land by the proclamation of the Evangelical Faith and declares its unfaltering resolve to be true to its Divinely appointed mission.

The Doctrines of the Evangelical Faith which Methodism has held from the beginning and still holds are based upon the Divine revelation recorded in the Holy Scriptures. The Methodist Church acknowledges this revelation as the supreme rule of faith and practice. These Evangelical Doctrines, to which the Preachers of the Methodist Church both Ministers and Laymen are pledged, are contained in Wesley's Notes on the New Testament and the first four volumes of his sermons.

The Notes on the New Testament and the Forty-four Sermons are not intended to impose a system of formal or speculative theology on Methodist Preachers, but to set up standards of preaching and belief which should secure loyalty to the fundamental truths of the Gospel of Redemption and ensure the continued witness of the Church to the realities of the Christian experience of salvation. . . .

(2) The Doctrinal Standards shall be unalterable, whether by the Conference or otherwise.

(3) The Conference shall be the final authority within the Church on all questions concerning the interpretation of the Doctrinal Standards.

SOUTH AFRICA

The section on "Doctrine" in *A Manual of the Laws and Discipline of the Methodist Church of South Africa*[16] is virtually identical in substance with the above paragraphs.

KOREA[17]

The fundamental principles of Christianity have been set forth at various times and in various forms in the historic creeds of the Church, and have been interpreted by Mr. Wesley in the *Articles of Religion* and in his sermons and *Notes on the New Testament*. This evangelical faith is our heritage and our glorious possession.

Upon those persons who desire to unite with us as members, we impose no doctrinal test. Our main requirement is loyalty to Jesus Christ and a purpose to follow Him. With us, as with Mr. Wesley in the earliest *General Rules* of the United Societies, the conditions of membership are moral and spiritual rather than theological. We sanction the fullest liberty of belief for the individual Christian, so long as his character and his works approve themselves as consistent with true godliness.

It is fitting, however, that we should state the chief doctrines which are most surely believed among us.

1. WE BELIEVE in the one God, Maker and Ruler of all things, Father of all men; the source of all goodness and beauty, all truth and love.

2. WE BELIEVE in Jesus Christ, God manifest in the flesh, our Teacher, Example, and Redeemer, the Savior of the world.

3. WE BELIEVE in the Holy Spirit, God present with us for guidance, for comfort, and for strength.

4. WE BELIEVE in the forgiveness of sins, in the life of love and prayer, and in grace equal to every need.

5. WE BELIEVE in the Word of God contained in the Old and New Testaments as the sufficient rule both of faith and of practice.

6. WE BELIEVE in the Church as the fellowship for worship and for service of all who are united to the living Lord.

7. WE BELIEVE in the kingdom of God as the divine rule in human society; and in the brotherhood of man under the Fatherhood of God.

8. WE BELIEVE in the final triumph of righteousness, and in the life everlasting. Amen.

Doctrinal Standards of British Methodism

The Deed of Union that was adopted by the Uniting Conference of the British Methodist Church in 1932 contains the definitive statement of doctrine held among British Methodists. This deed brings together a series of previous deeds— all patterned after the original Model Deed of 1763: the Wesleyan Methodist Chapel Model Deed of 1832, the United Methodist Free Churches Model Deed of 1842, the Methodist New Connexion Model Deed of 1846, the Model Chapel Trust Deed of the Primitive Methodist Connexion of 1864, the United Methodist Free Churches Reference Deed of 1865, the Model Deed of the United Methodist Church of 1908, and the Model Deed of the Methodist Church of 1932 (Buckley, *CPD,* 41).

The first purpose of the Methodist Church of Britain has been stated since the time of union as "the advancement of the Christian faith in accordance with the doctrinal standards and the discipline of the Methodist Church" (Ibid., 10).

The Deed of Union, Section 30, defines Doctrinal Standards, while Section 31 prevents their amendment, analogous to the First Restrictive Rule of American Methodism:

The doctrinal standards of The Methodist Church are as follows:

The Methodist Church claims and cherishes its place in the Holy Catholic Church which is the Body of Christ. It rejoices in the inheritance of the Apostolic Faith and loyally accepts the fundamental principles of the historic creeds and of the Protestant Reformation. It ever remembers that in the Providence of God Methodism was raised up to spread Scriptural Holiness through the land by the proclamation of the Evangelical Faith and declares its unfaltering resolve to be true to its Divinely appointed mission.

The Doctrines of the Evangelical Faith which Methodism has held from the beginning and still holds are based upon the Divine revelation recorded in the Holy Scriptures. The Methodist Church acknowledges this revelation as the supreme rule of faith and practice. These Evangelical Doctrines to which the Preachers of The Methodist Church both Ministers and Laymen are pledged are contained in Wesley's Notes on the New Testament and the first four volumes of his sermons.

The Notes on the New Testament and the 44 Sermons are not intended to impose a system of formal or speculative theology on Methodist Preachers, but to set up standards of preaching and belief which should secure loyalty to the fundamental truths of the Gospel of Redemption and ensure the continued witness of the Church to the realities of the Christian experience of salvation.

Christ's Ministers in the Church are Stewards in the household of God and Shepherds of His flock. Some are called and ordained to this sole occupation and have a principal and directing part in these great duties, but they hold no priesthood differing in kind from that which is common to all the Lord's people, and they have no exclusive title to the preaching of the gospel or the care of souls. These ministries are shared with them by others to whom also the Spirit divides His gifts severally as He wills.

It is the universal conviction of the Methodist people that the office of the Christian Ministry depends upon the call of God, who bestows the gifts of the Spirit, the grace and the fruit of which indicate those whom He has chosen.

Those whom The Methodist Church recognizes as called of God and therefore receives into its Ministry shall be ordained by the imposition of hands as expressive of the Church's recognition of the Minister's personal call.

The Methodist Church holds the doctrine of the priesthood of all believers and consequently believes that no priesthood exists which belongs exclusively to a particular order or class of men, but in the exercise of its corporate life and worship special qualifications for the discharge of special duties are required and thus the principle of representative selection is recognized.

The preachers itinerant and lay are examined, tested, and approved before they are authorized to minister in holy things. For the sake of Church Order and not because of any priestly virtue inherent in the office the Ministers of The Methodist Church are set apart by ordination to the Ministry of the Word and Sacraments.

The Methodist Church recognizes two sacraments, namely Baptism and the Lord's Supper, as of Divine Appointment and of perpetual obligation of which it is the privilege and duty of Members of

The Methodist Church to avail themselves.

31. Doctrinal Standards Unalterable. (a) The Conference shall not have any power to alter or vary in any manner whatsoever the clauses contained in this Deed which define the doctrinal standards of The Methodist Church.

(b) The Conference shall be the final authority within the Methodist Church with regard to all questions concerning the interpretation of its doctrines (*CPD, 61, 62*).

Under Book III, Standing Orders, paragraph 010 on Doctrinal Qualification reads: "No person shall be appointed to office in the Church who teaches doctrines contrary to those of the Church, or who holds doctrines likely to injure the peace and welfare of the Church" (*CPD*, 110).

Included in *The Constitutional Practice and Discipline of the Methodist Church* are the "Liverpool Minutes of 1820." They commend frequent reading and study of "Mr. Wesley's 'Twelve Rules of a Helper.'" These disciplinary rules of the itinerant preachers were first formulated in the Conference held by Wesley in 1744. They were revised by the Conference of 1753 and later were associated with the Liverpool Minutes, commended to be read annually in the pastoral session of the May synod.[18] One section of the Liverpool Minutes concerns the cardinal doctrines of Methodist preaching:

RESOLUTIONS ON PASTORAL WORK

(Commonly referred to as the "Liverpool Minutes 1820," adopted by the Wesleyan Methodist Conference in 1820 and revised in 1885.)

The Pulpit

Let us preach constantly the leading and vital doctrines of the Gospel; repentance toward God; a present, free, and full salvation from sin;—a salvation flowing from the grace of God alone, "through the redemption that is in Christ Jesus," and apprehended by the simple exercise of faith;—a salvation which begins with the forgiveness of sins (this forgiveness being certified to the penitent believer by the Holy Spirit) and (by means of this witness, but by the power of that Divine Spirit who bears the witness) a change of heart;—a salvation which is itself the only entrance to a course of practical holiness.

And let us preach these cardinal doctrines in our primitive method,—evangelically and experimentally, with apostolical and earnestness and zeal, and with great simplicity. Let us "labour in the word and doctrine," applying our discourses closely and lovingly to the various classes of our hearers, and "by manifestation of the truth, commending ourselves to every man's conscience in the sight of God."

Remembering that the prominence which is properly given in the Methodist pulpit to the doctrine of present salvation is ever liable to Antinomian abuses, let us diligently and evangelically preach the precepts as well as the privileges of the Gospel, expounding them carefully and applying them faithfully.

Let us build up our people in knowledge and holiness; urging them to fidelity in family duties, and especially in the godly training up of their children; and, in general, to "follow after the things which make for peace, and things where-with one may edify another."

In every place, let us speak plainly and pointedly on the duty and advantage of Christian communion, and exhort all who are seeking salvation to avail themselves, without delay, of the help of our more private Means of Grace.

In particular, let us urge upon all our people a conscientious and frequent observance of the Sacrament of the Lord's Supper; expounding its nature; instructing the young, and reasoning with the timid and the doubting; and setting forth the duty and blessedness of "showing the Lord's death till He come."

The Doctrines of the Salvation Army (1878)[19]

1. We believe that the Scriptures of the Old and New Testaments were given by inspiration of God and that they only constitute the Divine rule of Christian faith and practice.

2. We believe that there is only one God who is infinitely perfect, the Creator Preserver and Governor of all things and who is the only proper object of religious worship.

3. We believe that there are three persons in the Godhead—the Father, the Son, and the Holy Ghost—undivided in essence and co-equal in power and glory.

4. We believe that in the person of Jesus Christ the Divine and human natures are united so that He is truly and properly God and truly and properly man.

5. We believe that our first parents were created in a state of innocency but by their disobedience they lost their purity and happiness and that in consequence of their fall all men have become sinners totally depraved and as such are justly exposed to the wrath of God.

6. We believe that the Lord Jesus Christ has by His suffering and death made an atonement for the whole world so that whosoever will may be saved.

7. We believe that repentance toward God, faith in our Lord Jesus Christ and regeneration by the Holy Spirit are necessary to salvation.

8. We believe that we are justified by grace through faith in our Lord Jesus Christ and that he that believeth hath the witness in himself.

9. We believe that continuance in a state of salvation depends upon continued obedient faith in Christ.[20]

10. We believe that it is the privilege of all believers to be "wholly sanctified" and that their "whole spirit and soul and body'" may "be preserved blameless unto the coming of our Lord Jesus Christ" (1 Thess. 5:23).[21]

11. We believe in the immortality of the soul, in the resurrection of the body, in the general judgment at the end of the world, in the eternal happiness of the righteous and the endless punishment of the wicked.

The Catechism of 1852, No. 1

In 1783 Wesley published certain instructions for children (WJW, 7:81ff.; cf. Sermon 95, WJW, 7:86–98), commending them to Methodist preachers in their ministry to children and youth. The American Conference of 1787 mandated that preachers procure and use these "Instructions." In the period of 1800–

1808, there are references to a catechism being used among American Methodist preachers—presumably the "Instructions"—recommending that they be committed to memory by the young. This pattern apparently persisted until 1824, when the General Conference made it a stated duty of preachers to introduce the Catechism in Sunday Schools.

The General Conference of 1848 instructed Daniel Kidder to prepare a church catechism, which was approved in 1851 by the Book Committee (composed of E. Hedding, N. Bangs, S. Olin, and J. Holdich) and submitted to the General Conference of 1852. The Conference unanimously approved and ordered the publication of two forms of the catechism (No. 1 and No. 2) and authorized the development of a third catechism, which would have additional study materials attached. In the period after 1852, many came to regard these three forms of catechism as a supplementary part of the standards of doctrine in the Methodist Episcopal Church: "The General Conference of 1852, indirectly, added to our doctrinal standards by authorizing the publication of a series of catechisms, now known as Catechisms Nos. 1, 2, and 3" (Wheeler, QA, 112; cf. Curtiss, SC, 119–21).

What follows are selections from the first three parts of the shortest form of the catechism (No. 1), which contained 112 questions and answers covering these topics: God; Creation; Man's Fall and Sinful State; Salvation; The Means of Grace; God's Law; and Death, Judgment, and Eternity. To these were appended the Beatitudes, the Lord's Prayer, the Ten Commandments, the Apostles' Creed, and a baptismal covenant. To indicate the nature of this catechism, we will include the first 28 questions:

CATECHISM NO. 1

I. GOD

A. Sec. 1. His Nature and Attributes

1. *Who made you?* God.
2. *Who is God?* The Creator of all things.
3. *What is God?* An uncreated Spirit.
4. *Where is God?* God is everywhere.
5. *What does God know?* God is all-wise: he knoweth all things, even the thoughts of our hearts (1 John 3:20).
6. *What can God do?* God is almighty; he doeth whatsoever he will.
7. *How long has God existed?* God is eternal; he has lived always, and will live forever.
8. *What is the character of God?* "God is love" (1 John 4).
9. *Is God holy?* God is holy; he hateth all workers of iniquity (Ps. 5:5).
10. *Is God merciful?* "The Lord is merciful and gracious, slow to anger, and plenteous in mercy" (Ps. 103:8).
11. *Is God just?* The Lord is just, rewarding the righteous and punishing the wicked.
12. *Is God true?* He is "the God of truth" (Isa. 65:16). He "cannot lie" (Titus 1:2).

B. Sec. 2. The Persons of God

13. *Are there more Gods than one?* "There is none other God but one" (1 Cor. 8:4).
14. *Are there more persons in the Godhead than one?* There are three persons in the Godhead, the Father, the Son, and the Holy Ghost, and these three are ONE (1 John 5:7).
15. *Is the Father God?* "To us there is but one God, the Father" (1 Cor. 8:6).
16. *Is the Son God?* Christ "is over all, God blessed forever" (Rom. 9:5). He is the true God.
17. *Is the Holy Ghost God?* The Holy Ghost is "the Eternal Spirit" (Heb. 9:14).
18. *In what name are Christians baptized?* In the name of the Holy Trinity—the Father, the Son, and the Holy Ghost (Matt. 28:19).

II. OF CREATION.

A. Sec. 1.—The World.
19. *Can you repeat the first verse of the Bible?* "In the beginning God created the heaven and the earth" (Gen. 1:1).
20. *Does God preserve all things which he has made?* He upholdeth all things by the word of his power (Heb. 1:3).

B. Sec. 2.—Man.
21. *Of what did God make man's body?* "Of the dust of the ground" (Gen. 2:7).
22. *How did God make man's soul?* God "breathed into his nostrils the breath of life, and man became a living soul" (Gen. 2:7).
23. *How do the soul and body differ?* The body is material and mortal, the soul is spiritual and immortal.
24. *Was man created good?* He was; God created man in his own image (Gen. 1:27).
25. *In what did this image of God consist?* "In righteousness and true holiness" (Eph. 4:24).
26. *What authority was given to man at the creation?* God gave him dominion over every living thing (Gen. 1:28).
27. *Where did God place our first parents?* In the garden of Eden (Gen. 2:15).
28. *What law was given them?* The law of perfect obedience (Gen. 2:16, 17). . . .

Doctrinal Traditions of the Evangelical Church and the United Brethren Church[22]

The unfolding of doctrinal concerns among the Albright Evangelicals and Otterbein's United Brethren in Christ has run a course roughly parallel to that of the Methodists— with such differences as there were springing largely from the different ecclesiastical heritage that they had brought from Germany and Holland, together with the mellowed Calvinism of the Heidelberg Catechism. In the German-speaking communities of America, Albright and Otterbein believed it more important to stress evangelism than theological speculation. Their constant and common stress was on "conversion," on "justification by faith confirmed by a sensible assurance thereof," on Christian nurture, on the priesthood of all true believers in a shared ministry of Christian witness and service, and on "entire sanctification" as the goal and crown of Christian life.

As with Wesley, their primary source and norm for Christian teaching was Scripture. Otterbein enjoined his followers "to be careful to preach no other doctrine than what is plainly laid down in the Bible." Each new member was asked "to confess that he received the Bible as the Word of God." Ordinands were required to affirm the plenary authority of Scripture "without reserve." Matched with these affirmations was the conviction that "converted" Christians are enabled by the Holy Spirit to read Scripture with a special "Christian consciousness," and this principle was prized as the supreme guide in biblical interpretation.

Jacob Albright was directed by the Conference of 1807 to prepare a list of Articles of Religion. Before he could attempt the task he died. George Miller then assumed the responsibility. He recommended to the Conference of 1809 the adoption of a German translation of the Methodist *Articles of Religion,* with the addition of a new one, "Of the Last Judgment." The recommendation was adopted. This suggests a conscious choice of the Methodist *Articles* as normative, since the added article was their only other borrowing—from the Augsburg Confession (Article 17), on a theme strangely omitted in the Anglican Articles. These Twenty-six Articles were generally interpreted among the Albright Evangelicals in a typically non-dogmatic temper.

In 1816, the original Twenty-Six Articles were reduced to twenty-one by the excision of five of the most polemical ones in the earlier text: Article 11 ("Of Works of Supererogation"), Article 14 ("Of Purgatory"), Article 19 ("Of Both Kinds"),[23] Article 21 ("Of the Marriage of Ministers"),[24] and Article 25 ("Of a Christian Man's Oath").[25] This act of deletion was a notable instance of a conciliar spirit in a time of bitter controversy (Disc., 1984, 49).

In 1839, a few slight changes were made in the text of 1816 and it was then stipulated that "the Articles of Faith . . . should be constitutionally unchangeable among us." In 1851, it was discovered that Article 1 had been altered without authorization, and this was promptly corrected. In the 1870s a proposal that the Articles be extensively revised touched off a flurry of debate; but the Conference of 1875 decisively rejected the proposal. In a later action the Twenty-one Articles were reduced to nineteen in number by combining several of them, but without omitting any of their original content. These nineteen were brought intact into the Evangelical United Brethren union of 1946.

Among the United Brethren in Christ, a summary of normative teaching was formulated in 1813 by the disciples and colleagues of William Otterbein, Christian Newcomer, and Christopher Grosch. Its first three paragraphs follow the order of the Apostles' Creed. Paragraphs four and five affirm the primacy of Scripture and the universal proclamation of "the biblical doctrine . . . of man's fall in Adam and his deliverance through Jesus Christ." An added section commends "the ordinances of baptism and the remembrance of the Lord" and approves foot-washing as optional. In the first General Conference of the United Brethren in Christ (1815) a slight revision of this earlier statement was formally adopted as their official Confession of Faith. A further slight revision was adopted in 1841, with the stipulation that there should be no subsequent changes in the *Confession*: "No rule or ordinance shall at any time be passed to change or do away with the Confession of Faith as it now stands."

Even so, agitation for change continued, and in 1885 a church commission was appointed to:

> prepare such a form of belief and such amended fundamental rules for the government of this church in the future as will, in their judgment, be best adapted to secure its growth and efficiency in the work of evangelizing the world.

The resulting proposal for a new Confession of Faith and Constitution was submitted to the general membership of the church (the first such referendum on a Confession of Faith in its history) and was then placed before the General Conference of 1889. The general membership and the Conference approved it by preponderant majorities, and it was thereupon enacted by episcopal "Proclamation." However, this action was protested by a minority as a violation of the restrictive rule of 1841 and became a basic cause for a consequent schism, resulting in the formation of the United Brethren Church (Old Constitution).

The *Confession of Faith* of 1889 was more comprehensive than any of its antecedents, with articles on depravity, justification, regeneration and adoption, sanctification, the Christian Sabbath, and "the future state." Its article on sanctification, though brief, is significant in its reflection of the doctrine of holiness of the Heidelberg Catechism. It was this *Confession* of 1889 that was brought by the United Brethren into their union of 1946.

In that union, the Evangelical *Articles* and the United Brethren *Confession* were both printed in the *Discipline* of the new Evangelical United Brethren Church. A dozen years later, however, the General Conference of the United church authorized its Board of Bishops to prepare a new *Confession of Faith*. This was done after extensive consultation. A new *Confession,* with sixteen Articles of a somewhat more modern character than any of its antecedents, was presented to the General Conference of 1962 and adopted without amendment. In it the influence of the Evangelical statement on "Entire Sanctification and Christian Perfection" is reflected as a distinctive emphasis. This *Confession* was declared to supplant both former *Articles* and *Confession,* and was brought intact into the *Discipline* of the United Methodist Church (1968).

The standard commentary on the United Brethren *Confession of Faith* was written by Jonathan Weaver in 1893. A commentary on the *Confession* of 1962 was published in 1964 and entitled *This We Believe*.[26]

UNITED BRETHREN IN CHRIST
CONFESSION OF 1815 (AMENDED)

The group that adhered to the Confession of Faith of 1815 and the

Constitution of 1841 under the leadership of Bishop Milton Wright adopted the name "Church of the United Brethren in Christ (Old Constitution)." Church headquarters were moved from Dayton, Ohio, to Huntington, Indiana, in 1897.[27]

What follows is the *Confession of Faith* of the Church of the United Brethren in Christ.[28] Phrases omitted from the 1815 *Confession* are placed in brackets and headings are added:

1. The Triune God

In the name of God, we declare and confess before men that we believe in the only true God, the Father, the Son, and the Holy Ghost; that these three are one—the Father in the Son, the Son in the Father, and the Holy Ghost equal in essence or being with both; that this triune God created the heavens and the earth and all that in them is, visible as well as invisible, and furthermore sustains, governs, protects and supports the same.

2. Jesus Christ, the Son

We believe in Jesus Christ; that He is very God and man; that He [by the Holy Ghost, assumed his human nature in Mary] became incarnate by the power of the Holy Ghost in the Virgin Mary and was born of her; that He is the Savior and [Redeemer] Mediator of the whole human race, if they [with faith] with full faith in Him accept the grace proffered in Jesus; that this Jesus suffered and died on the cross for us, was buried, [rose] arose again on the third day, ascended into heaven, and sitteth on the right hand of God to intercede for us; that He shall come again at the last day to judge the quick and the dead.

3. The Holy Spirit, Comforter and Guide

We believe in the Holy Ghost; that He is equal in being with the Father and the Son, [that he proceeds from both; that we are through him enlightened; through faith justified and sanctified] and that He comforts the faithful, and guides them into all truth.

4. The Church

We believe in [a holy church] a holy Christian church, the communion of saints, the resurrection of the [flesh] body, and life everlasting.

5. The Holy Bible and Salvation

We believe that the Holy Bible, Old and New Testaments, is the Word of God; that it contains [the true way to our salvation] the only true way of our salvation; that every true Christian is bound to [receive it] acknowledge and receive it with the [influences] influence of the Spirit of God as [his only rule] the only rule and guide; and that without faith in Jesus Christ, true [penitence] repentance, forgiveness of sins and following after Christ, no one can be a true Christian.

6. The Salvation Message

We also believe that [the doctrine which the Holy Scriptures contain, namely] what is contained in the Holy Scriptures, to wit: the fall in Adam and redemption through Jesus Christ, shall be preached throughout the world.

7. The Christian Ordinances

We believe that the [outward means of grace are to be in use in all Christian societies, namely: that baptism and the remembrance of the death of the Lord in the distribution of the bread and wine are to be in use among his children, according to the command of the Lord Jesus; the mode and manner, however, shall be left to the judgment of every one. Also, the example of feet-washing remains free to every one] ordinances, viz., baptism and the remembrance of the sufferings and death of our Lord Jesus Christ, are to be in use and practiced by all Christian societies; and that it is incumbent on all the children of God particularly to practice them; but the manner in which ought always to be left to the judgment and understanding of every individual. Also the example of washing feet is left to the judgment of every one to practice or not; but it is not becoming of any of our preachers or members to traduce any of their brethren whose judgment and understanding in these respects is different from their own, either in public or in private. Whosoever shall make himself guilty in this respect shall be considered a traducer of his brethren, and shall be answerable for the same.

This *Confession* is protected constitutionally by the following rule: "No rule or ordinance shall at any time be passed to change or do away with the Confession of Faith as it now stands, nor to destroy the itinerant plan."[29] Not included in the *Confession,* but later appearing in the United Brethren in Christ *Discipline* is the following paragraph:

Official Doctrinal Positions: Depravity

All men are born, because of the fall of the race in Adam, with an inherent tendency toward evil. This depravity has negatively affected and is operative in every faculty of one's being. Each person, because of the inherited depravity, when confronted by the world, the flesh and the devil, will follow his sinful nature, deliberately choosing to ratify sin, and thus assumes the guilt and condemnation belonging to a sinner.[30]

8.
Outline Syllabus of a Course on the Articles of Religion

Part One:
God's Saving Action

Session 1: God Our Source: Father, Son, and Spirit
  Article 1. Triune God
  Article 4. The Holy Spirit
Session 2: Christ Our Savior
  Article 2. The Son of God
  Article 3. The Resurrection
Session 3: Scripture Our Guide
  Article 5. Sufficiency of Scripture
  Article 6. The Old Testament
Session 4: Sin Our Predicament
  Article 7. Sin
  Article 8. Free Will
Session 5: The Cross Our Reconciliation
  Article 20. Christ's Atoning Sacrifice
  Article 9. Justification

Part Two: The Church's Response—The Christian Life

Session 6: Faith Active in Love
  Article 10. Good Works
  Article 11. Works Seeking to Accrue Merit
  Article 14. Purgatory
Session 7: The Body of Christ
  Article 13. The Church Defined

Article 15. The Church's Language: Speaking in a Tongue Understood
Article 21. The Church's Ministry: Marriage of Ministers
Article 22. The Church's Traditions
Session 8: Baptism and Communion
  Article 16. Sacraments Defined
  Article 17. Baptism
  Article 18. The Lord's Supper
  Article 19. Of Both Kinds
Session 9: The Christian in Society and the Christian Life
  Added Article: The Duty of Christians to the Civil Authority
  Article 23. Legitimate Government
  Article 24. Legitimate Use of Possessions
  Article 25. Oaths
Session 10: Growth in Grace
  Article 12. Sin After Baptism
  Added Article: Sanctification

Introduction

Since the *Articles of Religion* were written as a concise confession, they are stated with extreme economy. The *Articles of Religion* were not written so as to prevent commentary but to encourage it.

This course seeks to present basic Christian teachings in ten sessions guided by Wesley's revision of the Anglican Articles of Religion. This course is adaptable also to the Articles as subsequently revised by various Wesleyan-related Churches (see collation and variants recorded in chapter 7). For convenience we will use the numbering system for the Twenty-five Methodist *Articles*.

Each session's questions for discussion are directed toward the interpretation of the *Articles* and their scriptural grounding. Each session's resources provide issues for one of ten one-hour discussions. Participants may range from young people or college inquirers to confirmation classes, or older adult church school classes. The course could be offered in two terms, the first on "God's Saving Action" and the second on "The Church's Response."

If desired, the course could easily be correlated with the Christian year: The first five sessions could be utilized as a Lenten sequence of study on basic Christian teachings, while the last five sessions on the Christian life could become a series for the Pentecostal season following Easter.

Not every point of the outline is found precisely in the text of the *Articles,* but all points made are implicitly grounded in or derived from the *Articles.* The outline seeks to provide a framework for commenting on the *Articles* that is accountable to their content yet leaving freedom to teachers to develop their own accents and interpretations. The outline is not a verbatim statement of the language of the *Articles* but a brief exposition and thematic organization of key points of the *Articles.*

Here are some suggestions for procedure: Read aloud a particular article and/or selected corresponding Bible passages, inviting discussion. The questions should enable the group's participants to grasp Christian teaching and its biblical foundation on each point taught by the *Articles.* The text of the *Articles* under discussion should be provided in advance to each participant.

Further resources for the leader's study may be found in Thomas F. Chilcote, Jr., *The Articles of Religion of the Methodist Church* (Nashville: Methodist Publishing House, 1960). The basic conceptual pattern for this study sequence is found in Anglican studies by W. H. Griffith Thomas, *The Principles of Theology: An Introduction to the Thirty-nine Articles* (London: Church Book Room Press, n.d.), and O. R. Johnston, *The Faith We Hold: Group Studies in Christian Belief* (London: Church Society, n.d.).

The Articles as a Source of Christian Teaching

The Twenty-five *Articles* were never intended to be a completely adequate or full-ranging statement of Christian teaching. (The work of the Holy Spirit, for example, is not described in detail.) They do not ask or answer all questions asked by modern parishioners. But they do go to the heart of the matter. Most of the great central Christian teachings are found in the Twenty-five *Articles.* They deal with questions that every reader of Scripture does well to consider—issues unavoidable for the Christian life (e.g., who God is, how God is revealed, how sin is met by grace, and how the life of the worshiping community is to be ordered). They can usefully form the basis for introducing laity to the central teachings of Christianity, including the Trinity, the person and work of Christ, the order of salvation, justification by faith through grace, the church as the body of Christ, and Christian social responsibility.

The *Articles* are internally systematic but not comprehensively so. Understandably, they are somewhat tilted toward certain questions that required clarification in the earlier Protestant period when they were formulated; yet these questions still demand our attention and critical reflection. They serve the purpose of setting the direction in which Christian teaching shall proceed and the boundaries which it does well not to transgress if it is to remain accountable to central attestations of Scripture.

The Twenty-five *Articles* can still be taught forcefully as a channel or framework for Christian teaching. They remain something like an "identity card" of Methodist or Wesleyan theology amid the divisions of Christianity, a kind of "title-deed" indicating our doctrinal inheritance and theological entitlement.

The *Articles of Religion* do not belong to one wing or party of Methodists or Wesleyans, but to all. Some have paid more, others less, attention to them. Generally, the more traditionally Wesleyan and more evangelical side of the family (including many United Methodists and most other Wesleyans) has prized the *Articles* as a valid, useful, condensed expression of vital biblical faith.

How to Use the Coke-Asbury Notes on the Articles

One special feature of this study is its constant reference to the original notes on the Twenty-five *Articles* by Thomas Coke and Francis Asbury. In the 1790s, Thomas Coke and Francis Asbury wrote a brief commentary on the *Articles of Religion* that exercised wide influence in the Methodist Episcopal Church. The notes appeared in the 1798 Methodist *Discipline,* along with other annotations upon various sections of the *Discipline,* largely biblical references. These notes have guided numerous subsequent Methodist writers and documents of church teaching, by demonstrating how each article is grounded in Scripture.

Widely adapted in the extended Wesleyan family, the Coke-Asbury notes are reproduced below. International Wesleyans have become linked together doctrinally through these annotations. Many of the same references now appear as annotations to the official statements of faith of the Wesleyan Church, the Church of the Nazarene, and other Wesleyan-rooted churches.

It is suggested that the Coke-Asbury notes be used as a resource for lay theological study with these assumptions:

1. These annotations can serve the teacher and the class as an intelligent and probing guide to Scripture sources of the *Articles.*

2. These notes (as well as the *Articles*) can be legally copied (because they are in the public domain, there is no need to request permission) and distributed to the class.

3. Some of the texts referred to in the notes can be read aloud and discussed by participants. A modern

"dynamic equivalence translation" (such as the New International Version, New English Bible, or Good News Bible) is recommended for use in pursuing these references.

4. It is better to discuss thoroughly two or three texts than to try to cover them all.

PART ONE: GOD'S SAVING ACTION

Session 1: God Our Source: Father, Son, and Spirit

Preparation: Genesis 1:1–23

The Living God (Article 1)

[The leader may wish to develop one or more of the following points as an introduction:]

A. Seven Essential Attributes of the Living God
  1. Unity: God is one
  2. Vitality: God is alive
  3. Eternality: God is everlasting
  4. Incorporeality: God is not reducible to physical matter
  5. Simplicity: God cannot be divided into pieces
  6. Omnipotence: God is infinite in power
  7. Omniscience: God is infinite in knowledge

B. Two Principal Moral Attributes of the Living God
  1. Veracity: God tells the truth
  2. Benevolence: God is infinite in goodness

C. The One God is the Creator: Maker of All Things
  1. God is Maker of the visible, physical world
    a. The mineral world
    b. The plant world
    c. The animal world
  2. God is Maker of the invisible, spiritual world
  3. God is Maker of humanity, astride physical and spiritual worlds
    a. Humanity is finitely free, grounded in nature
    b. Humanity is capable of self-transcendence

D. The One God is the Preserver of All Things (Divine Providence)
  1. Thus, faith engages in the study of physics, chemistry, and geology
  2. Faith engages in the study of biology, zoology, and anthropology
  3. Faith engages in the study of history

E. The One God is Triune
  1. He is one God (the unity of the Godhead)
    a. One in substance, essentially united
    b. One in power
    c. One in eternity
  2. The One God Exists in Three Persons
    a. Father (Creator)
    b. Son (Redeemer, Word of the Father)
    c. Spirit (Consummator)

[The discussion leader may select and make reference to one or more of the following 1798 Coke-Asbury notes:]

Coke-Asbury Notes

This article is proved from the following scriptures, viz.,

(1) John 4:24—God is a spirit. Eph. 3:9—God, who created all things by Jesus Christ.

(2) John 1:14—We beheld his glory, the glory as of the only *begotten of the Father*. John 8:54—Jesus answered, "It is *my Father* that honoureth me."

(3) John 1:1—The *Word* was God. Isa. 9:6—Unto us *a child* is born, unto us *a Son* is given, and his name shall be called . . . *the mighty God*. John 20:28—Feed the church *of God*, which he hath purchased *with his own blood*. Rom. 9:5—Christ, who is over all, *God* blessed for ever. Phil. 2.6—Who [Christ Jesus] being in *the form of God*, thought it not robbery to be *equal with God*. Tit. 2:13—The glorious appearing of *the great God* and our Saviour, *Jesus Christ*. Heb. 1:8—Unto *the Son* he saith, Thy throne, O *God*, is for ever and ever. 1 John 5:20—His Son *Jesus Christ*: This is *the true God*, and eternal life.

(4) John 14:26—*The Comforter*, which is *the Holy Ghost*, . . . shall teach you all things, and bring all things to your remembrance, whatsoever I have said unto you. John 20:26—When *the Comforter* is come, whom I will send unto you from the Father . . . he shall testify of me. John 16:8—When he [the Comforter] is come, he will reprove the world of sin, and of righteousness, and of judgment.

(5) 1 John 5:7—There are *three* that bear record in heaven, *the Father, the Word*, and *the Holy Ghost; and these three are one*. Matt. 28:19—Go ye, therefore, and teach all nations, baptizing them in the name of *the Father*, and of *the Son*, and of *the Holy Ghost*. Luke 3:23—The *Holy Ghost* descended in a bodily shape, like a dove, upon *him* [Christ] and a *voice* came from heaven, which said, Thou art *my beloved Son*, in whom I am well

pleased. 2 Cor. 13:14—The grace *of our Lord Jesus Christ*, and the *love of God*, and the communion *of the Holy Ghost*, be with you all. Amen.

The Holy Spirit (Article 4)

A. The Person of the Holy Spirit
  1. The Holy Spirit proceeds from the Father and the Son (dual procession)
  2. The Holy Spirit is truly God
    a. Of one substance (consubstantial) with the Father
    b. Of one substance (consubstantial) with the Son
    c. Sharing in the divine majesty
    d. Sharing in the divine glory
  3. The Holy Spirit is eternal

B. The Work of the Holy Spirit is to complete the mission of the Son

Coke-Asbury Notes

(1) John 14:16, 17—I will pray *the Father*, and he shall give you *another Comforter*, that he may abide with you for ever, even *the Spirit* of truth. John 14:26—*The Comforter*, which is *the Holy Ghost*, whom *the Father* will send in my name. . . .

(2) Rom. 8:9—Ye are not in the flesh, but in the Spirit, if so be that *the Spirit of God* dwell in you: now if any man have not *the Spirit of Christ*, he is none of his. Gal. 4:6—Because ye are sons, God hath sent forth *the Spirit of his Son* into your hearts.

(3) 2 Cor. 3:3—*The Spirit of the living God*. 2 Cor. 3:17—Now *the Lord* is *that Spirit*; and where *the Spirit of the Lord* is, there is liberty. 1

Pet. 4:14—*The Spirit of glory and of God* resteth upon you.

Discussion Questions for Session 1:

Do the attributes of God indicated in Article 1 possess an intrinsic order? May one or another be said to be more crucial? Why? Do they complement each other?

What are the principal moral attributes or qualities of God?

What is that liberty that is said to be present with the Spirit of the Lord? By whom and to whom is the Comforter sent?

Is the Son equal to God the Father?

Is the Holy Spirit of God or God?

Which New Testament passages imply a triune God? Do other world religions share Christianity's trinitarian belief? Does Scripture attest that all the Persons of the Trinity are active in the creation?

Was it necessary to God to create the universe? Are the biblical concepts of Creation and Providence reconcilable with scientific views?

Session 2: Christ Our Savior

Preparation: John 1:1–18

The Son of God (Article 2)

A. The Son
1. He is the Word of the Father
2. He is truly God (of one substance with the Father)
3. He is eternal

B. The Incarnation of the Son
1. He assumed human nature
2. He was born of the blessed Virgin

C. The Person of Christ: God-head and Humanity in Union
1. He is truly God (His divine nature)

2. He is truly human (His human nature)
3. The two natures—divine and human—are united in Him
4. He is one person, undivided

D. The Work of Christ
1. Christ's work was consummated in His atoning deed. He:
   a. Suffered for us
   b. Was crucified for us
   c. Died for us
   d. Was buried
2. His death gained our reconciliation with the Father
3. His atoning sacrifice expunged:
   a. Original guilt
   b. Actual sins

Coke-Asbury Notes

This article is proved by many of the above-quoted as well as by the following scriptures, viz.

(1) John 1:14—And *the Word* [who was God, v. 1] was made *flesh.* Phil. 2:7, 8—Christ Jesus, [who thought it not robbery to be equal with God, *vv. 5, 6*] was made *in the likeness of men;* and being found in fashion *as a man,* he humbled himself, and became obedient unto death, even the death of the cross. 1 Tim. 3:16—Without controversy, great is the mystery of godliness, *God* was manifest *in the flesh.*

(2) Col. 1:14—In whom [God's dear Son] we have *redemption* through his blood, even *the forgiveness of sins.* Eph. 2:13, 16—Now, *in Christ Jesus,* ye who sometimes were far off, are *made nigh* by the *blood of Christ.* For he is *our peace,*—that he might *reconcile* both [Jews and Gentiles] *unto God* in one body

by *the cross,* having slain the enmity thereby. 1 Tim. 2:6—Who [Christ Jesus] gave himself a *ransom for all.*

The Resurrection (Article 3)

A. The Resurrection: Christ Rose from the Dead
   1. The resurrection of Christ is a central truth of our faith
   2. He now lives in His resurrected body
     a. A real body
     b. A glorified body
     c. A body having all things pertaining to the perfection of human nature

B. Christ's Ascension, Session, and Intercession
   1. Christ ascended into heaven
   2. Christ sits at the right hand of the Father
   3. Christ presently intercedes for the faithful

C. Christ's Return to Execute Judgment at the Last Day

Coke-Asbury Notes

Matt. 28:6—He [Jesus] is not here; for he is *risen,* as he said. Luke 24:39—Behold my hands and my feet, that it is I myself. Handle me, and see: for a spirit hath not flesh and bones, as ye see me have. Mark 14:19—After the Lord had spoken to them, he was received up into heaven, and sat on the right hand of God.

Discussion Questions for Session 2:

How is Jesus the Word of God? What is meant by *incarnation*?

What is the significance of the phrase, the Son "took man's nature in the womb of the blessed Virgin"? Does Jesus share fully our human nature? What New Testament texts help bring this point home?

What evidence does the New Testament present for the premise that Jesus is truly God? If Jesus is truly God, how could He be truly human? Are these two natures inseparably united in a single person? Could He reconcile us to God if He were not fully human, fully God?

Why is it necessary to Christianity to say that He truly suffered and was crucified, dead and buried? And how did this happen "for us"? In what sense may it be said that one may suffer for another?

Why is the bodily resurrection of Christ so central to Christian belief? What kind of evidence does the New Testament present for the statement that Jesus rose from the dead? What is the import or meaning of Christ's resurrection?

Why is it significant that the Son intercedes before the Father for the faithful?

Session 3: Scripture Our Guide

Preparation: 2 Timothy 3:14–16

Sufficiency of Scripture (Article 5)

A. Scripture as Norm
   1. Scripture contains all the testimony necessary for salvation
   2. All true articles of faith are derived from Scripture
   3. No article is required if not contained in Scripture

B. The Canon Defined
   1. The canon is based on long-term ecumenical, consensual reception
   2. Canonical books were listed by early church

councils; the list is repeated in the *Articles*

3. The principal divisions of the Old Testament are:
   a. Pentateuch
   b. Historical Books
   c. Wisdom, Psalms, and Proverbs
   d. Major Prophets
   e. Minor Prophets
4. New Testament:
   a. Synoptic Gospels and Acts
   b. John's Writings
   c. Paul's Epistles
   d. General Epistles
   e. Hebrews

Coke-Asbury Notes

2 Tim. 3:16, 17—All scripture is given by inspiration of God, and is profitable for doctrine, for reproof, for correction, for instruction in righteousness; that the man of God may be perfect, thoroughly furnished unto all good works. 2 Pet. 1:19, 20, 22—We have also a more sure word of prophecy, whereunto ye do well that ye take heed, as unto a light that shineth in a dark place, until the day dawn, and the Daystar arise in your hearts: Knowing this first, that no prophecy of the Scriptures is of any private interpretation. For the prophecy came not in old time by the will of man, but holy men of God spake as they were moved by the Holy Ghost. Isa. 8:20—To the law and to the testimony: if they speak not according to *this word,* it is because there is *no light* in them. 1 Pet. 4:11—If any man speaks, let him speak *as the oracles of God.* Ps. 119:72—The law of thy mouth is better unto me than thousands of gold and silver. Ps. 119:97—O how I love thy law! It is my meditation all the day. Ps.

138:2—Thou hast magnified *thy word above all thy name.*

By the word *canonical* is meant *whatever* reflects, or is confirmed by, the laws of the church; and here it particularly refers to the decisions of the councils in the *first* and *purest* ages of Christianity concerning the holy Scriptures; in which times the inspired writings were collected into one volume. The Scriptures of the *Old* Testament had indeed been published in one volume long before by the Jews; but the Scriptures of the *New* were then added to them.

We could enter minutely into the proofs of the divine authority of each book, both of the Old and New Testament, and into an account of the times in which they were written, and the persons by whom: but it would require a treatise of itself, to do justice to so extensive a subject.

The Old and New Testaments (Article 6)

A. Complementarity of Old and New Testaments
   1. The two Testaments are not contrary but mutually edifying
   2. The revelation of God's will is set forth in both Testaments

B. Christ the Only Mediator
   1. He is the God-man
   2. He was promised in the Old Testament
   3. God's covenant promises were not transitory, nor culturally determined

C. Mosaic Law: Given by God for Various Times and Purposes

1. The ceremonial law is not binding upon Christians
   a. Levitical sacrificial rites
   b. Civil precepts
2. The moral law is binding upon Christians
   a. The Decalogue
   b. The Law and Prophets

Coke-Asbury Notes

(1) Luke 24:27—And beginning at Moses and all the prophets, *he* [Christ] expounded unto them, *in all the scriptures,* the things concerning himself. John 5:39—*Search the scriptures* [of the Old Testament, which alone were then in being] for in them ye think ye have eternal life; and they are they *which testify of me.*

(2) Job 19:25–27—I know that my Redeemer liveth, and that he shall stand at the latter day upon the earth; and though, after my skin, worms destroy this body, yet in my flesh shall I see God; whom I shall see for myself, and mine eyes shall behold, and not another. Ps. 17:15—As for me, I will behold thy face in righteousness. I shall be satisfied when I awake with thy likeness.

(3) Matt. 22:40—On these two commandments [the love of God, and the love of man] hang *all the law and the prophets.* Matt. 7:12—All things, whatsoever ye would that men should do to you, do ye even so to them; for this is *the law and the prophets.*

Discussion Questions for Session 3:

Are the *Articles of Religion* themselves to be judged according to Scripture, or is their authority detachable from Scripture?

According to 2 Tim. 3:14–17, what can we expect from Scripture?

What is the essential nature of Scripture? Is it uniquely inspired by God?

What is the meaning of Matt. 5:17–18 (read aloud)?

How is the apostolic preaching related to Old Testament promises? Must Christians follow in detail all of the ceremonial law of the Old Testament? State reasons for your answer.

Why cannot highly debatable books whose authenticity is questionable also be included in the canon?

How are the varied writings of the Bible organized?

Session 4: Sin, Our Predicament

Preparation: Rom. 1:18–2:5

Sin (Article 7)

A. The Meaning of "Original Sin"
   1. The Pelagian definition is inadequate
   2. It involves a deeper corruption of human nature
   3. Sin is universal—everywhere in human history

B. Adam and Eve as Types of the Human Predicament
   1. Sin has been transmitted to all the descendants of Adam and Eve
   2. Sin has become second nature to us
   3. We have a resultant impairment of our original righteousness
      a. Very far gone
      b. Yet not without grace
      c. Not left without God's witness

C. The Human Inclination to Evil

1. Evil is invasive of the very nature of fallen humanity
2. Evil is unremitting, continual, and ubiquitous

Coke-Asbury Notes

Gen. 6:5—God saw that the wickedness of man was great in the earth; and that every imagination of the thoughts of his heart was only evil continually. Jer. 17:9—The heart is deceitful above all things, and desperately wicked: who can know it? Ps. 14:3—They are all gone aside; they are altogether become filthy; there is none that doeth good, no, not one. Ps. 53:3—Every one of them is gone back; they are altogether become filthy; there is none that doeth good, no, not one. Rom. 3:10—As it is written, There is none righteous, no, not one. Ps. 51:5—Behold, I was *shapen* in iniquity, and in sin did my mother *conceive* me. Eph. 2:1–3—And you hath he quickened, who were *dead in trespasses and sins:* wherein in times past ye walked according to the course of this world, according to the prince of the power of the air, the spirit that now worketh in the children of disobedience; among whom also we all had our conversation, in times past, in the lusts of our flesh, fulfilling the desires of the flesh and of the mind; and were, *by nature, the children of wrath,* even as others. Mark 7:21–23—From within, out of *the heart* of men, proceed evil thoughts, adulteries, fornications, murders, thefts, covetousness, wickedness, deceit, lasciviousness, an evil eye, blasphemy, pride, foolishness: All these evil things come from within, and defile the man.

Free Will (Article 8)

A. The Alienated Human Condition
1. We were alienated from God after the Fall
2. We remain in a maze of self-deception

B. The Resultant Impairment
1. We are unable to change ourselves or turn ourselves around
2. We are unable to do good works; our natural strength to do good is radically diminished
3. We are unable to trust God
4. We are unable to call upon God
5. We are unable to envision or execute good work
6. We are unable to do God's will
7. We are unable to please God
8. We are unable to act acceptably to God

C. Prevenient Grace
1. God's gift is prior to our faith
2. God's grace precedes regeneration
3. God's grace elicits our good will

D. Cooperating Grace
1. God's grace works with human freedom
2. God's grace enables the human will to be responsive to His good will

Coke-Asbury Notes

(1) 2 Cor. 3:5—Not that we are sufficient of ourselves, to think any thing as of ourselves, but our sufficiency is of God. Eph. 2:5—Even when we were dead in sins

[God] hath quickened us together with Christ (by grace ye are saved). Eph. 2:8, 9—By grace are ye saved through faith; and that not of yourselves, it is the gift of God, not of works, lest any man should boast.

(2) John 15:5—Without me [Christ] ye can do nothing. Phil. 2:12, 13—Work out your own salvation with fear and trembling; for it is God which worketh in you both to will and to do, of his good pleasure.

Discussion Questions for Session 4:

What is sin? Is it universally found in human history? Where is the plausible evidence that the human heart is deceitful and desperately wicked? How profoundly is this poignant Christian view of sin anticipated in the Old Testament (see Ps. 51)?

What is Pelagianism and is it alive today? Is sin the result of ignorance? Do the heirs of Adam and Eve start with a corrupted human nature?

What does the sinner deserve, according to Paul?

How may excessively optimistic or pessimistic views of human nature lead to injustice? Is fallen humanity ever left without grace?

How is the human will impaired by sin? Can the natural will, without grace, trust or please God, or offer God good works?

How does God's grace continue to operate amid the conditions of sin? Does grace eliminate or displace the human will?

Session 5: The Cross Our Reconciliation

Preparation: Romans 3:9–31

Christ's Atoning Sacrifice (Article 20)

A. The Self-offering of Christ for Sinners
  1. His death was a once-for-all offering
    a. No other satisfaction possible
    b. No other satisfaction required
  2. His sacrifice was perfect, complete, and sufficient
    a. As a redemption of sinners from the bondage of sin
    b. As a conciliation of the divine anger against sin
    c. As a satisfaction of the divine justice
  3. The truth of the atonement contradicts medieval teaching:
    a. That Christ is offered anew sacrificially in each Mass
    b. That human guilt is remitted through the Mass itself

B. The Scope of Redemption
  1. A. Christ's sacrifice is offered for all the sins of the world
    a. For original sin
    b. For actual sin

Coke-Asbury Notes

Heb. 7:26, 27—Such an high priest became us, who *needeth not daily* as those high priests [of the tribe of Levi] to offer up sacrifice, first for his own sins, and then for the people's: *for this he did once, when he offered up himself.* Heb. 10:11–14—Every priest standeth *daily* ministering and offering *oftentimes the same sacrifices,* which can never take away sins: But this man [Christ] after he had offered *one* sacrifice for sins, for ever sat down on the right hand of God. . . . For by *one* offering he hath perfected for ever them that are sanctified. John 19:30—He [Jesus] said, *It is finished;* and he bowed his head, and gave up the ghost.

The sacrifice of Masses, in which Christ is supposed to be offered again, is wholly grounded on the doctrine of transubstantiation: and it must be granted, that if the wafer after consecration, be the *real* body of Christ, the priest may offer it, or crucify it, or do what he please with it.

Justification (Article 9)

A. Justification Defined
   1. *Justification* means "to be accounted righteous."
   2. *Justification* means "to stand upright or uprighted before God."

B. The Means of Justification
   1. Justification is obtained only through the merit of our Lord and Savior Jesus Christ
   2. It is received by trusting in God's grace
   3. We are justified by faith only

C. The Exclusion of Self-earned Merit
   1. Justification is not by anything one does
   2. It is not by anything one imagines to deserve

D. A Comforting Doctrine
   1. Justification by faith is a wholesome doctrine, enabling spiritual health
   2. It is a consoling doctrine, edifying and strengthening the downcast

Coke-Asbury Notes

(1) Rom. 3:24–26—Being justified freely by his grace, through the redemption that is in Christ Jesus; whom God hath set forth to be a propitiation through faith in his blood, to declare his righteousness for the remission of sins that are past, through the forbearance of God: to declare I say, at this time, his righteousness, that he might be just, and the justifier of him which believeth in Jesus. Rom. 5:18—Therefore as by the offence of one, judgment came upon all men to condemnation; even so, by the righteousness of one, the free gift came upon all men unto justification of life. Rom. 10:4—For Christ is the end of the law for righteousness to every one that believeth. Gal. 2:16—Knowing that a man is not justified by the works of the law, but by the faith of Jesus Christ, that we might be justified by the faith of Christ, and not by the works of the law; for by the works of the law shall no flesh be justified.

(2) Ps. 32:1—Blessed is he whose transgression is forgiven, whose sin is covered. Rom. 5:1—Being justified by faith, we have peace with God through our Lord Jesus Christ.

Discussion Questions for Session 5:

What sort of "redemption" has occurred in the Cross? Did Christ die for all or some? In what sense did Christ perform a priestly function for us on the Cross?

Why is it said to be a "finished work"?

Can you describe one who seeks to justify oneself by one's works?

For those who understand themselves to be standing in the presence of God the Judge, what quality is most urgently needed? What do we typically try to do when we become conscious of our shortcomings in the divine presence?

God's requirement is clear from the law; but what is the regrettable outcome of the sinner's knowing the law?

What does Scripture mean when it says that we are justified by God's grace? How can a sinner be "accounted righteous"?

What key terms does Paul use in Rom. 3:24–26 to stress that justification has nothing to do with what we earn or merit? How is this a "comforting doctrine"?

How do the themes of justification and peace (serenity, blessedness) correlate? In what sense is Christ the "end of the law"?

PART TWO: THE CHURCH'S RESPONSE— THE CHRISTIAN LIFE

Session 6: Faith Active in Love

Preparation: James 2:14–26

Good Works (Article 10)

A. Faith Active in Love
1. The Christian life is lived in response to God's grace
2. The fruits of faith are good works

B. The Right Ordering of Faith and Good Works
1. Good works are ordered:
    a. Follow after faith
    b. In response to God's justifying grace
2. Good works are limited:
    a. Egocentrically distorted without faith
    b. Cannot put away our sins
    c. Cannot endure the severity of God's judgment

C. The Sole Basis of Works Pleasing to God
1. Good works spring out of faith
    a. True faith (grounded in sound teaching of grace)
    b. Lively faith (living out of God)
    c. Knowable faith (known through evidence of works)
2. Analogy of fruit: As fruit comes naturally from a tree, so works spring naturally from a living faith

D. The Value of Good Works
1. Good works are pleasing to God
2. Faith's works are acceptable to God in Christ

Coke-Asbury Notes

(1) Gal. 5:6—In Jesus Christ neither circumcision availeth anything, nor uncircumcision, but faith which *worketh* by love. James 2:22—Seest thou how faith wrought with his [Abraham's] *works*; and by *works* was faith made perfect. James 2:26—As the body without the spirit is dead, so faith without *works* is dead also.

(2) Heb. 13:16—To do good and to communicate, forget not; for with such sacrifices God is well pleased. James 1:27—Pure religion and undefiled before God and the Father, is this, To visit the fatherless and widows, in their affliction, and to keep himself unspotted from the world. Tit. 3:8—This is a faithful saying, and these things I will that thou *affirm constantly*, that they which have believed in God, might be careful to maintain *good works*.

The Vain Attempt to Do More Than is Required (Works of Supererogation) (Article 11)

A. Works of Supererogation Defined:
   1. Works of "supererogation" are supposed "super-works," exceeding God's command
      a. Trying extra-hard to give God more than is required
      b. Voluntary attempts to "pile up" good works
      c. Works presumably added to God's work
      d. Works seeming to exceed God's commandments

B. What God Requires
   1. Christ's humble way resists this pretense
   2. Do what God asks
   3. Then confess: "We are unprofitable servants."

Coke-Asbury Notes

Job 22:2, 3—Can a man be profitable unto God, as he that is wise may be profitable unto himself? Is it any pleasure to the Almighty that thou art righteous? Or is it gain to him that thou makest thy ways perfect? 1 Cor. 4:7—Who maketh thee to differ from another? And what hast thou, which thou didst not receive? Now, if thou didst receive it, why dost thou glory as if thou hadst not received it? Tit. 3:5—*Not by works of righteousness,* which we have done, but according to his mercy he saved us, by the washing of regeneration, and renewing of the Holy Ghost.

Abuses of Medieval Scholasticism Rejected (Article 14)

A. Medieval Teachings and Practices Unsupported by Scripture
   1. The Scholastics taught that a period of purgation is required:
      a. After death
      b. Before coming into Christ's presence
      c. In which added merit can accrue
   2. The Scholastics taught that pardon is mediated only through the Mass, regarded as a propitiatory sacrifice
   3. The Scholastics taught that visible images of divine things are to be worshiped and adored

B. Why These Teachings Are Rejected
   1. They appeal to our idolatry-prone fallen nature
   2. They tend toward excessive fondness for the temporal
   3. They are vainly invented
   4. They have no scriptural warrant
   5. They are repugnant to the Word of God

Coke-Asbury Notes

(1) Exod. 20:4, 5—Thou shalt not make unto thee any graven image, or any likeness of any thing that is in heaven above, or that is in the earth beneath, or that is in the water under the earth: *thou shalt not bow down* thyself to them. Matt. 4:10—Jesus saith unto him, . . . It is written, Thou shalt worship the Lord thy God, and him *only* shalt thou serve. Col. 2:18—

Let no man beguile you of your reward, in a voluntary humility, and *worshiping* of angels, . . . 1 Tim. 2:5—There is one God, and *one* Mediator between God and men, the man Christ Jesus. Rev. 19:10—I [John] fell at his feet to *worship* him; and he said unto me, *See thou do it not*; I am thy fellow-servant, and of thy brethren that have the testimony of Jesus. *Worship God.* Rev. 22:8, 9—I fell down to *worship* before the feet of the angel which shewed me these things. Then saith he unto me, *See thou do it not,* for I am thy fellow-servant, and of thy brethren, the prophets, and of them which keep the sayings of this book. *Worship God.*

(2) Luke 16:26—Besides all this, between us and you there is a great gulf fixed, *so that they which would pass from hence to you, cannot: neither can they pass to us, that would come from thence.* John 8:21—Then said Jesus again unto them, I go my way, and ye shall seek me, and shall die in your sins. Whither I go, ye *cannot* come.

(3) Mark 2:5ff. — When Jesus saw their faith, he said unto the sick of the palsy, Son, thy sins be forgiven thee. But there were certain of the scribes sitting there, and reasoning in their hearts, Why doth this man thus speak blasphemies? *Who can forgive sins but God only?* And immediately, when Jesus perceived in his spirit, that they so reasoned within themselves [he did not deny the justness of their reasoning, in ascribing to God *only* the power of forgiving sins, but] he said unto them, Why reason ye these things in your hearts? Whether it is easier to say to the sick of the palsy, thy sins be forgiven thee; or to say, Arise, and take up thy bed, and walk? But that ye may know that

the son of man [he does not add, *and the pope and his priests*] hath power on earth to forgive sins, He saith to the sick of the palsy, I say to thee, arise and take up thy bed, and go thy way into thine house. And immediately he arose, . . . See also Matt. 9:2ff. and Luke 6:18ff.

Discussion Questions for Session 6:

Is there a hidden danger in the Christian teaching of free grace, that we are justified without human merit?

How does Scripture correlate genuine faith and good works? Can faith in God's pardoning love leave life unaffected?

How is it best to answer the question: "Shall we sin that grace may abound"? Did Paul's teaching in any way promote or allow license?

Why is faith without works dead? How does Article 10 balance what good works are unable to do and what they are able to do?

Can we do good works so as to exceed the divine requirement? Why do we always remain "unprofitable servants"?

Why is the doctrine of purgatory objectionable?

Why should prayer be directed only to God, rather than to the saints?

Session 7: The Body of Christ
Preparation: Eph. 4:1–16; 1 Cor. 12

The Church (Article 13)
A. The Church Defined
   1. The church is the visible body of Christ
   2. The church is any congregation of the faithful

B. Marks of the Church

1. The church is present
where:
   a. The Word of God is
   preached
      (1) Purely and com-
      pletely
      (2) Without distortion,
      admixture, corrup-
      tion, or deficit
   b. The Sacraments are administered
      (1) According to
      Christ's ordinance
      (2) Duly, dutifully, and
      fittingly according
      to good order
   c. Where that which is
   required for preaching
   is provided
   d. Where that which is
   requisite to the Sacraments is provided

Coke-Asbury Notes

Matt. 18:20—Where *two or three*
are gathered together in my name,
there I am in the midst of them.
Rom. 16:5—Greet *the church,* which
is *in their house.* 1 Cor. 16:19— *The
churches of Asia* salute you. 1 Cor.
11:18—When *ye* come together *in
the church,* . . .

The Church's Language: Speaking in a Tongue Understood (Article 15)

A. Rejection of Speaking in a
Tongue Not Understood By
the People
   1. Ministers are not to
   preach in a tongue not
   understood
   2. No one is to pray in a
   tongue not understood
   3. No one is to administer
   the Sacraments in a
   tongue not understood

B. Why Rejected

1. Confusion is plainly repugnant to the Word of
God
2. Speaking in unknown
tongues was not the cus-
tomary practice of the
primitive church
3. Worship must be con-
ducted in the language of
the people

Coke-Asbury Notes

1 Cor. 14:11—If I know not the
meaning of the voice, I shall be unto
him that speaketh, a barbarian; and
he that speaketh shall be a barbarian
unto me. 1 Cor. 14:14— *If I pray* in
an *unknown* tongue, my spirit pray-
eth, but my understanding is un-
fruitful. 1 Cor. 14:16—When thou
shalt bless with the spirit, how shall
he that occupieth the room of the
unlearned, say Amen at *the giving of
thanks,* seeing *he understandeth not*
what thou sayest. 1 Cor. 14:19—In
the church I had rather speak five
words with my understanding, that
by my voice I might teach others
also, than ten thousand words in an
unknown tongue. (See the whole
chapter of 1 Cor. 14.)

A Special Question of the Church's Ministry: Freedom for Marriage or Singleness (Article 21)

A. Two Ways for Ministers to
Understand Their Vocation
   1. They may minister as
   married people (assuming
   covenant fidelity in marriage)
   2. They may minister as celibate people (exhibiting
   the single-mindedness of
   the single life)
   3. There is no third way

B. Some Clerics' Preference of Celibate State
1. Is either state preferred?
2. Either state is lawful
3. Neither of the two states is specifically commanded by God's law (Especially note: No scriptural requirement to vow celibacy)
4. Preference for celibacy grew out of medieval practice

C. Grounds for Making the Choice
1. Servants of God are free to use their best judgment
2. Proviso: That their choice serves best to elicit godliness

Coke-Asbury Notes

1 Tim. 4:1–3—Now, *the Spirit speaketh expressly,* that in the latter times some shall depart from the faith, giving heed to seducing spirits, and *doctrines of devils;—forbidding to marry, . . .* 1 Cor. 9:5—Have *we* not power to lead about *a sister, a wife,* as well as *other apostles,* and as *the brethren of the Lord,* and *Cephas?* Heb. 13:4—Marriage is *honourable in all.*

Limits and Possibilitites of Amending the Church's Traditions (Article 22)

Preparation: 1 Cor. 12

A. Variety of Church Traditions
1. Rites and ceremonies of various churches may differ
   a. From place to place
   b. From time to time
2. It is not necessary that they be absolutely uniform; rites and ceremonies

may be changed when appropriate
   a. According to diverse countries
   b. According to diverse morals and manners

B. The Limiting Principle of Church Governance
1. Nothing shall be ordained contrary to God's Word— the danger of applying one's private judgment over against church order
2. The breaking of rites and ceremonies may consist of:
   a. Publicly breaking
   b. Personally and secretly breaking
3. Duly ordained rites are those not repugnant to God's Word

C. The Problem of Overturning Rituals
1. One's private preference outweighs the church's due ordering
2. Rites are legitimately ordained and approved by duly constituted common authority

D. Proper Admonition Against Such Divisive Private Judgment
1. The admonition shall be open, not private. Why?
   a. That others may not follow, fearing rebuke
   b. The common order of the church has been offended
   c. The conscience of the weak has been offended

E. Church Order for Edification
1. Church polity may be amended for edification

2. Particular forms may be abolished for edification
3. Every congregation shall seek to apply the criterion of edification in its own context

Coke-Asbury Notes

(1) Heb. 13:17—Obey them that have rule over you, and submit yourselves; for they watch for your souls, as they that must give account, that they may do it with joy, and not with grief. 1 Cor. 11:16— But if any man seem to be contentious, we have no such custom, neither the churches of God.

(2) Rom. 2:8—Unto them that are *contentious,* indignation and wrath. Rom. 16:17, 18—Now, I beseech you, brethren, *mark* them which *cause divisions and offences,* contrary to the doctrine which ye have learned, and *avoid them.* For they that are such serve not our Lord Jesus Christ, but their own belly; and *by good words and fair speeches* deceive the hearts of the simple. 1 Cor. 1:10—Now *I beseech you, brethren, by the name of our Lord Jesus Christ,* that ye all speak the same thing, and *that there be no divisions* among you; but that ye be perfectly joined together in the same mind, and in the same judgment.

Discussion Questions for Session 7:

How can one identify where the church exists? What is the church?

Why are Word and Sacrament so decisive to the definition of the church?

Should worship proceed by using a language unfamiliar to the common people?

Is marriage or celibacy preferred in Scripture?

Are adultery, promiscuity, and homosexuality ruled out by Scripture and by the *Articles*? Must that sexual choice that best elicits godliness be the same for everyone?

Why does the church need to be ordered? Under what circumstances may private judgment overrule church order or accepted practice? How shall offenders against rightly constituted church order be appropriately counseled and guided?

Session 8: Baptism and Communion

Preparation: 1 Cor. 10:1–5, 11:23–32

The Sacraments (Article 16)

A. The Sacraments Defined
   1. The Sacraments are:
      a. Ordained of Christ
      b. Signs of grace
      c. Signs of God's good will toward us
      d. Working invisibly in the faithful
   2. The Sacraments have the purpose of enlivening, awakening, and quickening our faith
   3. The Sacraments are not merely:
      a. Badges of subjective faith
      b. Tokens of Christian profession

B. Five Practices "Commonly Called" Sacraments
   1. Only two Sacraments were ordained by Christ:
      a. Baptism
      b. The Supper of the Lord
   2. Five remaining "commonly called" Sacraments were derived from medieval practice:

a. Confirmation
b. Penance
c. Orders
d. Matrimony
e. Extreme Unction
3. Why these practices are rejected as valid Sacraments:
   a. Not regarded as Sacraments in Scripture
   b. Not instituted by Christ
   c. Partly derived from corruptions of apostolic teaching
4. Yet these practices are not to be completely rejected, because they are allowed in Scripture:
   a. Confirmation in Scripture
   b. Repentance in Scripture
   c. Ordination in Scripture
   d. Marriage in Scripture
   e. Care for the dying in Scripture
5. These five lack essential qualities of Sacraments:
   a. Not visible signs specified by Christ
   b. Not dominically ordained of God

C. Misuses of the Sacraments
   1. They are not for exploitation (not to be "gazed at")
   2. They are not for show (not to be "carried about")
   3. They are intended to be duly used as means of grace

D. Reception of the Sacraments
   1. What constitutes a worthy rejection of the Lord's Supper?

a. Having wholesome effect
b. Working to make one whole
2. What constitutes an unworthy reception of the Lord's Supper?
   a. Eats and drinks without recognition of the Lord
   b. Fails to meet the living Lord
   c. Brings judgment on himself (1 Cor. 11:29)

Coke-Asbury Notes

(1) Matt. 28:19; Mark 16:16—He that believeth and *is baptized,* shall be saved. Acts 2:38—Peter said unto them, Repent, and *be baptized,* every one of you, in the name of Jesus Christ, for the remission of sins. Acts 8:12—When they believed Philip preaching, . . . they were *baptized,* both men and women. Acts 8:16—As yet he [the Holy Ghost] was fallen on none of them, only they were *baptized* in the name of the Lord Jesus. Acts 16:15—When she [Lydia] was *baptized,* and *her household,* . . . Acts 19:5—They were *baptized* in the name of the Lord Jesus. Acts 22:16—And now why tarriest thou? Arise, and *be baptized,* . . . Rom. 6:3, 4—Know ye not that so many of us as were *baptized into Jesus Christ, were baptized* into his death? Therefore we are buried with him *by baptism* into death: that like as Christ was raised up from the dead by the glory of the Father, even so we also should walk in newness of life. 1 Cor. 1:16—I *baptized* also *the household* of Stephanus. 1 Pet. 3:21—The like *figure* whereunto even *baptism* doth also now save us; not the putting away of the filth of the flesh, but the

answer of a good conscience towards God, by the resurrection of Jesus Christ.

(2) Luke 22:19—He [Jesus] took bread and gave thanks, and brake it, and gave unto them, saying, This is my body which is given for you: *this do in remembrance of me.* 1 Cor. 11:24-26—When he had given thanks, he brake it, and said, Take, eat; this is my body which is broken for you; *this do in remembrance of me.* After the same manner also he took the cup, when he had supped, saying, this cup is the new testament in my blood; *this do ye, as oft as ye drink it, in remembrance of me.* For *as often* as ye eat *this bread,* and drink *this cup,* ye do shew the Lord's death, *till he come.* 1 Cor. 10:16—The cup of blessing, which we bless, is it not *the communion* of the body of Christ?

(3) 1 Cor. 11:27—Whosoever shall eat this bread, and drink this cup of the Lord unworthily, shall be guilty of the body and blood of the Lord. See also 1 Cor. 11:29.

In respect to the five additional *sacraments,* which the church of Rome has been pleased to adopt, there is not the least imaginable authority from the word of God to consider them *as such.* They want the *essential* requisites of a sacrament; and have been *imposed* on a considerable part of mankind by a most corrupt priesthood, whose only aim was to enrich and aggrandize themselves.

And from the same corrupt fountain sprung the gaudy, superstitious custom of carrying about the Host, that the poor blinded multitude might gaze at it, and worship it, to the degradation of human nature, as well as the dishonor of God.

Baptism (Article 17)

Preparation: Romans 6

A. Baptism Defined
   1. Baptism is not:
      a. Essentially a psychological event
      b. Merely a sign
      c. An indication of one's profession of faith
      d. Essentially a sociological phenomenon
      e. Merely a mark of difference, distinguishing those baptized from those not
   2. Baptism is:
      a. A sign of God's giving new life to the soul
      b. A sign of the regenerating of the Christian
      c. An anticipation of the "new birth"

B. Warrant for the Baptism of Infants
   1. Infant baptism points toward the new birth
      a. To be initiated through prevenient grace
      b. To be completed by justifying grace
   2. A sign which points to something that follows will retain the significance of what follows

Coke-Asbury Notes

Matt. 3:11—I [John the Baptist] indeed baptize you with water unto repentance; but he that cometh after me . . . *shall baptize you with the Holy Ghost, and with fire.* John 3:5—Jesus answered, Verily, verily, I say unto thee, except a man be born of water and *of the Spirit,* he cannot enter into the kingdom of God. Mark 10:13-16—They brought young children to him [Christ] that he should teach them, and his disciples rebuked those that brought them; but when Jesus saw it, he was much displeased, and said unto them, Suffer the little children to come unto me, and forbid them not; for of such is the kingdom of God. . . . And he took them up in his arms, put his hands upon them, and blessed them.

The preceding scripture evidently demonstrates that the *little children* were entitled to all the privileges of *the kingdom of grace.* They must, therefore, be entitled to the benefit of *that ordinance,* which initiates the members of Christ's kingdom into his church below. See also the texts concerning baptism on the preceding article, particularly those which respect the baptizing of whole households or families.

The Lord's Supper (Article 18)
Preparation: Matt. 26:26–29

A. The Lord's Supper Defined
  1. The Supper of the Lord is not:
    a. Merely an outward sign
    b. An external testimony that Christians love one another
  2. The Supper of the Lord is a Sacrament, hence:
    a. Ordained of Christ
    b. A sign of God's good will, quickening our faith
    c. A proof of our redemption by Christ's death

B. The Means of Reception
  1. The symbols of Christ's body and blood are to be received:
    a. With faith
    b. According to due order

c. Worthily, as prepared by self-examination

C. The Meaning of the Bread
  1. According to Scripture, the bread represents the body of Christ. Therefore:
    a. Only the faithful partake
    b. Sharing in Christ's bodily death
  2. The bread reminds us of God's gift of His Son. It is:
    a. Given—by God
    b. Received—by the faithful
    c. Eaten—a bodily and spiritual act
    d. Yet not merely a physical act—received in a heavenly and spiritual manner

D. The Meaning of the Cup
  1. The cup represents the blood of Christ
    a. A cup of blessing
    b. A partaking of (sharing in) Christ's suffering

E. Abuses to Be Avoided
  1. The Sacrament is not to be reserved or held for future use
  2. The Sacrament is not to be carried about or displayed
  3. The Sacrament is not to be lifted up or worshiped in itself
  4. These practices are not ordained in the New Testament

Coke-Asbury Notes

Matt. 26:28—This is *my blood* of the New Testament, which *is shed* for many, for the remission of sins. Mark 14:24—This is *my blood* of the

New Testament, which *is shed* for many. Luke 22:19—This is *my body,* which *is given* for you. 1 Cor. 11:24—This is *my body,* which *is broken* for you. 1 Cor. 11:7—For even *Christ our passover, is sacrificed for us.* (See also the notes on Article 16.)

In respect to the doctrine of transubstantiation, or the change of the bread and wine in the Lord's supper into the *real* body and blood of Christ, so that the divinity as well as humanity of Christ is contained in the transubstantiated elements, we have little hopes of convincing those of their error, who can hold so absurd a notion. If they can credit the assertion that a man can put his God into his mouth and swallow him down his throat, or that he can even swallow the whole humanity of the blessed Jesus, "whom the heavens must receive until the times of restitution of all things" [Acts 3:21], they must indeed be prepared to receive any error, which a corrupt and interested clergy may think proper to impose upon them, however absurd or monstrous it may be. Nor do we know of any opinion of the heathen mythologists, concerning their Jupiters, Junos, and Venuses, so astonishingly monstrous as the doctrine of transubstantiation.

At the same time, we are well assured that the true believer does, in a *spiritual* manner, feed upon the body and blood of Jesus Christ, and in this *spiritual* sense we take those words of our Lord (John 6:51–58), "I am the living bread which came down from heaven: if any man eat of this bread, he shall live for ever: and the bread that I will give, is my flesh, which I will give for the life of the world. . . . Verily, verily, I say unto you, Except ye eat the flesh of the Son of man, and drink his blood, ye have no life in you. Whoso eateth my flesh, and drinketh my blood, hath eternal life, and I will raise him up at the last day. For my flesh is meat indeed, and my blood is drink indeed. He that eateth my flesh, and drinketh my blood, dwelleth in me, and I in him." Faith is the grand instrument, whereby we thus *spiritually* discern the Lord's Body and *spiritually* eat his flesh, and drink his blood.

The Bread and the Cup (Article 19)

A. Communion in Both Kinds
   1. There are two parts of the Lord's Supper—the bread and the cup
   2. Both bread and cup ought to be given to the laity
   3. Both kinds are offered by Christ's specific ordinance and command

Coke-Asbury Notes

It is indubitable, from the 11th chapter of St. Paul's last Epistle to the Corinthians, that the Lord's supper was administered in *both* kinds to all the communicants in the apostolic age. The apostle, addressing himself to *the Corinthians,* observes in the 20th, 21st, and 22nd verses, "When *ye* come together, therefore, into one place, this is not to eat the Lord's supper. For in eating, every one taketh before other his own supper: and one is hungry, and *another is drunken.* What! Have ye not houses to eat and to *drink in?"* Here St. Paul does not complain of their *drinking the wine* at the Lord's supper, which he certainly would, if the cup was to be confined to the ministers; but of their both *eating* and *drinking* most intemperately. He adds, in v. 26ff., "As often as *ye [Corinthians]* eat this bread, and *drink this cup, ye* do shew the Lord's death, till he come. Wherefore, *whosoever* shall eat this bread, and *drink this cup* of the Lord unworthily, shall be guilty of the body and blood of the Lord. But let a man [any Christian, not a priest only, for neither priest nor minister is here mentioned] examine himself; and so let him eat of that bread, and *drink of that cup. . . .*" The whole passage removes all possibility of dispute, where the scripture is the rule of judgment. And indeed the refusal of the cup to the people is, even in the church of Rome, of very late date: however, it shews much of that wisdom which is from beneath; for it requires much more faith to believe in the transubstantiation of *the wine* after consecration, than of *the wafer* which has little or no taste.

Discussion Questions for Session 8:

Why are only two sacraments regarded as authentic in the Wesleyan tradition? How do confirmation, penance, ordination, matrimony, and extreme unction (recognized as sacraments in medieval scholasticism) differ from baptism and holy communion?

What is a sacrament? How is it possible that the sacraments remain effective when the minister is ungodly?

What does the water of baptism signify?

What does the bread of the Lord's Supper signify? What does the cup signify?

Why are the sacraments more than an outward sign or symbol of the profession of our faith—What is the "more"?

Who authorized baptism and why? What is the relation of baptism and the new birth? Does the baptism of young children have a valid biblical basis?

What reason did Jesus give for the Supper He instituted? How did He instruct His disciples to understand it?

What is the single qualification necessary for receiving the Supper properly? What is meant by receiving the Supper "in both kinds"?

Session 9: The Christian in Society

Preparation: Rom. 13:1–7

The Duty of Christians to Civil Authority (Article 23)

A. The Political Duty of Christians
  1. Christian ministers especially are asked to take note of their political duty
  2. All Christians are obliged to obey political authorities
     a. Observe the civil laws
     b. Obey established order and constituted governance
     c. Be accountable to the powers that be
  3. In whatever place a citizen resides, a duty is owed to preserve just order
  4. This political accountability is to be commended to all
     a. Using all laudable means to increase justice
     b. Encouraging legitimate authority
     c. Enjoining to political responsibility

B. Legitimate Civil Authority in America

1. There is wisdom in having several branches of governance (a division of powers)
   a. Federal government (executive, legislative, judicial branches)
   b. State government (governors and councils of state)
2. This authority is constitutionally delegated by the people
3. These civil authorities are legitimate powers to be respected. They are constitutionally grounded:
   a. By the federal constitution
   b. By the state constitutions
4. The national experiment is to be affirmed by Christians
   a. Its sovereignty
   b. Its independence
   c. Its freedom from intrusive colonializing powers

Coke-Asbury Notes

Rom. 13:1–7—Let every soul be subject unto the higher powers; for there is no power but of God; the powers that be are ordained of God. Whosoever, therefore, resisted the power, resisteth the ordinance of God; and they that resist shall receive to themselves damnation; for rulers are not a terror to good works, but to the evil. Wilt thou then not be afraid of the power? Do that which is good, and thou shalt have praise of the same; for he is the minister of God to thee for good. But if thou do that which is evil, be afraid; for he beareth not the sword in vain; for he is the minister of God, a revenger to execute wrath upon him that doeth evil. Wherefore, ye must needs be subject, not only for wrath, but also for conscience' sake. For this cause pay ye tribute also; for they are God's ministers, attending continually upon this very thing. Render, therefore, to all, their dues; tribute, to whom tribute is due; custom, to whom custom; fear, to whom fear; honour, to whom honour. Tit. 3:1—Put them in mind to be subject to principalities and powers, to obey magistrates. 2 Pet. 2:9–11—The Lord knoweth how . . . to reserve the unjust unto the day of judgment to be punished; but *chiefly them* that walk after the flesh in the lust of uncleanness, and *despise government.* Presumptuous are they, self-willed, *they are not afraid to speak evil of dignities;* whereas angels, which are greater in power and might, bring not railing accusation against them before the Lord. Jude 8—Likewise, also, these filthy dreamers defile the flesh, *despise dominion,* and *speak evil of dignities.* 1 Tim. 2:1, 2—I exhort, therefore, that first of all, supplications, prayers, intercession, and giving of thanks, be made for all men, . . . and *for all that are in authority.*

The Right to Possessions and Duty to the Poor (Article 24)

A. The Use of Goods in the Christian Community
   1. Being always subject to abuse, is the use of property intrinsically evil?
   2. Many types of property are held legitimately by Christians:
      a. Accumulated resources
      b. Goods acquired
      c. Right of possession
      d. Titles to land and real property

3. These are not to be abolished or presumptuously seized
   a. Not on equalitarian premises
   b. Not on supposed rationalistic premises
4. Property is not to be artificially held in common
   a. Communal ownership not a biblical injunction
   b. An invention of imagined rationality

B. Claims of Communal Advocates
   1. Christians must not fall prey to the false and boastful claims of those who advocate communal ownership:
      a. Those who wish to seize the property of others
      b. Those who presume to have the ability to redistribute fairly

C. Distribution to the Poor
   1. Property is to be liberally given away to the poor
      a. Voluntarily, not by force
      b. According to a reasonable assessment of ability and need
   2. Everything one possesses is subject to this rule of charity
   3. The Christian duty to offer constant succor and help to the poor and needy requires:
      a. Giving liberally
      b. Giving according to one's ability

c. Giving gratefully as one has received God's gifts

Coke-Asbury Notes

(1) Acts 5:3, 4—Peter said, Ananias, why hath Satan filled thine heart to lie to the Holy Ghost, and to keep back part of the price of the land? While it remained, *was it not thine own?* and after it was sold, *was it not in thine own power?* 1 Cor. 16:2—Upon the first day of the week, let every one of you lay by him in store, as God hath prospered him, that there be no gatherings when I come. 1 Tim. 6:17, 18—Charge them that are rich in this world [not, that they throw their property into a common stock with the other members of the church, to which they belong, but] that they do good, that they be *rich in good works,* ready to distribute, willing to communicate.

(2) Matt. 25:34–40—Then shall the king say unto them on this right hand, Come, ye blessed of my Father, inherit the kingdom prepared for you from the foundation of the world; for I was an hungered, and ye gave me meat; I was thirsty, and ye gave me drink; I was a stranger, and ye took me in; naked, and ye clothed me; I was sick, and ye visited me; I was in prison, and ye came to me. . . . Verily, I say unto you, Inasmuch as ye have done it unto one of the least of these my brethren, ye have done it unto me.

Oaths Forbidden and Permitted (Article 25)

A. Oaths Prohibited
   1. That swearing is forbidden which is:
      a. Vain—hollow, empty, futile, self-indulgent

b. Rash—reckless, lacking wise counsel and clear judgment
2. Such oaths are forbidden by Jesus and James the apostle

B. Oaths Permitted
1. That swearing is permitted which is:
   a. Required by the law or courts
   b. Required by a justifiable cause
2. Such oaths should be for the purpose of:
   a. Attesting fidelity
   b. Seeking charity
3. Such oath-making is done according to the prophet's teaching:
   a. In justice—swearing according to law
   b. In judgment—swearing prudently with wise counsel
   c. In truth—swearing honestly

Coke-Asbury Notes

(1) Matt. 5:34–37—I say unto you, Swear not at all; . . . But let your *communication* be yea, yea; nay, nay; for whatsoever is more than these, cometh of evil. James 5:12— Above all things, may brethren, swear not; neither by heaven, neither by earth, neither by any other oath; but let *your yea be yea; and your nay, nay;* lest ye fall into condemnation.

(2) Matt. 26:63, 64—The high priest answered, and said unto him, *I adjure thee by the living God,* that thou tell us whether thou be the Christ, the Son of God. Jesus saith unto him, Thou hast said; [or, as St. Mark expresses it 16:2] Jesus said, I am. [Jesus answered the high priest

on being solemnly adjured or *sworn* by him *in the name of the living God;* though he would not answer him, when questioned without an oath; and we may also observe, that the Jews always considered themselves *upon oath,* when thus adjured by the high priest. Why then should our Saviour give sanction to an oath by answering the adjuration, if no person ought to swear or take an oath before a magistrate?] 2 Cor. 1:18— *As God is true,* our word toward you was not yea and nay. 2 Cor. 1:23—Moreover, *I call God for a record upon my soul,* that to spare you I came not as yet unto Corinth. Gal. 1:20—Now, the things which I write unto you, behold, *before God,* I lie not. [St. Paul, in each of these instances, calls God to witness the truth which he asserted, which. has in it the nature and properties of *a solemn oath.*] Heb. 6:13—When God made promise to Abraham, *because he could swear by no greater, he sware by himself.* Heb. 6:16, 17—For men verily swear by the greater; and *an oath for confirmation is to them an end of all strife.* Wherein God, willing more abundantly to shew unto the heirs of promise the immutability of his counsel, confirmed it by an oath.

When we candidly compare together the texts quoted above, we do not see the possibility of reconciling them but by allowing, on the one hand, that it is sinful (it "cometh of evil") to use any asservation in common discourse, stronger than the simple *yes* and *no;* and, on the other hand, that it is *perfectly lawful to make an oath,* before the magistrate, on all important occasions.

Nevertheless, we do not object to any of our brethren, who still have doubts on this subject, and demand, where it can be obtained, an affirmation instead of an oath.

Discussion Questions on Session 9:

What duty, according to Paul, do Christians owe the civil government? Are there limits to this duty? Did Jesus affirm the same principle (see John 19:10–11)?

Are there dangers in "civil religion," wherein a religious faith becomes too closely identified with a government?

To what scriptural texts have advocates of Christian communism appealed, and how have these views been answered?

Should one follow Matthew 5:33–37 absolutely, by refusing to take an oath in a court of law? How is that swearing which is permitted distinguished from that swearing which is forbidden?

Session 10: Growth in Grace

Preparation: Rom. 12

Sin After Justification (Article 12)

A. Sin in Believers
1. Sin may occur in believers:
   a. After Baptism
   b. After receiving the Holy Spirit
2. A departure may occur from whatever grace God has given:
   a. Prevenient grace
   b. Justifying grace
   c. Sanctifying grace
3. Having walked in faith, one may fall into sin

B. Repentance Needed
1. Repentance may occur after justification, as well as before

2. Repentance is possible only by God's grace
   a. Not based on one's own natural power
   b. Not from one's own initiative
2. Having fallen, one may rise again
3. Forgiveness is offered to all who truly repent
4. Amendment of life is required to authenticate repentance

C. Rejection of Extreme Views
1. The church rejects various extreme views of sin:
   a. That no believer can ever return to sin
   b. That sinlessness in believers always continues uninterrupted
   c. That such a condition lasts until death
   d. That forgiveness is impossible after receiving justifying grace
   e. That sin after justification is unpardonable
   f. That it is sin against the Holy Spirit

Coke-Asbury Notes

(1) 2 Sam. 12:13—David said unto Nathan, I have sinned against the Lord. And Nathan said unto David, The Lord also hath put away thy sin; thou shalt not die. Matt. 26:75—Peter remembered the words of Jesus, which said unto him, Before the cock crow, thou shalt deny me thrice. And he went out, and wept bitterly [and Peter certainly was pardoned].

(2) Jer. 3:22—Return, ye backsliding children, and I will heal your backslidings. Hosea 14:4—I will heal their backsliding, I will love them freely. 1 John 2:1—My little

children, these things write I unto you, that ye sin not. And if *any man* sin, we have an Advocate with the Father, Jesus Christ the righteous.

Added Article on Sanctification

(From the Methodist Protestant *Discipline,* placed in the *Discipline of the Methodist Church* by the Uniting Conference of 1939 and in all subsequent United Methodist *Disciplines*)

A. Sanctification Defined
   1. Sanctification may be defined as the renewal of our fallen nature,
     a. Occurring by the power of the Holy Spirit
     b. Received through faith in Christ's atoning sacrifice
     c. Cleansing us from all sin
B. Extent and Consequence
   1. The full extent and consequence of sanctification includes:
     a. Deliverance from the guilt of sin
     b. Cleansing from the pollution of sin
     c. Salvation from the power of sin
     d. Enabling one to love God with the whole heart
     e. Enabling one to walk blameless in God's holy commandments

Discussion Questions for Session 10:

Once baptized, is one ever thereafter prevented from falling?

Does God continue to offer forgiveness, even after the believer has backslidden? Is one given only a single opportunity for repentance, or may it occur repeatedly? What if one appears to receive forgiveness, but one's life does not change at all—nothing is amended—has repentance occurred?

How is God's justifying grace distinguishable from God's sanctifying grace? How is our fallen nature renewed in sanctification? Is this only a partial renewal? What is the full extent of this renewal promised in the New Testament?

APPENDIX:
THE WARD MOTION

Much of the current debate about the Methodist doctrinal standards hinges on one curious incident: the defeat of Francis Ward's motion during the General Conference of 1808. It has been argued that this case stands as "conclusive evidence that the General Conference did not understand its standards of doctrine to include Wesley's *Sermons* and *Notes*" (*Heitz.*, 18). It appears that other hypotheses for explaining the evidence may have been neglected. We will review this intriguing case and its circumstances.

Alternative Hypotheses for Interpreting Its Meaning

Francis Ward was the assistant secretary of the 1808 General Conference. On Tuesday, May 24, 1808, at 3:00 P.M., it was "moved by Francis Ward and seconded by Lewis Myers, that it shall be considered as the sentiment of this Conference, that Mr. Wesley's Notes on the New Testament, his four first volumes of Sermons, *and Mr. Fletcher's Checks,* in their general tenor, contain the principal doctrines of Methodism, and a good explanation of our articles of religion; and that this sentiment be recorded on our Journal without being incorporated

in the Discipline" (manuscript journal, General Conference of 1808, 68, italics added).

In the original manuscript of the minutes of the Conference at the United Methodist archives at Drew University, however, the motion is merely noted as "lost" and there is a note in the margin in the same hand: "NB: It was voted that this motion be struck out of the Journal" (manuscript journal, General Conference of 1808, 68). The motion has a single large "X" through it. That is all we know, with no further explanation. It is clear that the Conference did not accept the motion, but it is not clear why.

For what possible reason could the 1808 Conference have preferred not to accept this motion at this time in this form? Why strike it from the record? One leading hypothesis is: "The General Conference was *not* willing to go on record defining its standards of doctrine in terms of documents other than the Articles" (*Heitz.*, 17). The implication is then drawn that no doctrinal standards other than the *Articles of Religion* are protected by the constitution. But is this the most likely explanation? If the Conference members had meant their defeat of the Ward motion to be a publicly declared positive rejection of its entire substance and intent, they would have been much more likely to have *left it in the record as acted upon*. The X-ing out suggests that a consensus of the group preferred to have the whole affair expunged, at best to be discussed later after more study and reflection.

We may imagine various reasons for the loss and deletion of this motion. We do not know whether any of the following hypotheses might be correct, because we do not have enough written evidence; but some combination is probable.

First, the motion asked for an enormous *innovation* never before suggested in the literature on Methodist doctrinal standards: that John Fletcher's writings be inserted into the well-known list of traditionally received standards provided by the deeds and Conference minutes since 1773. This would have been a controversial proposal at any time; but at this delicate time it was unthinkable. The motion asked that the constitution protect against any future amendment not only those doctrines contained in Wesley's *Sermons* and *Notes* but also those in Fletcher's "Checks"! This constituted an intrusive *innovation* inconsistent with the rigorously conserving spirit evident elsewhere in the Conference—a fact that alone was enough to defeat the motion.

Second, there are other technical reasons why a motion of this sort might be defeated: Perhaps the motion was rejected not because it was too strong, but too weak; or not because it was too decisively Wesleyan, but not decisive enough. It was proposed as a mere "sentiment of the Conference"; hence it could be taken frivolously. Perhaps the

Ward motion was simply thought unnecessary; or it could have been regarded as poorly worded or inappropriately formulated.

Third, in any event, the motion was exquisitely *ill-timed*. The Conference was not ready at that time to act on such a broadly stated and potentially controversial motion made without due consideration, referral, and deliberate study. At this critical stage of primary constitution-building when many votes had been extremely close, alliances fragile, and other issues yet to be faced, the deliberative body may have felt (without any demeaning of theological debate) that it was more prudent not to enter this hazardous territory and try to settle upon delicate language at this stage.

The Ward motion, asking for an abrupt and radical change in doctrinal standards (to include Fletcher), appears to have been too much to handle under these sensitive circumstances. It was very poorly timed, but not rejected for the reason that Dr. Heitzenrater has proposed (i.e., that the Conference was deliberately setting aside Wesley's *Sermons* and *Notes* as established doctrinal standards). Had that been the case, there surely would have been some residue of debate recorded in the minutes.

The Ward motion itself contains circumstantial evidence that Wesley's *Sermons* and *Notes* were in fact being regarded as the established standards of the 1808 Conference, because they were the only doctrinal standards mentioned by Ward, other than Fletcher's "Checks." Is not the evidence clear that it was the *Sermons* and *Notes*—and nothing else—to which the Conference was comparing Fletcher's "Checks"? Accordingly, the *Sermons* and *Notes* remained. the established standard against which Fletcher was being measured, by both Ward and the Conference.

Borgen's Analysis

Ole Borgen, former president of the United Methodist Council of Bishops, proposed another explanation of this curious record, in three steps. First:

> The inclusion of Fletcher's Checks may have been, at least in part, a reason for the defeat of the motion. However, the most likely reason for not adopting the Ward motion is the opposite of what is proposed by Heitzenrater: The motion was defeated (a) because the matter was already cared for in the second part of the rule, and (b) because it was not a proposal to *strengthen* the place of the *Sermons* and *Notes*. Just the contrary: it was proposed to be "the sentiment" of the Conference, not a decision; the *Notes* and the *Sermons* were not said to *contain* the principal doctrines, but only "in their general tenor" to contain them (Borgen, *SDUMC*, 13).

The second step of Borgen's explanation returns to the intriguing question of why the language first proposed for the First Restrictive Rule on May 16, 1808 was turned down. The Conference's journal recorded this initial wording: "The General Conference shall not revoke, alter, or change our Articles of Religion, nor establish any new standards of doctrine" (*JGC, 1808,* 82). This preliminary language for the Rule was defeated, precisely because it lacked reference to the other "established standards." This

was corrected by the language later accepted on May 24, 1808, which added the statement, "or rules [of doctrine] contrary to our present existing and established standards of doctrine" (Ibid., 312). Borgen says, "This motion from the floor carried, clearly showing that the General Conference was not willing to reduce the doctrinal standards to include only the Articles of Religion" (Borgen, *SDUMC,* 14).

The third step of Borgen's explanation hinges on the technical "use of the word 'nor' instead of the coordinating 'or' before the last part of the rule" (Ibid.):

> The original text of 1808 of the first restrictive rule had "revoke, alter, or change our articles of religion, *nor* establish. . . ." This remained unchanged until 1884, where the "or"–"nor" were changed to "nor"–"nor." The 1939 Discipline of the Methodist Church changed the two conjunctions again, to "or"–"or," which then has remained unchanged till today, giving the two parts of the rule a coordinative place, instead of the parallel place given through the use of the word "nor" (Ibid., 36n).

Speculations about the Ward motion may only deepen its irony. Much recent debate has focused upon why the Conference struck the Ward motion from the record. Could it have been struck precisely to avoid the kind of speculation that has been advanced? A Pandora's box has been opened by basing a constitutional argument upon speculation about a motion that was stricken intentionally from the record. What if the record was altered to circumvent precisely this sort of conjecture as to its meaning? Then might it not be unwise for current legislators to bring the Ward motion to the center stage of awareness, let alone make it a linchpin of a new hypothesis with far-reaching ramifications?

Since there is no record of the discussion surrounding this issue, and since the motion itself was stricken from the record, would it not be more respectful of the intent of the original constitution writers if we too would avoid such discussion? And is it not more prudent to avoid basing a major reversal of a long-held constitutional interpretation on such speculation?

LIST OF ABBREVIATIONS

CBTEL   John M'Clintock and James Strong, eds., *Cyclopedia of Biblical, Theological, and Ecclesiastical Literature* (New York: Harper, 1890).

CCG   Holland N. McTyeire, *A Catechism of Church Government* (Nashville: Southern Methodist Publishing House, 1878, 1883).

CH   John J. Tigert, *A Constitutional History of American Episcopal Methodism*, 2nd ed. (Nashville: Smith and Lamar, 1904).

COC   Philip Schaff, ed., *The Creeds of Christendom*, 3 vols. (New York: Harper, 1919).

CPD   *The Constitutional Practice and Discipline of the Methodist Church* (London: Methodist Publishing House, 1976).

CPH   James Monroe Buckley, *Constitutional and Parliamentary History of the Methodist Episcopal Church* (New York: Eaton and Mains, 1912).

CR   T. A. Kerley, *Conference Rights* (Nashville: Barbee and Smith, 1898).

DCA   *Daily Christian Advocate, Reports of General Conference Proceedings.*

DDS   William Shaw, *Digest of the Doctrinal Standards of the Methodist Church* (Toronto: William Briggs, 1895).

Disc., 1785   *Minutes of Several Conversations Between the Rev. Thomas Coke, the Rev. Francis Asbury and others, at a Conference begun in Baltimore, December 27th, 1784, Composing a Form of Discipline,* (Philadelphia: C. Cist, 1785). The full text of this *Discipline* is reprinted in J. Tigert, *CH*, pp. 532–602; see also Robert Emory, *HD*.

Disc., 1792   *The Doctrines and Discipline of the Methodist Episcopal Church, 1792* (Philadelphia: P. Hall, 1792).

Disc., 1798   Frank Norwood, ed., *The Methodist Discipline of 1798, including the Annotations of Thomas Coke and Francis Asbury* (reprint, Rutland, Vt.: Academy Books, 1979).

Disc., 1804   *The Doctrines and Discipline of the Methodist Episcopal Church,* 12th ed. (New York: T. Kirk, 1804).

Disc. with date   *Discipline of the Methodist Episcopal [or United Methodist] Church.*

205

DML   Stephen M. Merrill, *A Digest of Methodist Law* (New York: Phillips and Hunt, 1885; Methodist Book Concern, 1912).

DSM   Thomas B. Neely, *Doctrinal Standards of Methodism* (New York: Revell, 1918).

DSMC   Edwin Lewis, "Doctrinal Standards of the Methodist Church" (Prepared for the Commission on a Proposed Union of the Methodist Church and the Protestant Episcopal Church, n.d.).

DT   W. H. Shipman, et al., *The Doctrinal Test* (New York: Methodist Book Concern, 1922).

EWM   Nolan B. Harmon, ed., *Encyclopedia of World Methodism* (Nashville: United Methodist Publishing House, 1974).

FWA   Frank Baker, *From Wesley to Asbury* (Durham: Duke University Press, 1976).

GAD   Osmon C. Baker, *A Guide-book in the Administration of the Discipline of the Methodist Episcopal Church* (New York: Carlton and Phillips, 1855). Revised after each General Conference, 1860, 1864, 1873, 1878, and 1884.

GCM   Thomas B. Neely, *A History of the Origin and Development of the Governing Conference in Methodism* (Cincinnati: Hunt and Eaton, 1892).

H&E   Henry Wheeler, *History and Exposition of the Twenty-five Articles of Religion of the Methodist Episcopal Church* (New York: Eaton and Mains, 1908).

HD   Robert Emory, *History of the Discipline of the Methodist Episcopal Church* (New York: Lane and Sandford, 1844). Revised 1845, 1851, and 1856.

Heitz.   Richard P. Heitzenrater, "At Full Liberty: Doctrinal Standards in Early American Methodism," *Quarterly Review* 5 (Fall 1985).

Hist. MEC Abel Stevens, *History of the M. E. Church* (New York: Carlton and Porter, 1859).

HM   Jesse Lee, *History of the Methodists* (Baltimore: Magill and Clime, 1810).

HMEC   Nathan Bangs, *History of the M. E. Church,* 4 vols. (New York, Mason and Lane, 1840).

HRD   David Sherman, *History of the Revisions of the Discipline of the Methodist Episcopal Church* (New York: Nelson and Phillips, 1874).

HSCC   Albert C. Outler, ed., "The Methodist Standards of Doctrine," in *A Handbook of Selected Creeds and Confessions* (Dallas: Perkins School of Theology, 1958).

J&L	Francis Asbury, *Journals and Letters,* ed. E. T. Clark, 3 vols. (Nashville: Abingdon, 1958).
JGC with date	*Journals of the General Conference, 1796–1836* (New York: Carlton and Phillips, 1855) and *Journals of the General Conference of the Methodist Episcopal Church* (separate volumes after 1836).
JGCS with date	*Journal of the General Conference of the Methodist Episcopal Church, South* (Nashville: Methodist Publishing House, 1846–1939).
LJW	John Wesley, *The Letters of the Rev. John Wesley,* ed. John Telford, 8 vols. (London: Epworth, 1931).
LM	*Minutes of Several Conversations Between John and Charles Wesley and others, From the Year 1744 to the Year 1780* (London: J. Paramore, 1780). These are commonly known as the "Large Minutes." See an earlier version in J. Tigert, *CH,* 532–602, and a later version in Robert Emory, *HD.* Also in WJW, 8:299–339.
MAC	*Minutes of the Annual Conferences of the Methodist Episcopal Church for the Years 1773–1828* (New York: T. Mason and G. Lane, 1840).
MD	Holland N. McTyeire, *Manual of the Discipline,* 1st ed. (Nashville: Southern Methodist Publishing House, 1870); 20th ed., 1931.
MMC	*The Minutes of the Methodist Conferences Annually Held in America, from 1771 to 1794* (Philadelphia: Henry Tuckness, 1795).
MQR	Methodist Quarterly Review.
NDS	Committee on Our Theological Task, "The New Doctrinal Statement: A First Draft Proposal," *Circuit Rider* 11 (February 1987), 9–16.
NTA	A. A. Jimeson, *Notes on the Twenty-five Articles of Religion as Received and Taught by the Methodists in the United States . . . Supported by the Testimony of the Holy Scriptures* (Cincinnati: A. H. Pounsford, 1853).
PP	Jerry L. Walls, *The Problem of Pluralism: Recovering United Methodist Identity* (Wilmore, Kentucky: Good News, 1986).
QA	Henry Wheeler, *One Thousand Questions and Answers Concerning the Methodist Episcopal Church* (New York: Eaton and Mains, 1898).
RA	Nathan Bangs, *The Reviewer Answered* (New York: Waugh and Emory, 1830).
SC	George L. Curtiss, *A Study of the Constitution of the Methodist Episcopal Church* (New York: Hunt and Eaton, 1889).
SDUMC	Ole Borgen, "Standards of Doctrine in the United Methodist Church: Never Revoked, Altered or Changed?" manuscript of Vosburgh Lecture (Madison, N.J.: Drew University, Oct. 8, 1986).

SJWN   John Lawson, *Selections from John Wesley's Notes on the New Testament: Systematically Arranged with Explanatory Comments* (London: Epworth, 1955).

SSO   John Wesley, *Sermons on Several Occasions.* Reprinted in WJWB, vols. 1–2: WJW, vols. 5–6; WS; and WDS.

TSC   Albert C. Outler, ed., "The Theological Study Commission on Doctrine and Doctrinal Standards: Interim Report to the General Conference," (N.p. 1970).

UUMC   Nolan B. Harmon, *Understanding the United Methodist Church* (Nashville: Abingdon, 1977).

WDS   Nathaniel Burwash, ed., *Wesley's Doctrinal Standards* (Toronto: William Briggs, 1881).

WJW   John Wesley, *Works of the Rev. John Wesley,* ed. Thomas Jackson, 14 vols. (London: Wesleyan Conference Office, 1872).

WJWB   John Wesley, *Works of John Wesley: Bicentennial Edition,* ed. Frank Baker (New York: Oxford, 1979–83; Nashville: Abingdon, 1984–).

WS   John Wesley, *The Wesleyan Standards: Sermons by the Rev. John Wesley,* ed. W. P. Harrison, 2 vols., 1st ed. (Nashville: Smith and Lamar, 1886; reprint, 1918).

WSS   John Wesley, *Wesley's Standard Sermons,* ed. Edward H. Sugden, 2 vols. (London: Epworth, 1921; reprint, Grand Rapids: Zondervan, 1986).

YACC   C. H. Jacquet, Jr., ed., *Yearbook of American and Canadian Churches* (Nashville: Abingdon, 1985).

NOTES

Introduction

1. *Oxford Universal English Dictionary*, 2:424; *Webster's Ninth New Collegiate Dictionary*, 1148.

2. John Wesley, "Thoughts Upon Methodism" (1786), *WJW*, 13:258.

3. Heitzenrater says that the *Articles of Religion* was the only document protected by the 1808 constitution (*Heitz.*, 6–27).

Chapter 1

1. Philip Schaff, *Creeds of Christendom*, 1:7; Richard Wheatley, *Methodist Quarterly Review*, 1883, 28.

Chapter 2

1. See J. B. Wakeley, *Lost Chapters Recovered from the Early History of American Methodism* (New York: n.p., 1858).

2. *Western Christian Advocate*, 4 (26 May 1837): 18.

3. The Conference of May, 1784 "recognizes the Large English Minutes as law in America" (Neely, *GCM*, 214).

4. Jesse Lee said that the preachers could pray better with their eyes shut than open.

5. *Certain Sermons or Homilies, Appointed to be read in the churches in the time of the late Queen Elizabeth* (Oxford: Oxford University, 1832).

6. "Asbury took no personal risk in the submission, but, on the contrary, by the submission made his position more secure" (Neely, *GCM*, 251).

7. William Watters, *A Short Account*, 104, italics added; cf. Kerley, *CR*, 70, and Buckley, *CPH*, 48.

8. Kerley, *CR*, 78.

9. *Disc.*, 1798, Preface; cf. Kerley, *CR*, 78.

10. *Minutes of Several Conversations* (Philadelphia: Cist, 1785), 1, italics added; also in Tigert, *CH*, 534.

11. John Emory, *Defense of Our Fathers* (New York: Bangs and Emory, 1827), 77–78.

12. Ibid., 124–25.

Chapter 3

1. Heitzenrater says, "During the decade prior to the Christmas Conference [of 1784], the American Methodist conference had on several occasions pledged itself to the Wesleyan scheme in both doctrine and polity. . . . But the Christmas Conference had established American Methodism as a separate organization with its own set of constitutive documents, similar in form but significantly different in content from the British counterparts" (*Heitz.*, 10–11).

2. Ibid., 24–25

3. John Lawson, ed., *Notes on Wesley's Forty-four Sermons* (London: Epworth, 1946).

4. The 1825 edition added Wesley's short *Treatise on Baptism* and omitted Peter Edwards' *A Short Method with the Baptists*, which in 1814 had replaced Hemmenway. The third edition also added William Wall's *History*

of *Infant Baptism* and H. S. Boyd's *Remarks on Infant Baptism.*

5. *The Doctrines and Discipline of the Methodist Episcopal Church, 1805* (New York: Ezekiel Cooper and John Wilson for the Methodist Connection). The 1805 edition was virtually identical to that of 1804.

6. See T. Neely, *Vital Points in the Methodist Episcopal Church* (Philadelphia: Yeakel, 1924), 117.

Chapter 4

1. Neely, *Vital Points,* p. 117.

2. For various amendments see *Disc., 1864,* 121 and the *Disciplines* of 1860, 1872, and 1880. Also see Sherman, *HRD,* 194–95.

3. A. B. Sanford, ed., *Reports of the Committee on Judiciary of the General Conference of the Methodist Episcopal Church,* (New York: Methodist Book Concern, 1924), 268.

4. "The Ritual," *The Methodist Hymnal* (Nashville: Methodist Publishing House, 1966), 829; also *Disc., 1984,* 114.

Chapter 5

1. Augustine, *The City of God,* bk. 11, sec. 17.

2. Tertullian, *On Prescription Against Heretics,* in *The Ante-Nicene Fathers,* ed. Alexander Roberts and James Donaldson, 10 vols. (Buffalo: Christian Literature, 1885–96; reprint, Grand Rapids: Eerdmans, 1950), 3:261.

3. Nolan B. Harmon, *Understanding the United Methodist Church* (Nashville: Abingdon, 1977), 23–24.

4. *Heitz.,* 20.

5. Ibid., 20–21.

6. "Doctrinal Statement: A First Draft Proposal," *Circuit Rider* (February 1987), 9–15.

Chapter 6

1. As noted earlier, the early American *Minutes of the Methodist Episcopal Church* would mandate that Methodist preachers study the Scripture twice daily, utilizing Wesley's *Notes* as a guide to interpretation.

2. John Deschner, *Wesley's Christology,* rev. ed. (Dallas: SMU Press, 1985; reprint, Grand Rapids: Zondervan, 1988), 7–9.

3. John Deschner, "Methodism's Thirteenth Article," *Perkins Journal* 13 (Winter, 1960) 2:6–8.

4. Forthcoming from Abingdon Press (Nashville).

5. The numbering discrepancy (43 sermons rather than 44) results from the later inclusion of "Wandering Thoughts," which is variously numbered as Sermon 36 or 41.

6. John Lawson, ed., *Notes on Wesley's Forty-four Sermons* (London: Epworth, 1946), xxi.

7. *Methodist Recorder,* Dec. 20, 1894.

8. *Minutes of Conference, 1914,* 614–26; cf. Sugden, *WSS,* 2:331–40.

9. 3rd ed. (London: Epworth, 1951; reprint, Grand Rapids: Zondervan, 1986).

10. Sugden, *WSS,* xii.

11. Paragraphs 15–18 continue with a further series of questions on Christian ethics—doing the will of God, serving God, loving the neighbor, doing all the good one can. All these doctrinal concerns are assumed in the condition pointed to by the phrase "that one's heart is right, as my heart."

12. Wheeler, *H&E,* 5, 6. For extended discussion of the Thirty-nine Articles, see Gilbert Burnett, *On the XXXIX Articles,* 1699; E. Harold Browne, *Exposition of the Thirty-nine Articles* (London: 1860); Charles Hardwick, *A History of the Articles of Religion* (London: Geo. Bell, 1876); Edgar C. S. Gibson, *The Thirty-nine Articles of the Church of England* (London: Methuen, 1904); E. J. Bicknell, *A Theological Introduction to the Thirty-nine Articles* (London: Longman,

1919); W. H. Griffith Thomas, *The Principles of Theology* (London: Church Book Room Press).

13. Wesley did not provide an explicit rationale for his amendments. For a ·more complete discussion of hypotheses on the reasoning underlying omissions and amendments, see Henry Wheeler (*H&E*) and H. M. DuBose (*SM,* 69ff.). Also see Albert Outler, *John Wesley* (New York: Oxford, 1970), 235ff., 389ff.

14. Abel Stevens, *History of Methodism,* 2:206.

15. See "A Resolution of Intent of the General Conference of 1970," *Journal,* 254–55, and *The Book of Resolutions, 1968,* 65–72; *Disc., 1984,* 58.

16. *Subscription and Assent to the 39 Articles* (London: S.P.C.K., 1968) sec. 97.

17. E. J. Bicknell, *Theological Introduction to the Thirty-nine Articles* (1955), 21.

18. The British Methodists at their Conference of 1806 adopted the same Articles that had been sent to the American church, except for necessary alteration of Article 23 on civil authority. However, the *Articles of Religion* never became well-established in British Methodist ordinal examination, which continues to focus upon the *Sermons* and *Notes.* The *Articles* were not included in the doctrinal definition of the British Methodist Union of 1932.

19. For further reading, several commentaries on the Twenty-five *Articles* have been written: William Phoebus (1817); A. A. Jimeson (Cincinnati: A. H. Pounsford, 1853); Silas Comfort (New York: Conference Office, 1847); William I. Shaw, *Digest of the Doctrinal Standards of the Methodist Church* (Toronto: Briggs, 1895); Henry Wheeler, *History and Exposition* (New York: Eaton and Mains, 1908); Horace M. Dubose, *The Symbol of Methodism* (Nashville: Publishing House of the Methodist Episcopal Church, South, 1907); John Tigert, *CH,* ch. 9; J. M. Buckley, *CPH, 1912,* ch. 22); and Thomas B. Neely, *Doctrinal Standards of Methodism* (New York: Revell, 1918). The most recent commentaries are those by Nolan B. Harmon, *UMC,* ch. 2, and Thomas F. Chilcote, *The Articles of Religion of the Methodist Church* (Nashville: Methodist Evangelistic Materials, 1962).

20. See also Robert Emory, *HD;* R. Sherman, *HRD*; dual-column comparisons are found in Henry Wheeler, *H&E,* and in the *Encyclopedia of World Methodism.*

21. St. Jerome, compiler of the Latin Vulgate version of the Bible.

22. Misprinted in the United Methodist *Discipline* until 1836 as *rights.* Note that twice in Wesley's revisions of this paragraph he shifts to non-sexist language.

23. The words "of the love" were omitted by a misprint in the Methodist *Discipline* of 1812 and were not restored until 1840.

24. Misprinted as *scriptural* in the Methodist *Discipline* of 1808 and corrected in 1844.

25. This was originally Mr. Wesleys' twenty-fifth Article.

26. For current language, see *Disc., 1984,* 63.

27. This was originally Mr. Wesley's twenty-third Article.

28. This was originally Mr. Wesley's twenty-fourth Article.

Chapter 7

1. C. H. Jacquet, Jr., ed., *Yearbook of American and Canadian Churches* (Nashville: Abingdon, 1985), hereafter *YACC.*

2. This group of denominations teaches the more Wesleyan "three-stage theory" of Christian experience (i.e., conversion, sanctification, and baptism of the Holy Spirit), as distinguished from the Baptistic-Pentecostal

denominations such as the Assemblies of God, Full Gospel Fellowship, and Pentecostal Church of God, which teach a "two-stage theory" (i.e., conversion and baptism of the Holy Spirit). See *YACC,* 111.

3. Current membership statistics, brief histories, and theological views of the various denominations are summarized in YACC and in the *Handbook of Denominations in the United States,* ed. F. S. Mead and S. S. Hill (Nashville: Abingdon, 1985).

4. For others the reader may consult *COC,* 3:487ff., or E. Gibson, *The Thirty-nine Articles* (London: Methuen, 1904), 90ff.

5. The preamble of this document states the doctrinal intent of the Free Methodist Church: "In order that we may wisely preserve and pass on to posterity the heritage of doctrine and principles of Christian living transmitted to us as evangelicals in the Arminian-Wesleyan tradition, insure church order by sound principles and ecclesiastical polity, and prepare the way for evangelization of the world and the more effective cooperation with other branches of the Church of Christ in the advancement of Christ's kingdom among men" (*Free Methodist Discipline, 1969,* 9). This preamble appears both in the 1969 version and following the revision of 1972. In what follows, the 1969 version will be marked with the symbol "F," while quotations from the version of 1972 and following will be indicated "Free Methodist, 1972." Where the two versions are identical, the symbol "F" will serve.

6. The primary doctrinal focus of the Church of the Nazarene is stated in the preamble of its *Articles of Faith*: "In order that we may preserve our God-given heritage, the faith once delivered to the saints, especially the doctrine and experience of *entire* sanctification as a second work of grace, and also that we may cooperate effectually with other branches of the Church of Jesus Christ in advancing God's kingdom among men."

7. The Augsburg Confession reads: "There is one divine essence which is called and is God, without body, indivisible (Ger., *ohne Stueck,* 'without part'), of infinite power, wisdom, goodness, the Creator and Preserver of all things, visible and invisible; and that yet there are three persons of the same essence and power, who also are co-eternal, the Father, the Son, and the Holy Ghost" (*COC,* 3:7).

8. The Nicene Creed confesses faith in "the one Lord Jesus Christ, the only-begotten God, Light of Light, Very God of Very God, begotten not made, being of one substance (Gk., *homoousion*) with the Father by whom all things were made, who for us men and our salvation came down from heaven and was incarnate by the Holy Ghost of the Virgin Mary, and was made man; he was crucified for us under Pontius Pilate, and suffered and was buried. . . . "

9. The phrase, "follow after justification," is from Augustine, "On Faith and Good Works," xiv.

10. Promulgated after the Council of Trent, Session 22, had anathematized those who said that "Mass ought only to be celebrated in the vulgar tongue."

11. See Augustine, "Epistles," 45 and "On Christian Doctrine," 3:9.

12. The following wording appears in the *Foundation Documents of the United Methodist Church* with the following annotation: "The following Article from the Methodist Protestant *Discipline* is placed here by the Uniting Conference (1939). It was not one of the Articles of Religion voted upon by the three churches" (*Disc., 1984,* 62).

13. *The Doctrine and Discipline of the Methodist Church, Canada* (Toronto: Methodist Book and Publishing House, 1922), 11.

14. *The Doctrines and Discipline of the Methodist Church of Japan* (Tokyo: Methodist Publishing House, 1907), 19.

15. *The Constitution and Discipline of the Methodist Church in the Caribbean and the Americas* (London: Cargate Press, 1967), 29–30.

16. *A Manual of the Laws and Discipline of the Methodist Church of South Africa* (Methodist Church of South Africa: 1973), 3, 4.

17. *Discipline of the Korean Methodist Church* (Seoul, Korea: General Board of the Korean Methodist Church, 1932), 25–26.

18. The full text appears in *CPD*, 527–28.

19. *The Salvation Army Handbook of Doctrine* (London: International Headquarters, n.d.).

20. *That is to say,* We believe that the Scriptures teach that not only does continuance in the favour of God depend upon continued faith in, and obedience to, Christ, but that it is possible for those who have been truly converted to fall away and be eternally lost.

21. *That is to say,* We believe that after conversion there remains in the heart of the believer inclinations to evil, or roots of bitterness, which, unless overpowered by divine grace, produce actual sin; but that these evil tendencies can be entirely taken away by the Spirit of God, and the whole heart, thus cleansed from everything contrary to the will of God, or entirely sanctified, will then produce the fruit of the Spirit only. And we believe that persons thus entirely sanctified may, by the power of God, be kept unblamable and unreprovable before Him.

22. From the United Methodist *Discipline* of 1984, 46–49.

23. The first three deleted articles were all aimed at Roman Catholics.

24. Aimed at both Roman Catholics and Anabaptists.

25. Aimed originally at sixteenth-century sectarians.

26. See William H. Naumann, "Theology and German-American Evangelicalism: The Role of Theology in the Church of the United Brethren in Christ and the Evangelical Association," Ph.D. diss., Yale University, 1967.

27. *Discipline, 1985–89* (Huntington, Ind.; Department of Church Services, 1985), 3.

28. Ibid., 6–10.

29. Ibid., 9.

30. Ibid., 10.

BIBLIOGRAPHY

No standard bibliography of Methodist constitutional interpretation exists, so readers seeking bibliographical roots may find this section exceptionally time-saving. These materials are listed in chronological groupings rather than alphabetical order. Abbreviations appear alphabetically in the List of Abbreviations and below at the end of each title abbreviated.

A. *Official Records of the Early American Methodist Tradition*

Wesley, John. *Works of John Wesley: Bicentennial Edition*. Ed. Frank Baker. New York: Oxford, 1979–83; Nashville: Abingdon, 1984– . WJWB.

——. *Works of the Rev. John Wesley*. Ed. Thomas Jackson. 14 vols. London: Wesleyan Conference Office, 1872. WJW.

——. *Letters of the Rev. John Wesley*. Ed. John Telford. London: Epworth, 1931. LJW.

——. *Sermons on Several Occasions*, WJWB 1, 2; WJW 5, 6; WS; WSS. SSO.

——. *Minutes of Several Conversations Between John and Charles Wesley and others, From the Year 1744 to the Year 1780*. London: J. Paramore, 1780. (Commonly known as the "Large Minutes."). Full text reprinted in J. Tigert, CH,

532–602, and in WJW, 8:299–339. LM.

——. *The Sunday Service*. London, 1784.

The Minutes of the Methodist Conference Annually held in America, from 1771 to 1794. Philadelphia: Henry Tuckness, 1795. MMC.

Minutes of the Annual Conference of the Methodist Episcopal Church for the Years 1773–1828, vol. 1. New York: T. Mason and G. Lane, 1840. MAC.

Minutes of Several Conversations Between the Rev. Thomas Coke, the Rev. Francis Asbury and others, at a Conference begun in Baltimore, December 27th, 1784, Composing a Form of Discipline. Philadelphia: C. Cist, 1785. Full text reprinted in J. Tigert, CH, 532–602. Disc., 1784.

"First Discipline of the Methodist Episcopal Church Compared with Large Minutes." In Emory, Robert. *History of the Discipline*. New York: Lane and Sandford, 1844, 26–79. HD.

The Arminian Magazine 1 (1789). Philadelphia: Princard and Hall, 1789.

The Doctrines and Discipline of the Methodist Episcopal Church, 1792. Philadelphia: Parry Hall, 1792. Disc., 1792.

Journal of the General Conference of 1792. Ed. Thomas B. Neely. New York: Methodist Book Concern, 1899.

215

The Doctrines of the Methodist Episcopal Church in America. Ed. John Tigert, 2 vols. New York, 1902.

The Methodist Discipline of 1798, including the Annotations of Thomas Coke and Francis Asbury. Ed. Frederick Norwood. Reprint. Rutland, Vt.: Academy Books, 1979. Disc., 1798.

The Doctrines and Discipline of the Methodist Episcopal Church. 12th ed. New York: T. Kirk, 1804. Disc., 1804.

Journals of the General Conference, 1796–1836. New York: Carlton and Phillips, 1855. Journals of the General Conference of the Methodist Episcopal Church, 1836–   JGC with date.

Journal of the General Conference of the Methodist Episcopal Church, South. Nashville: Methodist Publishing House, 1846–1939. JGCS with date.

B. *Early Interpreters*

Asbury, Francis. *Journals and Letters.* Ed. E. T. Clark. 3 vols. Nashville: Abingdon, 1958. J&L.

Whatcoat, Richard. *Memoirs, 1806,* in J. Telford, *Wesley's Veterans.* Salem, Ohio: Schmul, n.d. 2:219–28.

Lee, Jesse. *History of the Methodists.* Baltimore: Magill and Clime, 1810. HM.

Emory, John. *Defense of Our Fathers, and of the Original Organization of the M. E. Church, against Rev. Alexander M'Caine and others.* New York: Bangs and Emory, 1827.

——, ed. *The Journal of John Wesley.* 2 vols. New York: Mason and Lane, 1837. Reprint. 1855–57.

——, ed. *The Works of John Wesley.* 7 vols. New York: Emory and Waugh, 1831–33, 1835, 1853, 1856.

Phoebus, William. *Memoirs of Bishop Whatcoat.* New York, 1828.

Youngs, James. *History of the most interesting events in the Rise and Progress of Methodism in Europe and America.* New Haven: D. McLeod, 1831.

Hedding, Elijah. *A Discourse on the Administration of the Discipline.* New York: Lane and Sandford, 1842.

Bangs, Nathan. *The Reviewer Answered.* New York: Emory and Waugh, 1830. RA.

——. *History of the M. E. Church.* 4 vols. New York: Mason and Lane, 1840. HMEC.

Ware, Thomas. *Life and Travels of Rev. Thomas Ware.* New York: Mason and Lane, 1839.

Emory, Robert. *History of the Discipline of the Methodist Episcopal Church.* New York: Lane and Sandford, 1844, 1845, 1851, 1856. HD.

Stevens, Abel. *Centenary Reflections on the Providential Character of Methodism.* New York, 1840.

Peck, George. *The Rule of Faith: An Appeal From Tradition to Scripture and Common Sense; or an Answer to the Question, What Constitutes the Divine Rule of Faith and Practice?* New York: Lane and Tippett, 1844.

Ralston, Thomas. *Elements of Divinity.* Louisville: Morton and Griswold, 1847.

C. *Historians and Interpreters (Late Nineteenth Century)*

Jimeson, A. A. *Notes on the Twenty-five Articles of Religion as Received and Taught by the Methodists in the United States . . . Supported by the Testimony of the Holy Scriptures.* Cincinnati: A. H. Pounsford, 1853. NTA.

Baker, Osmon C. *A Guide-book in the Administration of the Discipline of* the *Methodist Episcopal Church.* New York: Carlton and Phillips, 1855. Revised after each General Conference, 1860, 1864, 1869, 1873, 1878, 1884. GAD.

Henkle, M. M. *Primary Platform of Methodism: Exposition of the General Rules.* Louisville, 1851.

_____. *Analysis of the Principles of Church Government.* Nashville: Stevenson and Owen, 1857.

Stevens, Abel. *History of the M. E. Church.* New York: Carlton and Porter, 1859. Hist. MEC.

_____. *The Life and Times of Nathan Bangs.* New York: Carlton and Porter, 1865.

Harris, William L. *The Constitutional Powers of the General Conference.* Cincinnati, 1860.

_____. *Ecclesiastical Laws and Rules of Evidence, with Special Reference to the Jurisprudence of the Methodist Episcopal Church.* Rev. ed., 1881.

Peck, Jesse T. "Methodism: Its Method and Mission." *Methodist Quarterly Review* 51 (April, 1869).

McTyeire, Holland N. *Manual of the Discipline.* 1st ed. Nashville: Southern Methodist Publishing House, 1870. 20th ed., 1931. MD.

_____. *A Catechism of Church Government.* Nashville: Southern Methodist Publishing House, 1878, 1883. CCG.

_____. *A History of Methodism.* Nashville: Southern Methodist Publishing House, 1884.

Peirce, William. *Ecclesiastical Principles and Polity of the Wesleyan Methodists.* London: Hamilton, Adams, 1854; City Road, 1873.

Sherman, David. *History of the Revisions of the Discipline of the Methodist Episcopal Church.* New York: Nelson and Phillips, 1874. HRD.

Marvin, E. M. *The Doctrinal Integrity of Methodism.* St. Louis: Advocate Publishing House, 1878.

Curry, Daniel. "Conservation of Methodist Orthodoxy: Editor's Study." *National Repository* 5 (1879): 356–63. See also articles in *The Independent,* Nov. 3, 1881 and Dec. 1, 1881.

Pullman, Joseph. "Methodism and Heresy." *Methodist Quarterly Review* (April 1879): 334–57.

Burwash, Nathaniel, ed. *Wesley's Doctrinal Standards.* Toronto: William Briggs, 1881. WDS.

Wheatly, Richard. "Methodist Doctrinal Standards." *Methodist Quarterly Review* 65 (1883): 26–51.

Merrill, Stephen M. *A Digest of Methodist Law.* New York: Phillips and Hunt, 1885; Methodist Book Concern, 1912. DML.

Harrison, W. P., ed. *The Wesleyan Standards: Sermons by the Rev. John Wesley.* 2 vols., 1st ed. Nashville: Smith and Lamar, 1886. Reprint. 1918. WS.

Curtiss, George L. *A Study of the Constitution of the Methodist Episcopal Church.* New York: Hunt and Eaton, 1889. SC.

Peterson, Peter Archer, *History of Revisions of the Discipline.* Nashville: Methodist Episcopal Church South, 1889.

M'Clintock, John, and Strong, James, eds. *Cyclopedia of Biblical Theological, and Ecclesiastical Literature.* New York: Harper, 1890. CBTEL.

Neely, Thomas B. *History of the Governing Conference in Methodism.* New York: Methodist Book Concern, 1892.

Shaw, William. *Digest of the Doctrinal Standards of the Methodist Church.* Toronto: William Briggs, 1895. DDS.

Kerley, T. A. *Conference Rights.* Nashville: Barbee and Smith, 1898. CR.

Wheeler, Henry. *One Thousand Questions and Answers Concerning the*

Methodist Episcopal Church. New York: Eaton and Mains, 1898. QA.

D. *Early Twentieth-Century Interpreters*

Tigert, John J. *A Constitutional History of American Episcopal Methodism*. 1st ed. Nashville: Smith and Lamar, 1894. 2nd ed. (quoted here), 1904. CH.

_____. *The Making of Methodism*. Nashville: Barbee and Smith, 1896.

_____. *The Doctrines of the Methodist Episcopal Church in America, as contained in the Disciplines of said Church from 1788 to 1808*. 2 vols. New York: Eaton and Mains, 1902.

Dubose, Horace Mellard. *The Symbol of Methodism*. Nashville: Methodist Episcopal Church, South, 1907.

Tillett, Wilbur F. *A Statement of the Faith of World-wide Methodism*. Nashville: Methodist Publishing House, 1907.

Hendrix, E. R. "The Creed of Ecumenical Methodism: Where Can it be Found?" *Southern Methodist Quarterly Review* (April 1907).

Wheeler, Henry. *History and Exposition of the Twenty-five Articles of Religion of the Methodist Episcopal Church*. New York: Eaton and Mains, 1908. H&E.

Buckley, James Monroe. *History of Methodism in the United States*. 2 vols. New York: Christian Literature, 1896.

_____. *Constitutional and Parliamentary History of the Methodist Episcopal Church*. New York: Eaton and Mains, 1912. CPH.

Bennetts, George Armstrong. *The Doctrinal Crisis in Wesleyan Methodism*. London, n.d.

Neely, Thomas B. *A History of the Origin and Development of the Governing Conference in Methodism*. Cincinnati: Hunt and Eaton, 1892. GCM.

_____. *Doctrinal Standards of Methodism*. New York: Revell, 1918. DSM.

_____. *Vital Points in the Methodist Episcopal Church*. Philadelphia: E. A. Yeakel, 1924.

The Conference Course of Study. Evanston: General Conference Commission on Sources of Study, 1918. (See other years.)

Sugden, Edward H., ed. *Wesley's Standard Sermons*. 2 vols. London: Epworth, 1921. Reprint, Grand Rapids: Zondervan, 1986. See especially the introduction, 1:13–26. WSS.

Cutshall, Elmer Guy. "The Doctrinal Training of the Traveling Ministry of the Methodist Episcopal Church." Ph.D. diss., University of Chicago, 1922.

Shipman, William H., et al. *The Doctrinal Test*. New York: Methodist Book Concern, 1922. DT.

Lewis, Edwin. "The Doctrinal Standards of the Methodist Church." Prepared for the Commission on a Proposed Union of the Methodist Church and the Protestant Episcopal Church, n.d. Mimeo. DSMC.

E. *Interpreters Since 1950*

Outler, Albert C., ed. "The Methodist Standards of Doctrine." In *A Handbook of Selected Creeds and Confessions*. Dallas: Perkins School of Theology, 1958. Mimeo. HSCC.

_____, ed. "The Theological Study Commission on Doctrine and Doctrinal Standards: Interim Report to the General Conference," 1970.

_____, ed. "The Theological Study Commission Doctrine and Doctrinal Standards: A Report to the General Conference," April 1972. TSC.

Chilcote, Thomas F. *The Articles of Religion of the Methodist Church.* Nashville: Methodist Evangelistic Materials, 1960.

Blankenship, Paul F. "The Significance of John Wesley's Abridgment of the Thirty-nine Articles as Seen from his Deletions." *Methodist History* (April 1964): 35ff.

Howard, Ivan C. "Controversies in Methodism over Methods of Education of Ministers up to 1856." Ph.D. diss., State University of Iowa, 1965.

Baker, Frank. *From Wesley to Asbury.* Durham: Duke University Press, 1979. See especially chapter 10, "The Doctrines in the *Discipline,*" *162–82, (previously published in the Duke Divinity School Review,* 31:39–55). FWA.

Stokes, Mack. *Major United Methodist Beliefs.* Nashville: Abingdon, 1971.

Harmon, Nolan B., *Understanding the United Methodist Church.* Nashville: Abingdon, 1977. UMMC.

——, ed. *Encyclopedia of World Methodism.* Nashville: United Methodist Publishing House, 1974. Includes articles by C. J. Harrell on "Deeds of Trust in American Methodism," 1:647; E. B. Perkins on "Trust Deeds in British Methodism," 1:646; Rupert E. Davies on "Doctrinal Standards of Methodism," 1:698ff. EWM.

Ogden, Schubert M. "Doctrinal Standards in the United Methodist Church," *Perkins Journal* (Fall 1974): 20–25.

Cushman, Robert E. "Doctrinal Standards and the Ecumenical Task Today," *Religion and Life* 45 (Winter 1975). Reprinted in amended form in *Faith Seeking Understanding.* Durham: Duke University, 1981, 317–27.

Campbell, Ted. *The Apostolate of United Methodism.* Nashville: Discipleship Resources, 1979.

Wainwright, Geoffrey. *Doxology.* New York: Oxford University, 1980.

Mickey, Paul A. *Essentials of Wesleyan Theology.* Grand Rapids: Zondervan, 1980.

Howe, Leroy T. "United Methodism in Search of Theology." *Perkins Journal* 28 (Fall 1974).

McCulloh, Gerold O. *Ministerial Education in the American Methodist Movement.* Nashville: United Methodist Board of Higher Education and Ministry, 1982.

Langford, Thomas A. *Practical Divinity: Theology in the Wesleyan Tradition.* Nashville: Abingdon, 1983.

——, ed. *Wesleyan Theology: A Sourcebook.* Durham: Labyrinth, 1984.

Runyon, Theodore, ed. *Wesleyan Theology Today.* Nashville: Kingswood Books, 1985.

"The Development of Wesleyan Theological Method," series of articles in the *Wesleyan Theological Journal* 20 (Spring 1985). The series includes Albert C. Outler on "The Wesleyan Quadrilateral in Wesley"; Leon O. Hynson on "The Wesleyan Quadrilateral in the American Holiness Tradition"; and William J. Abraham on "The Wesleyan Quadrilateral in the American Methodist-Episcopal Tradition."

Heitzenrater, Richard P. "At Full Liberty: Doctrinal Standards in Early American Methodism." *Quarterly Review* 5 (Fall 1985). Heitz.

Walls, Jerry L. *The Problem of Pluralism: Recovering United Methodist Identity.* Wilmore, Ky.: Good News, 1986. PP.

Borgen, Ole E. "Standards of Doctrine in the United Methodist

Church: Never Revoked, Altered or Changed?" Vosburgh Lecture. Madison, N.J.: Drew University, Oct. 8, 1986. SDUMC.

Committee on Our Theological Task. "The New Doctrinal Statement: A First Draft Proposal." *Circuit Rider* 11 (February 1987): 9–15. NDS.

F. *Sources of Official Doctrinal Definition in the Wesleyan Family of Church Bodies*

The Book of Discipline of the American Methodist Episcopal Church. Nashville: A.M.E. Sunday School Union, 1976.

A Catechism of the Christian Religion. Salem, Ohio: Schmul, 1980.

The Church of God Book of Doctrines. Huntsville, Ala.: Church of God Publishing House, 1970.

The Constitution and Discipline of the Methodist Church in the Caribbean and the Americas. London: Cargate Press, 1967.

Constitution and Government of the Congregational Methodist Church. Dallas: Messenger Press, 1960.

The Constitutional Practice and Discipline of the Methodist Church. London: Methodist Publishing House, 1976. CPD.

Discipline of the Evangelical Church. Medicine Hat, Alberta: H.C.C. Printshop, 1982.

Discipline of the Evangelical Methodist Church. Wichita: Evangelical Methodist Church, 1985.

The Discipline of the Evangelical United Brethren Church. Harrisburg and Dayton: Evangelical Press, 1959.

Discipline of the Korean Methodist Church. Seoul: Korean Methodist Church, 1932.

The Discipline of the Wesleyan Church, 1980. Marion, Ind.: Wesleyan Publishing House, 1980. W.

The Doctrine and Discipline of the Methodist Church, Canada. Toronto: Methodist Publishing House, 1922.

The Doctrines and Discipline of the African Methodist Episcopal Zion Church. Charlotte: AME Zion Publishing House, 1981. Z.

The Doctrines and Discipline of the Christian Methodist Episcopal Church. Memphis: CME Publishing House, 1976. C.

The Doctrines and Discipline of the Methodist Church of Japan. Tokyo: Methodist Publishing House, 1907.

The Doctrines and Discipline of the United Evangelical Church. Harrisburg, Pa.: United Evangelical Church, 1894.

Doctrines, Character, and Ritual of the Free Methodist Church: Part 1, Book of Discipline. Winona Lake, Ind.: Free Methodist Publishing House, 1985. F.

Handbook of the Methodist Protestant Church. N.p.: T. H. Lewis, 1925.

In the Last Days: An Early History of the Assemblies of God. Springfield, Mo.: Assemblies of God, 1962.

Manual of the Church of the Nazarene. Kansas City: Nazarene Publishing House, 1980. N.

The Manual of the Churches of Christ in Christian Union. Circleville, Ohio: C.C.C.U., 1985.

Manual of Doctrine and Government of the Brethren in Christ Church. Nappanee, Ind.: Evangel Press, 1984.

Manual of the Laws and Discipline of the Methodist Church of South Africa. N.p.: Methodist Church of South Africa, 1973.

Origin, Doctrine, Constitution and Discipline of the Church of the United Brethren in Christ, 1985–1989. Huntington, Ind.: Department of Church Services, 1985.

Salvation Army Handbook of Doctrine. London: International Headquarters, 1969. S.

INDEX OF PERSONS

INDEX OF SUBJECTS

Eucharist. *See* Lord's Supper
Evangelical Christian Church, 128
Evangelical Church, 46, 129, 131
Evangelical Church of North America, 128, 131
Evangelical faith, 110, 162, 164
Evangelical Friends Alliance, 128
Evangelical Methodist Church, 128, 131
Evangelicals, 76–77, 80, 108. 127–29, 156, 169
Evangelical United Brethren (E.U.B.), 12, 15, 26, 72, 80, 127, 129, 131–59, 170
Evangelism, 148, 160, 168, 170
Evil, 181–82, 196
Ex animo, 36, 107, 110
Exception of 1832, 59–61
Excommunication, 67, 103, 123
Exegesis, 24, 82, 84
Experimental religion, 59, 73, 91–92, 106
Explanatory Notes upon the New Testament. See *Notes*
Extreme Unction, 120, 149, 191, 195
Faddism, 110
Faith, 92, 94, 95, 98, 112, 132, 157, 173, 174–76, 179, 183–85, 193–95, 199–200
False prophets, 96
Fasting, 96
Fellowship, 30, 69, 148
Feminist theology, 71
Fifty-two Sermons. *See* Sermons
Fire-Baptized Holiness Church, 130
Foot washing, 170–72
Forgiveness, 117, 163, 171, 178, 187, 199
Formalist, 84, 92
Forty-two Articles (1553), 104, 133, 140, 145, 147–59
Free Methodist Church of North America, 12, 127–30, 132–59, 161
Free will, 115, 140–41, 173, 176, 182
Fruit of the Spirit, 95, 185
Fundamentalism, 82
Fundamental Methodist Church, Inc., 128, 131
General Councils, 104, 118–19

General Rules, 25, 27, 45, 54, 67, 163
Gifts of the Spirit, 146–47
Gnomon Novi Testamenti, 86
Good News Bible, 176
Good works, 115, 144–45, 173, 182, 184–87, 197
Goods, 158. *See also* Property
Grace, 26, 94, 104, 106, 117, 120, 141, 151, 165–66, 173–75, 182–85, 187, 191–93, 199
Guilt, 88
Happiness, 88–90, 98, 117
Healing, 155
Hegemony, 154
Heidelberg Catechism, 168, 17ᴜ
Hell, 92
Heresy, 62, 70–71, 105
Holiness, 24, 26, 47, 51, 59, 88, 95–96, 127, 129, 140–41, 151, 157–58, 162, 164–65, 168, 170
Holiness Church, 127, 129–30
Holiness Church of God, Inc., 130
Holiness Methodist Church, 131
Holy Catholic Church, 162–63
Holy Spirit, 26, 112, 173–74, 176–78, 199–200
Homilies, 35–37, 103, 105, 124
Homily of Justification, 106, 115
Homo unius libri, 38, 82, 90–91
Hope, 95
Hymnal, 57, 61–62, 68, 74
Immortality, 166
Incarnation, 136, 179
Inclusivism, 77
Independent Assemblies of God, International, 130
Independent Episcopal Church, 41
Indifferentism, 73, 97
Inerrancy, 138
Infant baptism, 150
Inspiration, 138, 180
Instruction. *See* Catechism
International Pentecostal Assemblies, 130
International Pentecostal Holiness Church, 129
Interpretation, 23–24, 37, 74, 83–84, 89, 162, 169, 180
Irish Methodist Conference, 131
Japan Immanuel Church, 128

John Street Methodist Church, 29
Judgment, 144, 159–61
Judicial Council, 56, 76, 155
Judiciary Committee, 68
Justification, 26, 94–96, 101, 105, 115–17, 142–43, 145, 168, 173, 175, 184–85, 199
King James Version, 82, 85, 87
Kingdom of God, 88, 159, 163
Laity, 27, 66–68, 84, 108–9, 122, 131, 153, 162, 164
Large Minutes, 30–31, 33, 44, 66, 68, 74
Last things. *See* Eschatology
Latitudinarianism, 33, 73, 97
Law, 96, 180. *See also* Civil government; Church government
Liberals, 109
Liberty, 109, 146
Liturgy, 70
"Liverpool Minutes," 165
"London Minutes," 72
Lord's Supper, 34, 35, 38, 95, 104–6, 120–22, 149–53, 164, 166, 171–73, 184, 186, 190–95
Love, 82, 92–93, 98, 142, 152, 156, 163, 173, 181
Love-feast, 59, 152
Marriage of ministers, 122, 153, 188–89
Mass. *See* Lord's Supper
Matrimony, 35, 120, 149, 189, 191, 195
Membership, 67–68, 159, 170, 193
Methodist Church, 15, 26, 72, 130–31
Methodist Church (Caribbean), 162
Methodist Church (Korea), 162
Methodist Church of South Africa, 162
Methodist Conference (British), 131
Methodist Episcopal Church, 36–39, 41, 58, 64–67, 105, 129–30, 167, 175
Methodist Episcopal Church, South, 128–31
Methodist New Connection (British), 46, 131, 162
Methodist Protestant Church, 128–30, 150, 156, 159, 161
Methodist Societies, 84

Methodist Union Act (1932), 46
Millenarianism, 104
Ministers. *See* Clergy
Minority Report, 68
Minutes, 25–26, 29–30, 32, 41, 44–45, 165
Missionary Church, 128, 131
Missionary Church Association, 131
Model Deed, 33, 43–44, 46–47, 50, 58, 72, 89, 93, 163
Modern translations, 87
Modernity, 83, 85
National Holiness Movement, 130
Nazarene Articles of Faith, 133, 136–38, 143, 151–52, 155, 158, 161
Neo-fundamentalism, 71
New English Bible, 176
New International Version, 176
New Stamps, 44
New Testament, 47, 83, 114, 180, 193–94, 200
New birth. *See* Regeneration
Nicene Creed, 99, 105, 133–35
Nippon Methodist Kyokwai (Japan), 162
Notes upon the New Testament, 12, 17, 31, 33, 35–39, 42, 43, 45, 47–48, 50, 52, 54, 56–59, 62–63, 66, 68, 71–77, 79, 81, 83–85, 87–89, 108, 111, 162, 164, 201–3
Oaths, 126, 159, 197–98
Obedience, 146
Old Methodist doctrines, 37, 42, 57, 61, 64
Old Testament, 114, 139
Ordinances, 35, 107, 110, 150, 164
Ordination and ordinands, 35, 73, 120, 149, 191, 195
Original sin, 101, 114, 139–40, 158, 181, 183
Orthodoxy, 99, 106
Pan-Orthodoxy, 128
Pan-Wesleyan dialogue, 79
Pan-Wesleyan doctrine, 128
Pantheism, 133
Papcy, 104, 156
Parsimony, principle of, 57
Pelagianism, 104, 115, 139–41, 181, 183
Penance, 120, 149, 191, 195

Pentecostal Alliance, 130
Pentecostal Church, 127, 129
Pentecostal Church of Christ, 130
Pentecostal Fire Baptized Holiness Church, 129–30
Pentecostal Holiness Church, 128, 130
Pentecostalism, 71, 129
Perfection, 24, 59, 97, 157
Pilgrim Holiness Church, 130–31
Pillar of Fire, 130
Plan of Union, 26, 66, 71–76
Pluralism, 12, 15–16, 69–71, 77, 99
Political and ethical theologies, 71
Polity. See Church government
Prayer, 95, 148–49, 155, 159, 163
Preaching, 32, 61–67, 74, 84, 89, 92, 96, 105, 111, 118–19, 126, 147–48, 155, 162, 164–72, 188
Predestination, 49, 104, 117
Presbyterian Church, 62
Prevenient grace, 36, 151, 182, 199
Priests, 35, 103, 107, 122
Primitive Methodist Church, USA, 128–29
Primitive Methodist Conference (British), 46, 131, 162
Principal Heads of Religion (1559), 149, 150, 153
Probation, 67
Property, 29, 44, 46, 51, 158, 173, 196–97
Propitiation, 153, 186
Protestantism, 99, 104
Providence, 176, 178
Punishment, 166
Purgatory, 119, 148, 187
Quadrilateral, 72
Rationalists, 95
Reconciliation, 142, 173, 183
Redemption, 121, 143, 147, 152–53, 165, 178, 183–84
Reformatio Legum Ecclesiasticarum, 133, 145, 147, 159
Reformation, the, 34, 37, 56, 100, 104, 149
Reformed Methodist Church, 129
Reformed Methodist Union Episcopal Church, 128–30
Reformed Zion Union Apostolic Church, 130

Reformed Zion Union Apostolic Faith, 128
Regeneration, 95, 142–44, 150, 156, 158, 166, 168
Repentance, 102, 117, 151, 165, 171, 191–92, 199
Republican Methodists, 129
"Resolution of Intent," 107
Restrictive Rule, 17–18, 26, 32, 49–61, 65, 67, 71–72, 74–75, 77, 105, 108, 163, 170, 203
Resurrection, 112, 135–36, 159–61, 166, 171, 173, 179
Return of Christ. See Eschatology
Revelation, 108
Revolutionary War, 30, 36, 38–40, 43
Righteousness, 88–89, 94–95, 98, 115, 141, 151, 163, 166, 168, 177, 180–81, 184, 186
Rites and ceremonies, 102, 106, 114, 124, 153–54, 181, 189
Roman Catholic Church, 24, 107, 127, 147, 152
Rule of doctrine, 21
Rule of faith, 21, 111, 137–38, 164, 166
Sabellianism, 133
Sacraments, 38, 70, 102, 106, 111, 118–20, 122, 125, 147–52, 164, 166, 173, 190–92, 195
Salvation, 35, 118, 137, 142, 162, 165, 173–75
Salvation Army, 12, 127–30
Sanctification, 35, 59, 94, 96, 136, 141, 149, 156–58, 170, 173, 200
Satan, 88
Satisfaction, 153
Schism, 12, 71
Scholasticism, 99, 145, 148, 153, 186, 195
Schwabach Articles (1529), 100
Scripture, 15, 21, 25, 64, 73, 82–84, 87, 91–92, 95, 104, 109, 113, 137, 166, 174–75, 179–81, 184, 187–88, 193, 195
Second Helvetic Confession, 145
Second Coming. See Eschatology
Secularity, 71
Sensus literalis, 82, 107

SCRIPTURE INDEX